personal training
theory and practice

personal training

theory and practice

JAMES CROSSLEY

Hodder Arnold
A MEMBER OF THE HODDER HEADLINE GROUP

Acknowledgements

Dedicated to my mother and father, my lifelong inspiration.

With thanks to Holmes Place, for use of their facilities and to Ian, Adele and Shaun for their help.

Orders: please contact Bookpoint Ltd, 130 Milton Park, Abingdon, Oxon OX14 4SB. Telephone: (44) 01235 827720. Fax: (44) 01235 400454. Lines are open from 9.00 – 5.00, Monday to Saturday, with a 24-hour message answering service. You can also order through our website www.hoddereducation.co.uk.

If you have any comments to make about this, or any of our other titles, please send them to educationenquiries@hodder.co.uk.

British Library Cataloguing in Publication Data
A catalogue record for this title is available from the British Library

ISBN–10: 0 340 913 495
ISBN–13: 978 0 340 913 499

First Edition Published 2006
Impression number   10 9 8 7 6 5 4 3 2 1
Year   2009 2008 2007 2006 2005 2004

Cover photo © Royalty-Free/Corbis

Hodder Headline's policy is to use papers that are natural, renewable and recyclable products and made from wood grown in sustainable forests. The logging and manufacturing processes are expected to conform to the environmental regulations of the country of origin.

Artwork by: Richard Morris and David Graham
Photo credits, pp.82: Top © David Gray/Reuters/Corbis, Bottom © Jessica Rinaldi/Reuters/Corbis
All additional photography by Sam Bailey
Typeset by Fakenham Photosetting Limited, Fakenham, Norfolk
Printed in Great Britain for Hodder Arnold, an imprint of Hodder Education, a member of the Hodder Headline Group, 338 Euston Road, London NW1 3BH by CPI Bath.

CONTENTS

INTRODUCTION

The health and fitness industry is growing rapidly in the UK, alongside a tide of weight-related illness such as heart disease, diabetes and back pain caused by inactivity and poor nutrition. We are also seeing a rise in the popularity of personal trainers to help people remain healthy and improve their body shape, and many of the large health club chains now offer personal training to their members. The number of people seeing personal training as a potential career is increasing. This book is aimed at personal trainers looking to start out or advance their skills in order to be successful in this competitive new field.

As a personal trainer in the UK you will be able to charge fees of anything between £15 and £100 per hour. This may sound like a lot of money and the one thing that will make your fee truly justifiable is *results*. Your clients will expect sufficient guidance and motivation to achieve their goals. A personal trainer has to deliver exercise sessions of a quality far and above that normally offered within any health club or gym.

At any one time you may have on your books clients with goals that vary widely, from improved posture, reduction of chronic pain, improved sport performance, weight loss, toning, to improved health and fitness. To deal effectively with these you must have an in-depth understanding of a broad range of topics and disciplines. You must be able to design effective programmes, provide guidance with regard to diet, help reduce chronic pain such as backache and, most importantly, be able to motivate your clients sufficiently to make them come back.

This book combines the underpinning theory and the practical application of topics such as *functional exercise* and *sport-specific training*. We provide insight into key issues involved in personal training such as *core stability* and *Swiss ball exercise*. We also provide core skills that a trainer should have at their disposal, such as *assisted/partner stretching* and *nutritional analysis*, as well as scientifically validated motivation tools to ensure you keep your clients on track.

A 'good' personal trainer will always know why they are asking the client to do what they are doing. They will have scientifically supported reasons for prescribing their exercises and will know the reasons behind everything that they say and ask. Unfortunately 'good' personal trainers are not always 'successful' ones. There are many trainers who are highly knowledgeable with regard to exercise science, but who simply lack the communication skills, sales technique and professionalism to find clients and make personal training a financially viable career. As well as providing advice on *sales and marketing* this text explains how to provide sessions that deliver far more than the usual gym induction or gym tours that are offered free of charge in most health clubs. This will enable you to bridge the gap in terms of quality of customer service, professionalism, skill and knowledge to warrant your fees.

By combining theoretical principles with practical applications this book is ideal for any instructor starting out, as well as for the established personal trainer looking to update their knowledge.

ANATOMY AND PHYSIOLOGY

THIS CHAPTER CONTAINS

- Anatomical and directional language
- The kinetic chain
- The nervous system
- The muscular system
- The skeletal system
- References and recommended reading

Before we start to cover aspects of exercise prescription, it is important to have a basic knowledge of how the body works. The better our anatomical and physiological knowledge, the better our exercise prescription will be. The following chapter provides a structural and functional insight into different aspects of the human body. Although the information is a brief overview, the areas covered are of particular importance to personal trainers.

ANATOMICAL AND DIRECTIONAL LANGUAGE

When we talk about a particular exercise it is common for people to have their own personal names for the exercises they do. It is important that exercise professionals have a common language and use common terminology so that communication is clear and concise. We should also have clear descriptive terms to describe what position the body is in or to pinpoint a particular part of the body. This is why it is important to use correct anatomical and directional language.

Whenever we talk about a part of the body, we generally talk as if the person is starting in the *anatomically correct position*. This is standing with head, eyes, toes and palms facing forwards.

Positional terminology

We generally refer to points in relation to a central midline or middle point. Here are some of the more common terms used to describe where a point is on the body.

- Proximal – Nearer the trunk
- Distal – Further away from the trunk
- Superior – Above (also known as cephalic)
- Inferior – Below (also known as caudal)
- Anterior – Towards the front of the body (also known as ventral)
- Posterior – Towards the rear of the body (also known as dorsal)
- Medial – Towards the midline of the body
- Lateral – Away from the midline of the body
- Superficial – Towards the surface of the body
- Deep – Being further from the surface of the body
- Internal – On the interior (inner)

- External – On the exterior (outer)
- Central – Towards the centre
- Peripheral – Further way from the centre
- Ipsilateral – The same side
- Contralateral – Opposite side
- Muscle origin – Proximal muscle attachment
- Muscle insertion – Distal muscle attachment
- Supine position – Lying facing upwards
- Prone position – Lying facing downwards
- Recumbent – Lying down
- Palmar surface – The anterior surface
- Plantar surface – The inferior surface.

Movement terminology

This is terminology used to describe certain movements at different joints of the body.

- Flexion – Bending or decreasing the angle between body parts
- Extension – Straightening or increasing the angle between body parts
- Abduction – Movement away from the midline
- Adduction – Movement towards the midline
- Rotation – Turning around an axis or pivot point
- Circumduction – Circular movement combining flexion, extension abduction and adduction
- Eversion – Moving sole of foot outwards
- Inversion – Moving sole of foot inwards
- Supination – Turning the palm to face anteriorly
- Pronation – Turning the palm to face posteriorly
- Internal rotation – Rotation towards the midline
- External rotation – Rotating away from the midline.

Planes of motion and axis of rotation

Anatomical descriptions can also be based on three imaginary planes or flat surfaces that pass through the body. These are called the sagittal, frontal and transverse planes. Imagine if we were looking straight onto a person in the anatomically

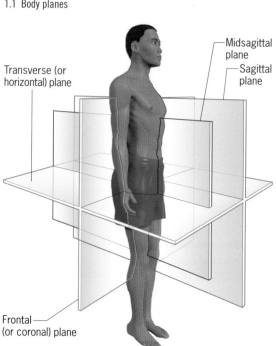

1.1 Body planes

Transverse (or horizontal) plane

Midsagittal plane

Sagittal plane

Frontal (or coronal) plane

correct position and cut through the body using these three different planes. The mid-sagittal plane would cut the body into two halves, left and right. The frontal plane separates us into front and back or anterior and posterior and the transverse plane runs parallel to the ground, separating us into superior and inferior (Figure 1.1).

Movement along these planes means that no body mass crosses this sheet. So, for example, movement along the sagittal plane only allows movement forwards and back (flexion and extension). Sagittal plane exercises might include crunches, chest presses, leg extensions or bicep curls. Exercises along a frontal plane would only allow movement side to side (abduction and adduction): a side-bend, for example. Exercises along the transverse plane would only allow turning or twisting (medial or lateral rotation).

An axis of rotation is simply a pivot point around which we move. There are three main axes:

the sagittal axis is like a rod going horizontally across our body from side to side, the frontal axis goes straight through our middle and the transverse axis passes straight through our body from head down through to the floor as if passing through our spine. Exercises can be classified according to which plane of motion and axis of rotation they involve.

The rest of this chapter looks at the anatomy and physiology of the body, providing brief descriptions about how each system works and relates to each other.

THE KINETIC CHAIN

The kinetic chain is a term used to describe all the nerves and muscles used to move bones and joints during movement (Figure 1.2).

kinetic chain: The sum total of the nervous action and muscular action to move bones and joints involved in any particular movement.

Kinetic refers to a force and the word *chain* suggests that all the different segments are linked or connected together. As a trainer it is essential that we know how these different segments of the chain work and how they interrelate and work together to produce human movement. The following information provides some basic information about each part of this kinetic chain.

1.3 Motor unit recruitment (M.U. = Motor Unit)

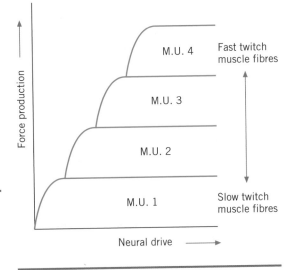

THE NERVOUS SYSTEM

The nervous system drives human movement. It ultimately determines when and how we move and the quality of these movements, as well as how much force our muscles can produce. The nervous system consists of both central (central nervous system, CNS) and peripheral (peripheral nervous system, PNS) branches. The CNS includes the brain and spinal cord and is effectively the decision-making part of the nervous system. The PNS is concerned with transmitting information between the CNS and other parts of the body.

1.2 The kinetic chain

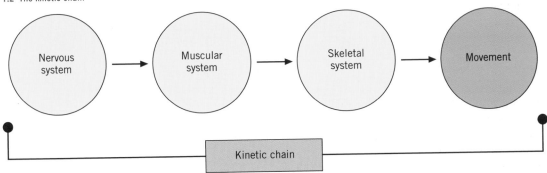

The afferent system (afferent means to 'carry toward') is composed of **sensory neurons** (or nerves) that detect changes in the environment and provide feedback to the brain. The efferent system (efferent means 'carrying from') sends information from the brain to different 'effector organs'. This includes **motor neurons** that transmit impulses from the brain to drive the muscles. **Interneurons** communicate information between the two.

KEY POINTS

Sensory neurons	Transmit information from the senses to the brain
Motor neurons	Drive muscles
Interneurons	Communicate between the two above.

The motor neuron and the muscle fibres it connects to are known as a **motor unit**. Each muscle fibre is connected to the brain by one motor neuron, but each motor neuron innervates many muscle fibres. The number of fibres that a single motor neuron innervates is dependent upon the level of control required in that muscle. A small muscle required for fine control will be controlled by far more motor neurons than a large muscle used for less accurate but more powerful movements.

The point at which the motor neuron connects to the muscle fibre is known as the **neuromuscular junction**. An electrical signal is sent through the motor nerve from the brain to activate the muscle fibres. This electrical signal is called an **action potential**. A single action potential causes a submaximal muscle action called a **twitch**. When action potentials are repeated rapidly, twitches combine to increase the level of force produced by the muscle.

The nervous system controls how much force a muscle produces. It achieves this by controlling the rate at which individual motor units are firing (rate coding) and by controlling how many motor units are involved in a muscle contraction (**recruitment**) (Enoka, 1988). Much of the improvements in strength in the initial stages of training for a novice will be improvements in the

1.4 Skeletal muscle structure

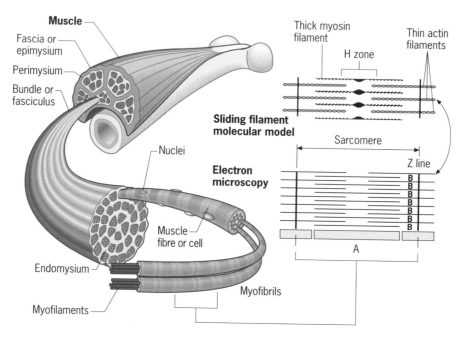

ability of their nervous system to increase rate coding and recruitment in muscles (Moritani and DeVries, 1979). The effort we put into muscle recruitment can be called **neural drive**. As neural drive increases, more muscle fibres are recruited and force production rises. Motor units or muscle fibres are generally recruited in accordance to their size – this is known as the **size principle** (Figure 1.3). Type I fibres are generally smaller, so are recruited first. They are said to have a low recruitment threshold; that is, the amount of effort needed to activate them is low. Type II fibres are larger, so are recruited second, when we require a more forceful movement (see below for details on muscle fibre type).

As we see in Chapter 7, the nervous system is the driving force behind movement, dictating how much muscle force we can produce, how we create movement and how accurate these movements are. Chapter 7 will also look at how we can train and improve the function of the nervous system with regard to producing movement.

THE MUSCULAR SYSTEM

Muscles comprise the largest group of tissues in the body, accounting for half of the body's weight (Sherwood, 1993). There are three main types of muscle: (1) skeletal muscle, which is known as **voluntary** because we have conscious control over its action; (2) cardiac muscle that forms the wall of the heart; and (3) smooth muscle that forms the walls of most vessels and organs. The latter two are both involuntary – they work without conscious effort. Under the control of the nervous system, voluntary skeletal muscles contract, creating forces that, if they are greater than external resistance, will produce movement in our skeletal system.

The structure of the skeletal system

Muscle is composed of many individual muscle fibres wrapped together in bundles (Figure 1.4). A type of connective tissue known as **fascia** covers these various bundles of fibres. The outer layer that covers the whole muscle is called the

epimysium. The epimysium runs into the **tendon** of the muscle that attaches and transmits force to the bone. Under the epimysium there are bundles of muscle fibres known as the fascicles, wrapped in fascia called the **perimysium**. Each of these muscle fibres is wrapped in a connective tissue called the **endomysium**. Each muscle fibre is made up of building blocks of muscle called **myofibrils**.

The myofibril contains specialized proteins that allow contraction of muscle called **myosin** and **actin**. Actin and myosin run parallel with each other. The thick myosin filaments have small heads called **cross-bridges**. Under an electrical stimulus from motor neurons these cross-bridges interact with, bind to and pull against the thin actin filaments. This pulls the actin and myosin filaments together to produce movement. This process is known as the **sliding filament theory** (Figure 1.4).

1.5 Muscle fibre arrangements

Gluteus medius

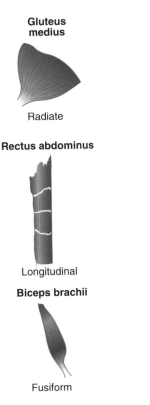

Radiate

Deltoid

Multipennate

Rectus abdominus

Longitudinal

Rectus femoris

Bipennate

Biceps brachii

Fusiform

Tibialis posterior

Unipennate

1.6 Major muscles of the lower leg, ankle and foot

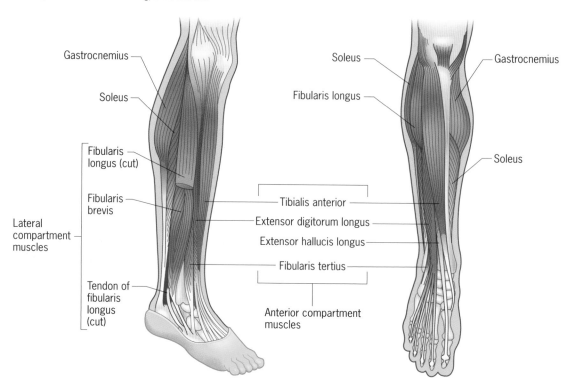

Gastrocnemius

Soleus

Fibularis longus (cut)

Fibularis brevis

Lateral compartment muscles

Tendon of fibularis longus (cut)

Soleus

Fibularis longus

Gastrocnemius

Soleus

Tibialis anterior

Extensor digitorum longus

Extensor hallucis longus

Fibularis tertius

Anterior compartment muscles

1.7 Major muscles of the trunk — vertebral column

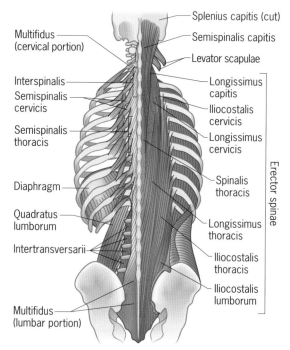

Multifidus (cervical portion)

Interspinalis

Semispinalis cervicis

Semispinalis thoracis

Diaphragm

Quadratus lumborum

Intertransversarii

Multifidus (lumbar portion)

Splenius capitis (cut)

Semispinalis capitis

Levator scapulae

Longissimus capitis

Iliocostalis cervicis

Longissimus cervicis

Spinalis thoracis

Longissimus thoracis

Iliocostalis thoracis

Iliocostalis lumborum

Erector spinae

1.8 Major muscles of the trunk — thoracic muscles

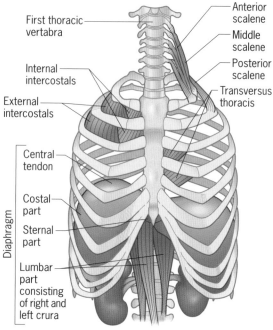

First thoracic vertebra

Internal intercostals

External intercostals

Central tendon

Costal part

Sternal part

Lumbar part consisting of right and left crura

Anterior scalene

Middle scalene

Posterior scalene

Transversus thoracis

Diaphragm

1.9 Major muscles of the trunk – abdominal wall muscles

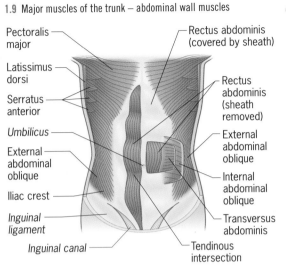

Pectoralis major

Latissimus dorsi

Serratus anterior

Umbilicus

External abdominal oblique

Iliac crest

Inguinal ligament

Inguinal canal

Rectus abdominis (covered by sheath)

Rectus abdominis (sheath removed)

External abdominal oblique

Internal abdominal oblique

Transversus abdominis

Tendinous intersection

Muscle fibre typing

Skeletal muscles are composed of many different fibres. Not all these fibres have the same characteristics. Fibres have been characterized based on the force they produce under a single action potential (see above). Some muscle fibres produce large amounts of force quickly and are quick to relax. These are known as *fast twitch fibres*. Some fibres produce lower levels of force, take more time to develop force and are slower to relax. These are known as *slow twitch fibres*.

Different fibres have different biochemical and physical properties. Muscle fibres have been categorized based on these different properties. Some have good resistance to fatigue, being able to produce low levels of force but over long periods of time. These muscle fibres are known as *type I*

1.10 Major muscles of the upper limb (a) anterior view (b) posterior view

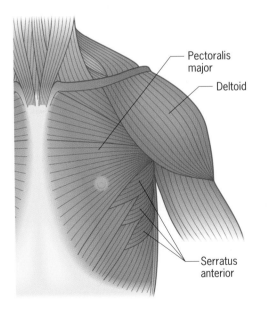

Pectoralis major

Deltoid

Serratus anterior

(a)

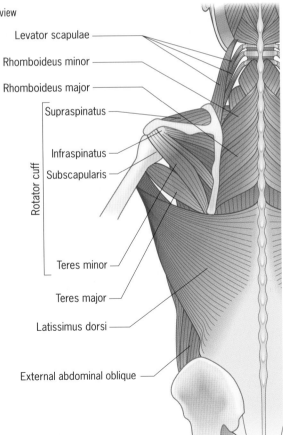

Levator scapulae

Rhomboideus minor

Rhomboideus major

Supraspinatus

Infraspinatus

Subscapularis

Rotator cuff

Teres minor

Teres major

Latissimus dorsi

External abdominal oblique

(b)

1.11 Major muscles of the upper arm

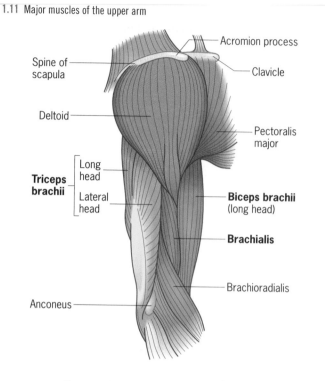

1.12 Major muscles of the lower arm and wrist (posterior, deep view)
(b) Anterior (superficial view)

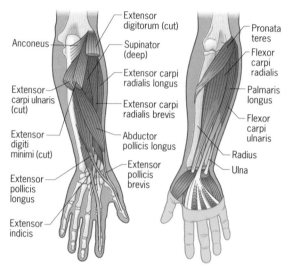

fibres. Others can develop force very quickly (fast twitch), and produce high levels of force due to their particular metabolic make-up. Unfortunately these fibres are often very quick to fatigue. They are called *type II* fibres. The type II fibres have been further broken down into type IIa and type IIb, with type IIa being almost a middle category combining properties from both extremes. Type I fibres are generally suited to performing more postural and stabilizing roles, whereas type II fibres are recruited when more explosive, powerful movements are required (Table 1.1).

Individuals who have muscles that are predominantly type I generally make better endurance athletes such as long-distance runners. Individuals with muscles that have a higher proportion of type II fibres are generally suited to more explosive activities such as sprinting, jumping or throwing. Training can alter our muscles' fibre types. There is little evidence to suggest that type II fibres will change into type I fibres with endurance training but there may be a gradual conversion of type IIb fibres to type IIa, increasing the aerobic or endurance capabilities of that muscle at the expense of speed and power (Kraemer *et al.*, 1995). There is no evidence for the conversion of type I fibres into type II with strength-to-power training (Jones and Round, 1995).

Table 1.1 Major characteristics of muscle fibre types

Characteristic	Type I	Type IIa	Type IIb
Twitch contraction time	Slow	Fast	Fast
Contraction speed	Slow	Fast	Fast
Force production	Low	Intermediate	High
Endurance	High	Intermediate	Low

Other factors determining muscle strength

Along with neural drive, other factors determining the amount of force our muscles can produce include the following:

- *Muscle cross-sectional area:* Larger muscles containing either more or larger muscle fibres are potentially able to generate more force than smaller muscles.
- *Length–tension relationships:* A muscle has a resting length at which its biomechanics are optimal and it is able to produce the largest amount of force. As a muscle's length becomes shorter or longer than this, the biomechanics become less efficient and the amount of force it can produce decreases.
- *Joint angle:* As we go through a movement the angle at the joint changes. This has the effect of changing lever arms (see below), changing muscle lengths and changing the muscles that have a mechanical advantage or that can take part in a movement. In this way the joint angle can have a large impact on the amount of force produced.
- *Load–velocity relationships:* It has been shown that as the velocity of contraction increases, the amount of force that can be produced by a muscle decreases. This is why highly explosive exercises such as Olympic lifting and jumping movements do not require great load.
- *Muscular fatigue:* There are three different types of fatigue; muscle fatigue, neuromuscular fatigue and central fatigue. Muscle fatigue may be due to the accumulation of waste products such as lactic acid (see Chapter 5) and depletion of energy stores, and is more likely to occur during endurance-based activities. Neuromuscular fatigue occurs when motor neurons cannot activate muscle fibres because they are unable to synthesize certain chemical transmitters quickly enough. This is more likely during faster, more powerful activities. Central or psychological fatigue occurs when the CNS can no longer activate motor neurons with which to drive muscles.
- *Muscle architecture:* Muscle fibres can be arranged in different patterns, and this affects the amount of force they can produce (Figure 1.5). Different muscles are usually adapted to perform specific functions. For example, fusiform muscles (e.g. biceps brachii) have parallel fibres, which produce very precise contractions, whereas in pennate muscles the fibres are arranged in a feather-like pattern, obliquely to the line of pull, making them very powerful (e.g. deltoid muscle). Fibres can even have a twist in them, giving them a lot of power in a very localized area (e.g. the latissimus dorsi). There are many different fibre arrangements affecting the properties and force production in muscle.

Muscle action

There are three basic types of muscle action during which a muscle generates force: concentric, eccentric and isometric. As muscles contract they do so against resistance. Although the term 'contract' suggests that the muscle shortens, this is not always the case.

- *Concentric muscle action:* The muscle overcomes the resistance against which it is applying force and as a result the muscle shortens.
- *Eccentric muscle action:* The resistance against which the muscle is working is greater than the muscular force produced and the muscle lengthens in a contracted state. This occurs when lowering a weight, for example. The mechanics of muscle action mean that it is possible to generate more force eccentrically than concentrically. This means that we can slowly lower a load greater than we can lift, which serves as a useful protective mechanism against excessive loads.
- *Isometric muscle action:* When the muscular force production is equivalent to the resistance, the result is a static contraction in which there is no movement.

1.13 Joint movements and muscle actions

Joint	Action	Plane	Muscles used	Diagram	Example
	Flexion	Median	Psoas Iliacus Rectus femoris		e.g. performing a 'tuck' jump in trampolining
	Extension	Median	Gluteus maximus Biceps femoris Semimembranosus Semitendinosus Gluteus medius (posterior)		e.g. preparation to kick a football
Hip	Abduction	Frontal	Gluteus medius Gluteus minimus Tensor fasciae latae		e.g. performing a cartwheel
	Adduction	Frontal	Adductor magnus Adductor brevis Adductor longus Pestineus Gracilis		e.g. the kick action in breast stroke
Hip	Medial rotation	Horizontal	Gluteus medius Gluteus minimus Tensor fasciae latae		e.g. rotational movement when throwing the discus
	Lateral rotation	Horizontal	Gluteus maximus Adductors		e.g. a side foot pass in football
	Flexion	Median	Semitendinosus Semimembranosus Biceps femoris Popliteus Gastrocnemius		e.g. preparing to kick a conversion in rugby
	Extension	Median	Rectus femoris Vastus medialis Vastus lateralis Tensor fasciae latae		e.g. rebounding in basketball
Knee	Medial rotation (when flexed)	Horizontal	Sartorius Semitendinosus		e.g. breast stroke 'kick' phase

1.13 continued

Joint	Action	Plane	Muscles used	Diagram	Example
	Lateral rotation (when flexed)	Horizontal	Tensor fasciae latae Biceps femoris		e.g. breast stroke recovery
	Dorsi flexion	Median	Tibialis anterior Extensor digitorum longus Peroneus tertius		e.g. landing from a lay up in basketball
Ankle	Plantar flexion	Median	Gastrocnemius Soleus Peroneus longus Peroneus brevis Tibialis posterior Flexor digitorum longus	Dorsiflexion Plantar flexion	e.g. pointing toes when performing a handstand
	Inversion	Frontal	Tibialis anterior Tibialis posterior Gastrocnemius Soleus	Eversion Inversion	e.g. line kicking in rugby (kicking a ball with outside of the foot)
	Eversion	Frontal	Peroneus longus Peroneus brevis		e.g. kick phase in breast stroke
	Flexion	Median	Anterior deltoid Pectoralis major Coracobrachialis	Extension Flexion	e.g. blocking of the net in volleyball
	Extension	Median	Posterior deltoid Latissimus dorsi Teres major		e.g. butterfly arm pull
	Adduction	Frontal	Latissimus dorsi Pectoralis major Teres major Teres minor	Abduction Adduction	e.g. landing phase of a straddle jump in trampolining
Shoulder	Abduction	Frontal	Medial deltoid Supraspinatus		e.g. straddle jump in trampolining
	Horizontal abduction	Horizontal	Posterior deltoid Trapezius Rhomboids Latissimus dorsi		e.g. preparing phase of throwing the discus

1.13 continued

Joint	Action	Plane	Muscles used	Diagram	Example
	Horizontal adduction	Horizontal	Pectoralis Major anterior deltoid		e.g. execution phase of throwing the javelin
	Medial rotation	Horizontal	Subscapularis		e.g. butterfly armpull
	Lateral rotation	Horizontal	Infraspinatus Teres minor		e.g. preparing for a forehand drive in tennis
	Flexion	Median	Biceps brachii Brachialis Brachioradialis		e.g. preparation for a set shot in basketball
Elbow	Extension	Median	Triceps		e.g. execution of a set short in basketball
Radio-ulnar	Pronation	Horizontal	Pronator teres Pronator quadratus Brachioradialis		e.g. putting top spin on a tennis ball
	Supination	Horizontal	Biceps trachii Supinator		e.g. recovery phase of the arms in breast stroke
Wrist	Flexion	Median	Wrist flexors		e.g. wrist snap in basketball shot
	Extension	Median	Wrist extensors		e.g. initial grip of a shot against neck
	Flexion	Median	Rectus abdominus Internal obliques External obliques		e.g. crouching at start of a swimming dive
	Extension	Median	Erector spinae Iliocostalis spinalis		e.g. a backflip in gymnastics
Movement of the trunk	Lateral flexion	Frontal	Internal oblique Rectus abdominis Erector spinae Quadratus laborum		e.g. a cartwheel

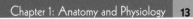

1.13 continued

Joint	Action	Plane	Muscles used	Diagram	Example
	Rotation	Horizontal	External oblique Rectus abdominis Erector spinae		e.g. follow through on a tennis serve
Move-ment of the scapulae	Elevation	Frontal	Levator sapulae Trapezius Rhomboids		e.g. recovery phase of butterfly armpull
	Depression	Frontal	Trapezius (lower) Pectoralis minor Serratus anterior (lower)		e.g. thrusting off a horse when performing a handspring
Move-ment of the scapulae	Protraction	Frontal	Serratus anterior		e.g. recovery phase in breast stroke
	Retraction	Frontal	Rhomboids Trapezius		e.g. pull phase in breast stroke
	Upward rotation	Frontal	Trapezius (upper) Serratus anterior		e.g. recovery phase in front-crawl
	Downward rotation	Frontal	Rhomboids Levator scapulae		e.g. front-crawl arm pull

1.14 Superficial muscles of the human body (a) anterior view (b) posterior view

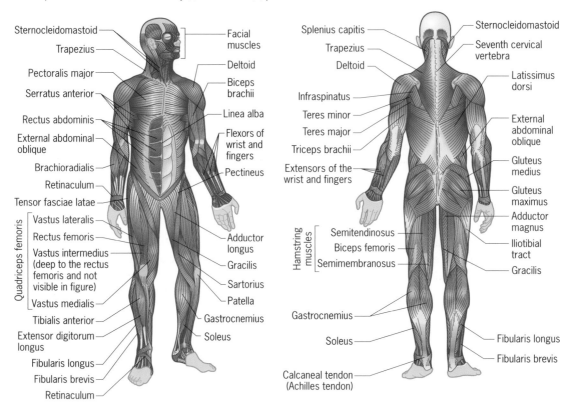

Ligaments

Ligaments attach bone to bone, providing static stability in order to prevent excessive joint range of motion that may lead to damage and injury. Ligaments are mainly made up of **collagen**, which is a substance with great tensile strength (i.e. it will resist large amounts of tension or pull). Ligaments also contain **elastin**, which provides some elasticity, enabling them to withstand bending and twisting movements. Because ligaments have a poor blood supply they often take a long time to heal and recover from injury.

Muscle actions: origins and insertions

Before prescribing any exercise regime it is important to know the movements available at each joint and what muscles create these movements. To understand truly how muscles are working we also have to know where individual muscles attach so that we can appreciate their lines of pull and their influence on different joints and bones of the body. Figure 1.13 shows which major muscles act at which joints and the main movements they perform.

It is also important to appreciate that the kinetic chain relies on the ability of the cardiovascular system to provide it with fuel for movement and to remove the waste products of movement (lactic acid, carbon dioxide and heat.) Without a constant supply of oxygen and sugar to the brain, damage occurs within minutes. If the oxygen supply is cut, brain damage occurs within 4–5 minutes and if the glucose supply is cut, it occurs within 10 minutes. This explains why we quickly suffer deficits in mental performance if blood-sugar levels fall. A more detailed description of components of the cardiovascular system is contained in Chapter 5.

THE SKELETAL SYSTEM

The skeleton of an adult is made up of an average of 206 bones and is, in effect, the framework for our bodies, determining our size and shape. The skeleton is divided into two clear parts with very different functions. The axial (central) skeleton includes the cranium, the spinal column and the rib cage. Its primary function is the protection of major organs. The appendicular skeleton includes the limbs, the pelvis and shoulder girdle. Its primary function is to enable movement.

The bones of the skeleton can be classified based on their shape.

Classification of bones

There are four major categories of bone:

1. *Long:* These have a long shaft with widened ends. Examples include the humerus and femur.
2. *Short:* These are cube-shaped. Examples are the carpals of the hand and the tarsals of the feet.
3. *Flat:* These are thin and designed to protect. Examples are the scapula and patella.
4. *Irregular:* These are unique in shape and function, for example the vertebrae.

Biomechanics of the skeleton

The appendicular skeleton aids movement by providing a system of levers to enhance the force produced by muscles in order to create movement. A lever is a rigid structure capable of moving

1.15 The skeletal system functioning as levers

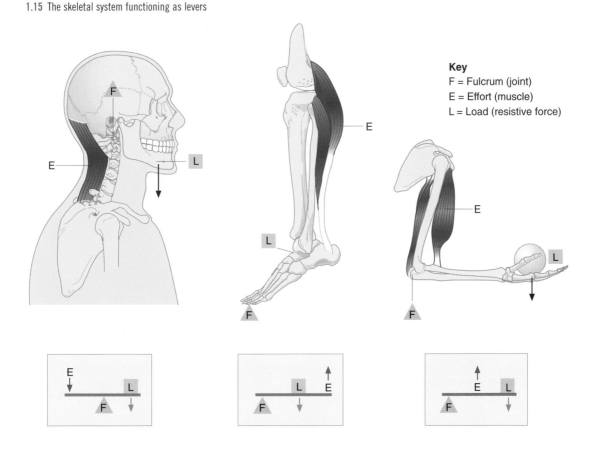

Key
F = Fulcrum (joint)
E = Effort (muscle)
L = Load (resistive force)

around a pivot point, known as a fulcrum (Sherwood, 1993). Bones function as levers, the joints as fulcrums. Muscles produce force against these levers. Due to the mechanical advantage provided by levers we can produce movement even against large external forces (Figure 1.15).

Joints

Junctions between bones are called joints (Baechle and Earle, 2000) and there are over 300 joints in the human body. There are different types: fibrous joints (e.g. sutures of the skull) that allow virtually no movement, cartilaginous joints (e.g. intervertebral discs) that allow limited movement, and synovial joints (e.g. elbow and knee) that are designed to allow considerable movement.

The most important joints in exercise training are the synovial joints. These have three distinguishing features: (1) a *joint cavity* or space within the joint, (2) *articular cartilage* that allows smooth movement and minimizes friction, and (3) a fluid-filled *articular capsule* that encloses the joint. The fluid is called *synovial fluid* and has an important function in lubricating the joint.

1.16 Types of synovial joints

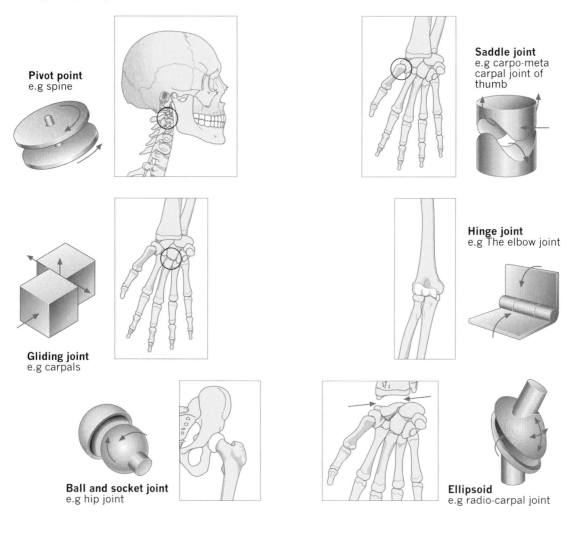

Pivot point
e.g spine

Saddle joint
e.g carpo-meta
carpal joint of
thumb

Gliding joint
e.g carpals

Hinge joint
e.g The elbow joint

Ball and socket joint
e.g hip joint

Ellipsoid
e.g radio-carpal joint

Ligaments and additional cartilage are also usually present in these joints to provide additional support.

Synovial joints can be classed as either *uniaxial*, allowing rotation in one direction such as the elbow, *biaxial*, allowing movement in two directions such as the ankle and wrist, or *multiaxial*, allowing movement in three directions. These tend to be called ball and socket joints and include the shoulder and the hip.

REFERENCES AND RECOMMENDED READING

1. Baechle, T.R. and Earle, R.W. (eds) (2000) *Essentials of Strength Training and Conditioning*, 2nd edn. National Strength and Conditioning Association. Champaign, IL: Human Kinetics.
2. Enoka, R.M. (1988) *Neuromechanical Basis of Kinesiology*. Champaign, IL: Human Kinetics.
3. Jones, D.A. and Round, J.M. (1995) *Skeletal Muscle in Health and Disease*. Manchester: Manchester University Press.
4. Kraemer, W.J., Patton, J., Gordon, S.E., Harman, E.A., Deschenes, M.R., Reynolds, K., Newton, R.U., Triplett, N.T. and Dziados, J.E. (1995) Compatibility of high intensity strength and endurance training on hormonal and skeletal muscle adaptations. *Journal of Applied Physiology* 78:976–989.
5. Moritani, T. and DeVries, H.A. (1979) Neural factors versus hypertrophy in the time course of muscle strength gain. *American Journal of Physical Medicine* 58:115–130.
6. Sherwood, L. (1993) *Human Physiology; From Cells to Systems*, 2nd edn. Minneapolis/St Paul: West Publishing Company.

2

EXERCISE PRESCRIPTION AND PROGRAMME DESIGN

THIS CHAPTER CONTAINS

- Fundamental training principles
- Acute exercise variables
- Structuring an exercise session

- Classification of exercises
- References and recommended reading

It is vital that, as instructors and personal trainers, we understand the fundamental principles underpinning exercise prescription and programme design. Without this foundation of knowledge we cannot progress with confidence into more advanced concepts and ideas. Within this chapter we explain these principles and how they influence the design of a client's programme, the structure of a workout and the classification of different exercises.

FUNDAMENTAL TRAINING PRINCIPLES

There are five fundamental training principles: *specificity, individualization, overload, progression* and *variation*. Adherence to these principles is vital if the client is to experience ongoing results and long-term success. These principles also form the basis of more advanced exercise concepts.

Principle of specificity

The principle of specificity states that the improvements and adaptations we make as a result of training are *specific* to the types of training that we perform. When talking about specificity we often refer to the '*SAID principle*', which states that we experience *specific adaptation to imposed demands*. In simple terms this means that we get good at what we do. When we perform resistance exercises, for example, the improvements in our strength will be specific to the particular muscles we use, the length and angles of the joints at which we work, and the speed at which we move. This has massive implications if we want to train for a particular task because our training should look as much like the task as possible.

Carryover is a term we can use to describe how our training leads to improvements in other tasks. Training on a bike, for example, will improve cycle times but will carry over less to our running performance. If we train for long distances it will improve our stamina but we will make little progress in speed. In fact, speed and agility might even drop as a result of endurance training. It is important to consider carefully the type of training we expose our clients to. We have to ask ourselves whether we should be asking a footballer to do long-distance runs during their competitive season when we want them to be fast and explosive.

The principle of specificity is very important when we talk about *functional training* (see Chapter 7).

Principle of individualization

As a result of our different genetic predispositions and hormone levels everyone reacts differently to exercise. For example, some clients will be **high responders** to exercise and will react very well to training. Other clients may be **low responders** who need to work a lot harder to achieve results. Clients will also respond differently to different types of training. We can prescribe certain exercise variables (sets, repetitions, weight) to achieve specific results (conditioning, hypertrophy, strength) but we must be aware that one size does not fit all. Although these recommendations are set because they apply to the majority of people, not everyone adheres to these guidelines. In essence, what works for one person may not work for the next.

We must also appreciate that because of age, medical history, posture, prior training, current fitness and so on, what is appropriate for one person might not be appropriate for the next. Before training a client, an in-depth **consultation** should form the basis of the first session. From there we can determine the client's training experience, how well they have responded to exercise in the past and what forms of exercise have been most effective for them. The more information you find out about them the better your exercise prescription will be and the more success your client will experience.

It is clear that no two exercise programmes will be the same.

Principle of overload

To stimulate some sort of training adaptation we have to expose our clients to *overload*. This means placing them under levels of physical stress beyond those that they are used to under normal circumstances. With correct levels of stress and recovery the body will adapt and grow stronger. This is known as *positive adaptation*. If the levels of exercise stress are too low we will fail to create an overload, the body will have insufficient drive to adapt and we will fail to create a training effect. On the other hand if levels of stress are too high or recovery is insufficient, adaptation will occur initially but eventually progress will slow or even stop and continued training may even cause damage, injury or illness. This is known as *negative adaptation*.

Optimal overload describes the maximal stress placed on the client for optimal training gains without increased risk of injury. This point will vary from person to person based on numerous factors, such as age, experience or genetics. During weight training the *point of failure* is the point at which form and technique deteriorate and the risk of injury increases. Optimal overload requires that we generally do not train our clients beyond this point. A key skill of the personal trainer is to assess and identify the point of optimal overload when a client is exercising.

Principle of progression

As we train we get stronger. *Progression* is the process of increasing the level of stress placed on the body in order to ensure an *overload* as the body adapts. If we do not make exercises more challenging as our clients get stronger, the difficulty of the exercise decreases to the point where there will be no overload and hence no training effect (Figures 2.1 and 2.2).

The classic example is the person going to the same aerobics class for years. When they started the class their body changed as it adapted to the new exercise, but after six weeks adaptation stopped and their body shape has not changed since. Exercise has to progress if we are to avoid *plateau*, the levelling-off of performance improvements.

Exercise can be progressed in a variety of ways, generally involving manipulation of *acute exercise variables*. These variables dictate how difficult an exercise is. They are discussed in more detail below. With respect to a resistance programme,

2.1 Plateau with no progression

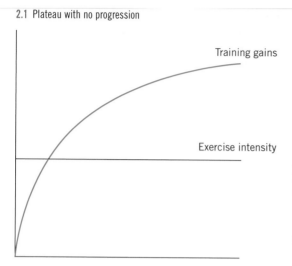

2.2 Continuing gains with progression

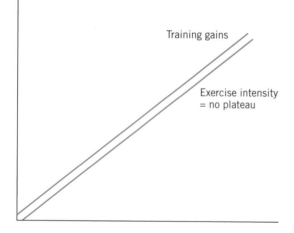

exercises are usually progressed by adding weight or repetitions, but this is extremely one-dimensional. Alternative methods of progressing exercise will be discussed below.

Principle of variation

While we may increase exercise difficulty in order to maintain overload, we see that the body fails to respond to a particular training stimulus after approximately 6–8 weeks. After this point, if we keep increasing the weight we try to lift, for

example, eventually the exercise will get too hard and we will inevitably pass the point of optimal overload, increasing our likelihood of injury. To avoid this point we have to alter the exercises we give to the client in order to challenge the body in different ways.

Periodization is the practice of systematically cycling acute exercise variables in order to fulfil the principle of variation, prevent performance plateau and avoid over-training. During periodized programmes we plan for progression and rest to ensure overload with sufficient recovery (see Chapter 4).

Adherence to all these principles is essential for effective programme design.

ACUTE EXERCISE VARIABLES

Acute exercise variables are the different ways we can alter an exercise to make it more or less challenging. When we looked at the principle of overload we talked about an appropriate amount of training stress. Another word to describe training stress is *intensity*. *Training intensity* describes how hard the person is working and is determined by a combination of acute exercise variables. *Load (weight)*, *sets* and *repetitions (reps)* are the most familiar acute exercise variables that most people tend to use to progress an exercise programme. As they get stronger they add more weight or perform more repetitions.

- *Load:* The resistance or weight used.
- *Number of sets:* A set is a group of consecutive repetitions.
- *Number of repetitions:* A repetition is one complete movement of an exercise.

The number of reps tends to be inversely proportional to load and sets. This means that if the number of reps is increased then the load and the number of sets tend to be decreased. The *total training volume* describes the total amount of weight lifted during a workout (reps times weight lifted) or the total distance travelled during a cardiovascular workout.

Although these are the most commonly known exercise variables they are far from being the only ones. *Rest, tempo, range of motion* and *neural demand* are alternative exercise variables that can be manipulated to alter the intensity of an exercise.

Rest

This is the time the client is given between sets to recover. The shorter the rest, the greater the intensity of the following set. Full recovery of short-term energy stores can require 3–5 minutes (Harris *et al.*, 1976).

Tempo and contraction velocity

The slower our muscles contract, the longer they have to work for or the more work they have to perform. The total time in which muscles have to produce force during a repetition is described as the *time under tension*. The greater the time under tension, the greater the exercise intensity. Try lifting a weight, then lift it twice as slowly and feel how much harder this is.

When performing a repetition of an exercise, each phase is characterized by a different type of muscular work. During the squat, for example, we have to lower, then hold, and then lift the weight. The three types of muscular contraction employed are:

- *Eccentric:* The muscle produces force whilst lengthening or whilst lowering a weight.
- *Isometric:* The muscle produces force whilst staying at the same length or holding a weight.
- *Concentric:* The muscle produces force whilst shortening or whilst lifting a weight.

All three of the phases of movement combine to constitute a full *muscle action spectrum*. When we are writing an exercise programme we can express the time in seconds spent in each one of the phases using three numbers; for example, 2/2/1 (= 2 seconds eccentric lowering, 2 seconds isometric hold and 1 second concentric lift).

Time under tension is frequently the least well-controlled acute exercise variable when people

train. For example, for a set in which we want to stimulate muscle growth (hypertrophy) we should have a time under tension of approximately 60–90 seconds. Next time you or a colleague is training, time how long your set lasts and how close you are to 90 seconds of work. You will probably find most people fall short because their time under tension for each repetition is not long enough.

Range of motion (ROM)

Range of motion is how far we move during an exercise or the *sum total of the angular movement* around a joint. There are different types of ROM:

- *Active range of motion (AROM):* This is the sum total of angular movement in which muscles are actually working (full ROM minus PROM).
- *Passive range of motion (PROM):* This is ROM in which there is little muscular work being performed. Times of PROM may be described as rest points.
- *Sticking points:* These are points within the AROM in which the person is at a mechanical disadvantage and the muscular work required to produce movement is greater.
- *Partial range of motion:* This is when ROM is limited to alter the intensity of the exercise.

ROM can be manipulated to increase or decrease intensity by removing PROM or by increasing overall ROM.

Neural demand or complexity

The neural demand is the degree of skill and control that is required to perform an exercise. A more complex exercise is said to have higher neural demand (this is different from neural *drive*, which is how hard we have to work our muscles; see Chapter 7). The term 'neural' relates to the nervous system. There are a number of ways in which the neural demand and complexity of an exercise programme can be increased.

- *Decreasing stability:* By making a person less

stable we increase the skill it takes to perform the exercise and the amount that muscles have to work to stabilize the body. This can be achieved by:

(a) using unsupported free weights instead of supported resistance machines
(b) reducing base of support (the area in contact with the ground) by bringing the feet together or balancing on one leg rather than two if standing
(c) adding unpredictable movement, by having the client sit or stand on an unstable surface, such as a Swiss ball or wobble board).

■ *Increasing the number of planes of motion* (see below for details about planes of motion): By adding sideways movement or rotation to an exercise such as a squat or lunge we increase neural complexity.

■ *Muscle integration:* Using the lower body muscles in conjunction with upper body muscles or vice versa increases the neural challenge of the exercise. For example, a seated shoulder press has less neural demand than a standing shoulder press.

■ *Alternating movement:* Most upper body exercises are classically performed using both arms at the same time (e.g. lateral raise, dumbbell press, bent over row). The neural challenge of the exercise can be increased by moving the arms one at a time (e.g. alternating dumbbell press).

■ *Unilateral loading:* Having a weight in one hand rather than two increases the load on the muscles of the core (those muscles around the middle of the body) as they work to keep good form and posture. This increases the neural complexity of the exercise (e.g. one arm dumbbell shoulder press).

■ *Combining movements:* By combining movements we greatly increase the neural challenge of an exercise. For example, progressing from a squat into a squat with dumbbell shoulder press greatly increases the neural demand of the exercise.

■ *Decreasing feedback:* Reducing the feedback to the client about performance makes the exercise more challenging. Feedback usually comes visually from the use of a mirror or by the personal trainer telling the client what he or she is doing right or wrong. Reducing this feedback increases the challenge of the exercise (e.g. you could tell the client to close one or both eyes, tilt the head, not use a mirror, or you, the personal trainer, could provide less guidance).

■ *Novelty:* Providing new and unlearned movements will make exercises far harder for the client. Simply by going from a familiar lat raise to an unfamiliar shoulder press will increase neural demand whilst still challenging similar muscles.

Adding neural demand can be achieved by using one or more of these methods together. As an example, take a squat and see how many different ways you can change the exercise to add neural demand (e.g. squat with rotation, one-leg squat, squat press, one-leg squat with bicep curl etc.). This type of progression can open up a new world of exercises for you and your client to use. Chapter 7 will go into further depth describing why this type of progression can be so effective.

Training frequency:

Increasing the frequency of exercise and reducing recovery time can make exercise sessions more challenging. It is during periods of recovery that we get stronger and it takes anywhere from 24 to 72 hours for a muscle to recover fully from a weights session, depending on the intensity and duration of the session and the quality of recovery. This means that we can optimally train a muscle group 2–3 times per week. Stretching, cold treatment, massage, correct rehydration and refuelling strategies can all enhance recovery. The conditioning of the client as well as factors such as genetics, age and the types of exercises performed will dictate the levels of recovery a client will need after a workout. If their frequency of training increases they may have to use a *split routine* to ensure sufficient recovery.

CASE STUDY: INCREASING NEURAL DEMAND

On starting a client on a set of squats it was soon clear that the exercise was not challenging enough and the intensity the client was working at was too low. We needed to progress the exercise without having to add additional load or perform more repetitions. I used the following methods to increase neural demand in an attempt to increase significantly the intensity at which the client was working.

During the set:
- I stopped providing feedback about technique and assessed form to ensure that technique remained high.
- I slowed the client's tempo down, increasing the eccentric phase by going from a 2–1–2 to a 4–1–2 tempo.
- I then asked the client to perform partial range of motion reps by not standing all the way up, indicating with my hand the range of motion I wanted.

During the next set, I wanted to increase the challenge of the exercise further, so:
- I got the client to squat on an unstable base (e.g. wobble board).
- I instructed the client to perform a shoulder press at the top of the squat.
- Then to rotate at the bottom of the squat.

Next session:
- I added variation by reducing the client's base of support, instructing him to perform a one leg partial squat (bending the leg to 20 degrees).
- I progressed this into a full squat (bending the leg to 90 degrees).

The exercise was progressed by increasing the neural demand and skill level of the client's movements until he felt significant challenge. I was careful to remember that if at any point form and technique deteriorated or stability or balance was lost, I would stop progressing and even regress the exercise.

Exercise prescription essentially involves manipulation of these exercise variables. The exercise variables we prescribe will dictate the type of training adaptations that our client experiences. Specific acute exercise variable prescription for alternative training adaptations is described in greater depth in Chapter 3.

STRUCTURING AN EXERCISE SESSION

An exercise session should be structured in order to minimize chances of injury and ensure that a client can perform optimally with maximal results. While there will be variations from client to client, the following general guidelines are recommended when designing an exercise session.

Warm-up and cool-down

A warm-up and cool-down should be included in any exercise session to prevent injury, enhance performance and promote recovery. A **warm-up** provides a smooth transition from resting state to a state of athletic readiness. The benefits of warm-up include:

- An increase in body temperature:
  - decreases the risk of muscular injury by increasing muscle extensibility (the degree of stretch in a muscle before injury occurs) and
  - increases the speed of muscular contraction.
- A gradual increase in stress on the cardiorespiratory system:
  - gradually increases heart rate and breathing rate
  - gradually increases blood flow to active muscles
  - gradually increases our oxygen exchange capacity (the ability of our lungs to take in oxygen for the body) and
  - reduces **oxygen debt**, which is the lag in

oxygen uptake we experience upon starting exercise.

- *An increased neural readiness:* This increases the speed and force with which we can activate and relax muscles by making the nervous system work more effectively.
- *Mobilization of joints:* This increases the *synovial fluid,* a lubricating fluid released around synovial joints, allowing fluidity of movement and increased range of motion.
- *Increased mental readiness for exercise:* Goals can be reviewed and attention focused on key elements to be achieved in the workout.

A general warm-up is a cardiovascular exercise meant to raise body temperature (e.g. walking, jogging, cycling). As well as a general warm-up, we should also include a *specific warm-up* that closely mimics the movements used in the main part of the programme. This prepares the neural system, including nervous pathways from the brain to the muscles, for the work to be performed and mobilizes muscles and joints in a way specific to the movements to be used in the main workout (see active and dynamic stretches in Chapter 11). A specific warm-up may involve a set of repetitions at a very low weight or even no weight at all. By neglecting a warm-up we increase our chances of injury and predispose ourselves to premature fatigue.

The *cool-down* provides a steady transition from a working state back to a rest. The cool-down should consist of a *general cool-down* involving a cardiovascular element, slowly decreasing in intensity, and a *post-stretch* designed to regain any range of motion lost throughout the workout due to contraction of muscles.

The benefits of cool-down include:

- Improved removal of waste products produced as a result of the workout (e.g. lactic acid).
- Improved or sustained flexibility depending on the time spent in each stretch.
- Possible reduction in *delayed onset muscular soreness* or DOMS (the muscle soreness typically felt 24–48 hours following a workout).
- Prevention of *blood pooling* (the accumulation of blood in the legs following exercise). Blood

pooling can cause a fall in blood pressure and dizziness.

The rest of the workout will typically consist of cardiovascular work and resistance training. The relative weighting of each will be determined by the goals of the client.

Exercise sequencing

When designing a resistance-training programme the following principles of exercise sequencing are generally applied.

- *Large to small:* Larger muscles should generally be trained first and to a larger degree (with increased volume) than smaller muscles.
- *High skill to low skill:* High-skill exercises should be performed first when concentration and skill levels are highest. High-skill exercises performed under conditions of fatigue increase the likelihood of injury.
- *Compound to isolation:* Exercises involving complex coordination of movement at more than one joint, i.e. *compound exercises* (e.g. squat), should be performed prior to exercises that isolate only one joint, i.e. *isolation exercises* (e.g. leg extension). Isolation exercises performed first will cause fatigue in muscles that may potentially be relied upon in compound exercises, predisposing your client to injury.
- *Prioritize:* Movements and exercises of increased importance or muscles in which we want the most improvement should be performed first, when mental energy is highest and fatigue is low, so that we achieve greatest intensity.
- *High danger to low danger:* Exercises with a high risk of injury should be performed first when energy and concentration are at their highest and fatigue is low. For example, it could be argued that a one-rep max squat should be performed before a one-leg squat even though we might consider a one-leg squat to be of higher skill level, because of the greater level of danger involved.
- *Stabilizing or core muscles last:* Muscles that stabilize joints, the muscles of the core in

particular, should be isolated only at the end of the workout. These muscles will probably be required throughout the entire workout. If they are *pre-fatigued* they are less able to stabilize joints, thereby increasing the likelihood of injury.

- *Muscle balance:* If a particular muscle (*agonist*) is stressed during an exercise, its opposite muscle (*antagonist*), usually found on the other side of the same joint, should also be stressed to produce a similar increase in functional capacity (strength, endurance etc.). Imbalance in functional capacity and flexibility in opposing muscle groups across a joint can cause changes in posture and postural stress (see Chapter 9 for more details).

---

agonist: The main force-producing muscle of a movement at a joint.

---

antagonist: The opposing muscle group usually found on the opposite side of the joint (e.g. the quads and hamstrings).

Although we cannot fulfil all these principles all of the time the key element is to try to ensure the safety of your client and maximize the effectiveness of your programme.

Training systems

There are many ways in which a resistance programme can be organized and structured. This list describes just some of them:

- *Single set system:*
  – Performing a single set of a number of exercises
  – Recommended for beginners.
- *Multiple set system:* Performing multiple sets of one or more exercises.
- *Circuit system:* Performing various exercises in rotation, either single sets of resistance exercises or alternating with cardio (resistance – cardio – resistance – cardio etc.).
- *Peripheral heart action (vascular shunt):* Circuit training alternating between upper and

lower body to place increased stress on the cardiovascular system as blood has to be shunted from lower to upper body to facilitate muscular work. Only to be performed with well-conditioned clients and contraindicated for those with heart problems. Can cause blood pooling; see below.

- *Pyramid system:* Involves a stepped system in which with each set weight is either increased and reps decreased (*ascending pyramid*) or weight is decreased and reps increased (*descending pyramid*), or one then the other (*triangular system*). For example, 12–15 reps then 8–12 reps then 4–6 reps and back down with a weight to achieve the point of failure by the end of each set. This ensures that all the different properties (strength and endurance) of the muscle are challenged.
- *Supersets:* One set composed of two different exercises; can include, for example:
  – *Agonist–antagonist* to cut down on workout time by reducing rest time; also known as push–pull (e.g. chest press and mid row).
  – *Agonist–agonist* to increase muscular fatigue in the same muscle (e.g. dumbbell chest press and dumbbell pec-fly).
  – *Pre-exhaust* in which an isolation exercise is performed prior to a compound exercise working the same muscle. Bodybuilders use this to help increase fatigue in a large muscle of the torso, the chest or back, for example (e.g. pec-fly into chest press).
  – *Stable–unstable:* a stable exercise followed immediately by an unstable, high-neural-demand exercise at reduced weight to continue to challenge stabilizing muscles.
  – *Strength–power:* a strength exercise followed immediately by a power exercise (see Chapter 8).
- *Active recovery:* This involves exercises performed during periods of rest. This may include other exercises, stretches, mobilization, balances, core work etc. Note that low-intensity cardiovascular work may facilitate recovery from high-intensity cardiovascular and resistance work by maintaining elevated levels of blood flow and venous return (blood flow

Table 2.1 Examples of split routines

	2-day split	3-day split	6-day split
Monday	Upper body	Chest/biceps	Chest
Tuesday	Lower body	Back/shoulders	Back
Wednesday	Rest	Legs/triceps	Shoulders
Thursday	Upper body	Rest	Biceps
Friday	Lower body	Chest/biceps	Legs/Triceps
Saturday	Rest	Back/shoulders	Legs/Triceps
Sunday	Rest	Legs/Triceps	Rest

back to the heart), which also aids removal of lactic acid from muscles. The optimal intensity of recovery exercise to promote blood lactic acid removal is approximately 30–40% of VO_2max (Dodd *et al.*, 1984).

■ *Split routine:* To allow optimal rest with increased volume of resistance training sessions, different muscle groups can be trained on different days of the week (Table 2.1).

Blood pooling

It is important to be wary of using vascular shunt – the practice of going straight from a lower body exercise to an exercise stressing muscles of the upper body. Blood supplied by the cardiovascular system is required for muscular work. Driving blood quickly from the lower body to the upper body can be an intense cardiovascular challenge. If the client is unconditioned and unused to this type of exercise they can experience a dramatic drop in blood pressure or loss of blood flow either to the stomach, causing them to feel sick, or to the head, causing them to feel dizzy and even pass out. Active recovery using a low-intensity cardiovascular exercise followed by mobilizing exercises in the upper body may prevent the blood pooling that causes these symptoms.

CLASSIFICATION OF EXERCISES

We can start to categorize the exercises that we prescribe in the following ways:

Compound and isolation

Compound exercises involve movement at more than one joint at the same time, involving more than one *prime mover. Isolation exercises* involve movements at only one joint and utilizing only one prime mover. Remember that we can isolate joints, the shoulder for example, but we cannot isolate muscles, as many muscles naturally work together whenever we move (see Muscle Synergy, Chapter 7).

---

the **prime mover** is the muscle primarily involved in producing force during an exercise, also known as the agonist.

Open and closed chain

An *open-chain* exercise is one in which we can overcome the resistance against which we are applying force (e.g. chest press, mid row, leg extension, leg curl, machine leg press in which the pad on which we push moves). A *closed chain* exercise is one in which we cannot overcome the resistance against which we are working and as a result the body moves away or towards it (e.g. pull-ups, squat, lunge). Although closed-chain exercises have classically been identified as being more functional, most movements in everyday life contain a complex interaction of both open- and closed-chain movements. For example, as we punch, we push against the floor (closed chain) and throw a fist (open chain). Even running can be classified as both open- and closed-chain. Our legs drive off the floor (closed chain) and our arms drive forwards and backwards (open chain).

Planes of motion

Movement occurs in three dimensions: forwards and back, side to side and twisting or turning.

Planes of motion and axis of rotation describe the different movements that are possible in our three-dimensional world. We can therefore classify exercises according to their dominant planes of motion: sagittal, frontal or transverse. A chest press is sagittal plane, side bend frontal plane and woodchop transverse plane. See Chapter 1 for more details on planes of motion.

CASE STUDY: TYPICAL WORKOUT

This is an example of a basic, very simple but time-efficient workout structured using the principles above and a 'cardio-resistance' circuit format.

1. General warm-up – 5 minutes treadmill, walking, building to a jog
2. Specific warm-up – Unweighted squat
3. Resistance lower body – Weighted squat and weighted dead-lift times 2 sets each
4. Cardiovascular – 1000m rowing
5. Active recovery – Mobilizing of the shoulder
6. Resistance upper body circuit – Mid row, bench press and lateral raise circuit, times 2
7. Cardiovascular – 5 minutes cross-trainer including 3 minutes gradually decreasing intensity for cool-down
8. Abdominal work – Crunch and dorsal raise
9. Post stretch

CHAPTER SUMMARY

You should now understand some of the fundamental rules underpinning your exercise programmes. These principles form the basis of how you will work with your clients and the exercises you will prescribe. You can see there are a variety of different ways to change how hard an exercise is even without altering sets, reps and load. You should also have a basic formula for structuring a client's workout, including general and specific warm-up, resistance work, cardiovascular exercise, cool-down and stretch. The following chapters will identify how to use these principles to get results for your clients and achieve their goals.

REFERENCES AND RECOMMENDED READING

1. American College of Sports Medicine (ACSM) (2001) *Resource Manual for Guidelines for Exercise Prescription*, 4th edn. Philadelphia: Lippincott Williams and Wilkins.
2. Baechle, T.R. and Earle, R.W. (eds) (2000) *Essentials of Strength Training and Conditioning*, 2nd edn. National Strength and Conditioning Association. Champaign, IL: Human Kinetics.
3. Dodd S., Powers, S.K., Callender, T. and Brooks, E. (1984) Blood lactate disappearance at various intensities of recovery exercise. *Journal of Applied Physiology* 57:1462–1465.
4. Harris, R.C., Edwards, R.H.T., Hultman, E., Nordesjo, L.O., Nylind, B. and Sahlin, K. (1976) The time course of phosphocreatine resynthesis during reovery of the quadriceps muscle in man. *Pflügers Archiv* 97:392–397.
5. Hernandez, J. and Salazar-Rojas, W. (2004) The effect of three lower-body training programs: a verification of the specificity principle. *Medicine and Science in Sports and Exercise* 36(5) Suppl:S353–S354.
6. Hultan, E. and Sjoholm, H. (1986) Biochemical causes of fatigue. In: Jones, N.J., McCartney, N. and McComas, A.J. (eds) *Human Muscle Power*. Champaign, IL: Human Kinetics.
7. Stone, J.S. and Stone, J.A. (2003) *Atlas of Skeletal Muscles*, 4th edn. New York: McGraw-Hill.

3

STRENGTH AND CONDITIONING TRAINING

THIS CHAPTER CONTAINS

- Muscular conditioning and muscular endurance
- Muscular hypertrophy
- Other factors influencing muscle mass

- Maximal strength
- Summary of acute exercise variables
- Examples of resistance training techniques
- References and recommended reading

In the previous chapter we looked at the basic principles underpinning programme design and identified some of the acute exercise variables which we can use to adapt our choice of exercises. As we alter acute exercise variables, such as sets, reps, tempo and rest, we change the demands placed on the body and therefore the specific adaptations that occur as a result of training. We can place the types of muscular adaptation experienced as a result of resistance training into five categories: muscular *conditioning*, *endurance*, *hypertrophy*, *strength* and *power*. In this chapter we look at how to prescribe exercise programmes to achieve the first four of these adaptations. We also look at some examples of resistance training techniques providing basic guidelines for their safe and effective execution. Power is looked at in further depth in Chapter 8.

In each of the following sections we break down what is meant by conditioning, hypertrophy and strength, and identify the acute exercise variables that are widely recommended to produce each one.

MUSCULAR CONDITIONING AND MUSCULAR ENDURANCE

Muscular conditioning is the process in which muscles, bones, cartilage and connective tissues (ligaments and tendons) are conditioned to be able to absorb and produce force. Without prior conditioning, sudden exposure to increased or repetitive loading can very easily result in injury. Shin splints are a classic example of over-exposure to running training without sufficient conditioning in the lower body. Conditioning training will increase the density of bone (Conroy *et al.*, 1992), increase the strength of connective tissue (ligaments and tendons) (Suominen and Heikkinen, 1975) and increase the blood supply to muscle through improved vascularization –increase in the number of veins, arteries and capillaries supplying muscle. The combination of these adaptations reduces the likelihood of injury. To allow connective tissue and bone to adapt, intensity and volume should generally start low and be increased gradually.

Acute exercise variables

- Volume is high (12–15 repetitions).
- Load is reduced to allow an increased number of repetitions.
- Tempo is slow (3–2–1 to 2–1–2).
- The use of a combination of increased reps and slow tempo increases time under tension, allowing connective tissue and bone to adapt without excessive increases in muscular strength.
- Rest is low to increase metabolic demand to improve muscular endurance and increase blood supply to muscle (approx. 45 seconds rest).
- There may be an emphasis on eccentric contraction (a controlled lowering of weight), improving the body's ability to absorb load and impact.

---

metabolic demand: the requirement for the body to supply muscle with oxygen via the cardiovascular system.

Muscular endurance is our ability to continue to produce force over an extended period of time. Imagine a tug of war in which you have to pull for a significant period of time – this is a classic example of a test of muscular endurance as well as strength. To train muscular endurance we have to sustain muscular work for long periods of time and limit our recovery.

Acute exercise variables

- Volume is high (15–20+ repetitions per set possible; more depending on the requirements of the client).
- Intensity is low.
- Time under tension is high.
- Rest periods are short.

Muscular conditioning should generally precede training of higher intensity and load to avoid injury (see Chapter 4).

MUSCULAR HYPERTROPHY

Building muscle is the goal of many individuals embarking on an exercise routine. Men generally ask to build muscle, often in the upper body for a better physique and in some instances to increase strength and gain weight to enhance sports performance.

From a physiological point of view it is generally accepted that muscles increase in size through a process known as *hypertrophy* (Goldberg *et al.*, 1975). This is an increase in the *size* of muscle fibres and is not to be confused with muscle *hyperplasia*, an increase in the *number* of muscle fibres. Muscular hypertrophy occurs when we work at high intensities, causing muscular fatigue and damage. It is this fatigue (reduction in energy stores such as ATP and glycogen, along with metabolic stress) and damage (microtrauma to individual muscle fibres) that stimulate the repair process that results in muscle growth (Jones and Round, 1995). Programmes designed to encourage hypertrophy have to maximize both load, to cause muscle damage, and volume, to stimulate muscular fatigue (Tesch and Larsson, 1982).

---

metabolic stress: levels of work exceeding the body's ability to supply muscle with oxygen via the cardiovascular system, causing build-up of waste materials such as lactic acid.

Muscle fibre type

An understanding of the composition of muscle helps our understanding of how to maximize hypertrophy. Muscles are composed of many individual fibres. Each of these fibres has different properties and muscles have been categorized based on these properties, the most common categorization being *types I* and *II* (see Chapter 1 for more details). Although all muscle fibres have the potential to undergo hypertrophy, type II fibres are more responsive to this type of training than type I and will hypertrophy to a greater extent (Hather *et al.*, 1991). Type II fibres are recruited at higher intensities. 8–12 repetitions, working to the point of failure is recommended for experienced exercisers. To stimulate muscle damage, the loads placed on the muscle should be very high. To allow this I recommend choosing exercises with lower *neural demand* (i.e. those exercises that are more complex and require higher skill and concentration) (see Chapter 2). This also ensures the safety of the client whilst lifting heavy loads.

Type I fibres also have the capacity to hypertrophy. As fatigue increases, type I fibres are stressed and they receive a stimulus to grow. This is one reason why increased fatigue is important to maximize muscle hypertrophy.

Muscular fatigue can be achieved by increasing the volume (number of sets and number of exercises), decreasing rest and increasing **time under tension** through slower tempos. Although some research demonstrates no significant benefit to doing more than three sets (Ostrowski *et al.*, 1997) some texts recommend as many as 12 or more sets per body part. Bodybuilders who try to optimize muscular hypertrophy perform numerous sets per body part with multiple exercises in order to maximise fatigue.

Acute exercise variables

- Intensity is high (8–12 reps with large load).
- Volume is increased through large numbers of sets (as many as 12 per body part).
- Rest is low (45–90 seconds).
- Time under tension is high through slow tempo (e.g. 3–1–2 or 2–1–2).
- Increased load is allowed through the use of stable exercises with low neural demand.

Increased intensity and volume cause great fatigue, meaning that we often have to split a client's workouts into different body parts to achieve sufficient rest and recovery. We should try to allow at least 2–3 days' recovery for a muscle working under these conditions of high intensity and high load. In Chapter 2 we gave some examples of split routines that can be used. Each individual will be different, so different splits should be experimented with to find the one that yields the best results.

OTHER FACTORS INFLUENCING MUSCLE MASS

There are many factors that influence our ability to put on muscle mass. These include the following.

Hormone levels

The higher a person's **testosterone** and **human growth hormone** (HGH) levels, the greater their potential for muscular growth. Women have lower levels of testosterone than men, which explains why it is harder for women to put on large quantities of muscle mass. Genetics are the main factor determining hormone levels, but testosterone and growth hormone levels can also be increased or decreased by environmental factors. For example, they have both been found to increase following intense exercise (Galbo, 1983).

We can enhance our clients' chances of building muscle by adapting our programme to increase the levels of testosterone and growth hormone circulating in their systems. Selecting exercises that require large amounts of muscle mass (compound exercises) and working at higher intensities with low levels of rest will maximize increases in testosterone following a workout (Galbo, 1983). Reducing **long steady distance** cardiovascular work, on the other hand, will optimize growth hormone levels, as low-intensity aerobic work can reduce the levels of this hormone in the system and hinder muscle development (Kraemer *et al.*, 1995).

Another factor that can be adjusted to optimize growth hormone levels is the diet. Clients should be encouraged to ensure a **positive energy balance** by eating sufficient quantities of carbohydrate and protein, especially before and after exercise (see Chapter 15 for other dietary guidelines for muscle gain).

Genetic predisposition

Some people are **responders** to exercise and others are **non-responders**, especially where weight training and muscular hypertrophy are concerned.

Genetics determine both the proportion of fast and slow twitch fibres an individual has and their hormones levels. This means that some people are genetically predisposed to respond more quickly to training than others and will find improving their muscle mass easy in comparison to non-responders.

Advanced techniques

Muscular damage and fatigue can be optimized using the following advanced training techniques.

- **Drop sets:** This involves reducing the load immediately after the point of failure so that more repetitions can be performed, thereby optimizing muscular fatigue.
- **Eccentric loading:** This involves giving the client a weight that they can lower with good technique but that is marginally too heavy for them to lift. The trainer can then help them through the lifting/concentric phase of each repetition. Muscle has a mechanical advantage when it lengthens under load during eccentric contraction, so the weight can be heavier than during normal repetitions. This allows us to put much more force through the muscle, enhancing muscle damage. Be aware that this type of eccentric loading increases delayed onset muscle soreness (DOMS), which is the soreness caused by muscle damage characteristically felt 24–48 hours after training. Make sure the client is aware of this prior to using this technique.
- **Forced reps:** This is when the trainer assists the client in lifting the weight after the point of failure, effectively reducing the load and allowing more repetitions to be completed. This increases the level of muscular fatigue the client achieves.

All of these techniques are highly advanced. They should not be performed by any inexperienced person and should not be overused even by an experienced athlete. There is an increased reliance on the client to ensure that their form and technique are satisfactory.

MAXIMAL STRENGTH

Developing maximal strength involves increasing **peak force production**, i.e. the most force an individual can produce in one effort or the most weight they can lift. As we have seen, muscles are made up of bundles of muscle fibres, each driven by nerves that connect to the brain. Muscular strength is based on how large these muscle fibres are (hypertrophy training should always precede strength training), how many muscle fibres we can recruit and how hard the muscles can be driven by the brain to produce force. Near-maximal intensities are required to train the nervous system to recruit as many muscle fibres as possible to produce as much force as possible. The neural components of maximal strength will be discussed in further detail in Chapter 7.

Acute exercise variables

- Intensities are extremely high (85–100 per cent) with very high loads.
- Number of repetitions therefore has to be low (1–6).
- Rest is high to allow complete recovery and near-maximal intensities in subsequent sets (complete recovery is thought to take about 3 minutes).
- Tempo is moderate to slow, to allow maximal force generation to occur (3–1–1 to 2–0–2).

Details of how to train for muscular power are contained in Chapter 8.

SUMMARY OF ACUTE EXERCISE VARIABLES

The acute exercise variables used to optimize endurance, conditioning, hypertrophy, strength and power are summarized in Table 3.1. The adaptations are ordered so as to represent an increasing level of intensity. As we see in Chapter 4, we generally move progressively through each of these types of training in order to receive most benefits and minimize risk of injury.

Table 3.1 Acute exercise variables summary

Adaptation	Endurance	Conditioning	Hypertrophy	Strength	Power
Reps	15–20	12–15	8–12	1–6	1–6
Sets per body part	1–3	1–3	2–4	3–4	3–6
Intensity (% of maximum effort)	50–70%	60–70%	70–85%	85–100%	85–100%
Rest	30–60 seconds	30–60 seconds	60–90 seconds	2–3 min	3–5 min
Tempo	Slow	Slow	Moderate	Moderate	As fast as possible

EXAMPLES OF RESISTANCE TRAINING TECHNIQUES

Every trainer has to know how to perform and teach a wide variety of exercise techniques. Here basic teaching points for the execution of some fundamental resistance exercise will be provided. These teaching points can be used in conjuncture with the generic pointers found in Chapter 10 to provide a more in-depth analysis and description of each exercise. Use the principles of core stability found in Chapter 13 to ensure stability through the spine.

Note that before performing any of these exercises with weight, the client's range of motion should be checked by performing an unweighted repetition. If the ROM cannot be completed with good technique then it should be limited to that in which good form can be maintained.

Barbell back squat

- Starting from a relaxed posture with feet shoulder-width apart and at a 0–30 degree angle.
- Place a bar on the shoulders below C7 (7th cervical vertebra) resting on the trapezius muscle of the shoulders and back.
- From start to finish the bar should remain over the feet.

- Bend from the hips and knees as if sitting into a chair until the legs reach 90 degrees.
- The back should remain straight (neutral, see Chapter 9) and the knees should not pass too far over the toes.

(Also see Dynamic assessment of posture during overhead squat in Chapter 9.)

Static lunge

- Take a large step forwards with the back heel in the air.
- Feet should be hip-width apart rather than in line with each other.

- Bend the front leg to 90 degrees and lower the back knee until it is at 90 degrees or several inches off the floor.
- Maintain an upright posture.

Barbell romanian dead-lift

- Hold a bar at arms' length in an upright posture.
- Lower the bar towards the knees by bending predominantly from the hip, the knees bending to approximately 20 degrees.

- The spine should remain straight with the head in line with the spine (see neutral head posture in Chapter 8).
- Return to start position.

Dumbbell press

- Lie on a bench, holding dumbbells with straight arms above the chest.
- Lower the dumbbells, keeping elbows in line

with the chest until the elbow passes slightly below the level of the shoulder.
- Return to start position.

Barbell bent over row

- Holding a barbell, move into the finishing position of the Romanian dead-lift.

- Maintain this position and draw the bar into the stomach.
- Return to start position.

Lateral raise

- Stand with feet shoulder-width apart holding dumbbells by your side, palms facing towards each other, with arms straight but elbows loose and not locked.

- Raise the arms up to level with the shoulders keeping shoulders, elbows and wrists in a straight line.
- Return to start position.

Dumbbell bicep curl

- From a standing posture, hold dumbbells by sides with palms facing forwards.
- Allow arms to rest in a natural position, not necessarily in line with the shoulders.

- Curl the dumbbells up as far as you can, keeping the elbows still and by the sides.
- Return to start position.

Each of these exercises can be progressed using the acute exercise variables highlighted in Chapter 1. We can simply add more repetitions, load or sets, or alternatively we can increase the neural complexity of the exercise. For example, we can decrease stability (e.g. by narrowing the stance or destabilizing the base using a Swiss ball or wobble board), increase motion in different planes of motion (i.e. by adding a twist or a sideways movement), perform alternating movements or provide unilateral load (just on one side). This is obviously just a handful of exercises out of the many available. It is the responsibility of the trainer to learn how to do a wide variety of exercises, learning their correct and safe execution.

CHAPTER SUMMARY

The information given here should provide the next step in building a client's programme based on what their goals are and what they want to achieve from their training. Although the exercise descriptions are brief we will expand the exercise guidelines in the following chapters on posture and the core. You should now understand which acute exercise variables should be selected to maximize the client's chances of the adaptations they are looking for in line with their goals.

REFERENCES AND RECOMMENDED READING

1. Conroy, B.P., Kraemer, W.J., Maresh, C.M. and Dalsky, G.P. (1992) Adaptive responses of bone to physical activity. *Medicine, Exercise, Nutrition and Health* 1:64–74.
2. Galbo, H. (1983) *Hormonal and Metabolic Adaptation to Exercise.* Stuttgart: Georg Thième Verlag.
3. Goldberg, A.L., Etlinger, J.D., Goldspink, L.F. and Jablecki, C. (1975) Mechanisms of work-induced hypertrophy of skeletal muscle. *Medicine and Science in Sports and Exercise* 7:248–261.
4. Hather, B.M, Tesch, P.A., Buchanon, P. and Dudley, G.A. (1991). Influence on eccentric muscle actions on skeletal muscle adaptations to resistance. *Acta Physiologica Scandinavica* 143:177–185.
5. Hedrick, A. (1995) Training for hypertrophy. *Strength and Conditioning Journal* 17(3):22–29.
6. Jones, D.A. and Round, J.M. (1995) *Skeletal Muscle in Health and Disease.* Manchester: Manchester University Press.
7. Kannus, P., Jozsa, L. and Jarvinen, A. (1997) Effects of training, immobilisation, and remobilisation on tendons. *Scandinavian Journal of Medicine and Science in Sports* 7:67–71.
8. Kraemer, W.J., Patton, J., Gordon, S.E., Harman, E.A., Descenes, M.R., Reynolds, K., Newton, R.U., Triplett, N.T. and Dziados, J.E. (1995) Compatibility of high-intensity strength and endurance training on hormonal and skeletal muscle adaptations. *Journal of Applied Physiology* 78:976–989.
9. Ostrowski, K.J., Wilson, G., Weatherby, R., Murphy, P.W. and Lyttle, A.D. (1997) The effect of weight-training volume on hormonal output and muscular size and function. *Journal of Strength and Conditioning Research* 11:148–154.
10. Tesch, P.A. and Larsson, L. (1982) Muscle hypertrophy in bodybuilders. *European Journal of Applied Physiology* 49:310.
11. Staron, R.S., Karaponda, D.L., Kraemer, W.J., Fry, A.C., Gordon, S.E., Falkel, J.E., Hagerman, F.C. and Hikida, R.S. (1994) Skeletal muscle adaptations during early-phase heavy-resistance training in men and women. *Journal of Applied Physiology* 76: 1247–1255.
12. Suominen, H. and Heikkinen, E. (1975) Effect of physical training on collagen. *Italian Journal of Biochemistry* 24:64–65.

4

PERIODIZATION: VARIATION AND RECOVERY FROM TRAINING

THIS CHAPTER CONTAINS

- Periodization explained
- The importance of rest and recovery
- Over-training, staleness and burnout
- Periodization theory
- Cycling of exercise variables
- Alternative systems

- Active rest
- Peaking
- Periodization and cardiovascular exercise
- Designing a periodized plan
- References and recommended reading

When we design an exercise programme we face a series of problems. The principle of *progression*, as discussed in Chapter 2, states that we have to make exercise progressively more challenging in order to achieve results, but we also have to ensure adequate rest and recovery. The principle of *specificity* says that we have to make exercises specific to our needs; at the same time the principle of *variation* says we have to change exercises in order to achieve continuing results (see Chapter 2). These contradictions pose a great challenge to the personal trainer looking to achieve long-term results for their clients. *Periodization* is one way to balance these different training demands in order to achieve best ongoing results. In this chapter we identify how we can design periodized programmes to balance these opposing principles of exercise. We shall see why rest and recovery are so important in achieving training gains and why the process of periodization is essential to maximize our clients' results.

PERIODIZATION EXPLAINED

As we have noted earlier, after a period of 6–8 weeks the body stops responding to a particular training stimulus. We have probably all had the same experience when starting a new training programme: initial improvements in performance are dramatic, with quick increases in the number of repetitions we can perform or the weight we can lift. Very soon these training gains start to level off as our body adapts to the training stimulus. The flattening of training gains is known as *plateau* and is one of the main reasons why people stop training and drop out. Because people stop getting results from their training they receive no reward for their efforts and they stop exercising. Lack of training variation is a major cause of training plateau. Periodization ensures both variation and progression in order to avoid training plateau and to maintain performance gains.

periodization: the systematic cycling of exercise variables with periods of planned rest to ensure maintenance of training gains.

In a periodized programme the exercises performed, along with their acute exercise variables, change every 4–8 weeks to coincide with the body's adaptive processes. The word 'systematic' simply implies that the changes are planned and that we have a schedule that we stick to. There will be periods of planned rest incorporated into the programme to allow recovery, and throughout each 4–8 week block intensity gradually increases to ensure overload.

The benefits of effective periodization therefore include:

- avoidance of *plateau* in gains by ensuring progression as well as variation
- avoidance of *over-training* via planned regular rest periods
- avoidance of *overuse* injuries caused by repetitive movements or doing the same exercises for long periods of time.

We shall also see how in a periodized programme training is split into *phases*. Each phase will be identifiable by different exercises and different acute exercise variables and therefore different performance adaptations. These phases are structured in a particular sequence in order to maximize results and prevent injury. They can also be organized to coincide with competitive events if your client is an athlete or sport performer.

THE IMPORTANCE OF REST AND RECOVERY

The Canadian biologist and endocrinologist Hans Selye formulated a model to describe how cells respond to stress. He called this three-stage process the *general adaptation syndrome (GAS)*, as summarized in Figure 4.1. He found that if living cells in laboratory conditions were exposed to stress (heat, chemicals etc.) they were damaged (*shock or alarm phase*) but they would be

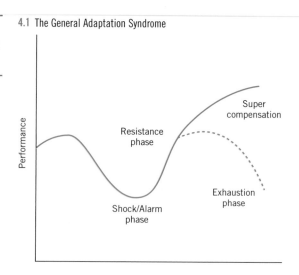

4.1 The General Adaptation Syndrome

repaired to pre-stress levels (*resistance phase*) and would even become stronger given sufficient time to recover (*super-compensation phase*). If the stress placed on these cells was too much or too prolonged the cells died (*exhaustion phase*).

These findings were later applied to resistance training to explain how the human body responds to exercise. Stress, whether physical, mental or emotional, is *catabolic*, i.e. it breaks the body down. Following the stress from a hard workout we experience fatigue, soreness from muscle damage and a drop in performance (*shock phase*). The body becomes *anabolic*, i.e. builds up, if levels of stress are reduced or there are periods of rest. At this point the body can repair itself and return to normal function (*resistance phase*). This repair process will only occur if we allow sufficient rest. During this rest time the body will repair itself and become stronger than previously, an effect known as *super-compensation* (Wathen, 2000). Sufficient rest is essential to allow super-compensation. This will represent our training gains after which we are stronger and our muscles become bigger. If the body is not allowed to rest and an athlete continues to train hard without recovery, the body reaches an *exhaustion phase* in which performance continues to deteriorate in a similar way as in the *alarm phase*. I try to explain to my clients that we do not get stronger when we train, we get stronger when we rest. Ask any marathon

4.2 The Training Stress Syndrome (Silva)

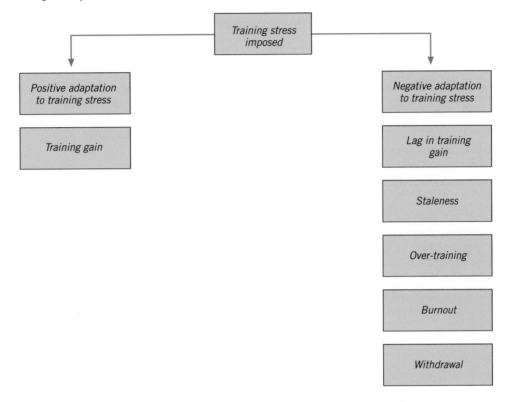

runner how fit they feel immediately after running their race. Only after rest and recovery does performance improve.

Full recovery, and therefore super-compensation, can take anywhere between 24 and 72 hours after a muscle has been trained, even longer with particularly intense resistance training. Time taken to recover will depend upon the intensity and volume of the work that muscle has performed, the genetics of the individual, their training experience and the quality of their recovery (recovery can be improved through effective cool-down, stretching and massage).

Failure to get sufficient rest is therefore detrimental to performance and adaptation to training. Some individuals get the balance wrong. They may see themselves working hard but getting nowhere. They mistake this for a lack of training stimulus or a failure to overload, and their reaction is to work even harder, their theory being that if they train harder they should get stronger, when in fact they are lacking sufficient rest and recovery. This continued exposure to even more training is known as ***over-training*** and may even cause burnout.

OVER-TRAINING, STALENESS AND BURNOUT

If someone's training stress exceeds their ability to cope, they experience what is known as a ***negative adaptation syndrome*** (Silva, 1990). As we see from Figure 4.2, negative adaptation syndrome can be extremely damaging because it starts a chain of negative consequences caused by over-training. First, we see a lag in training; this is an initial failure to adapt to the training stress, causing a condition known as ***staleness*** (Cox, 1994). Common symptoms of staleness include a loss of enjoyment or enthusiasm for the activity in question and a loss of performance gains. Often the natural response to a loss of gains is to train even harder. This increase in training stress, or over-training, will make the athlete's condition even worse and they may even experience deterioration in performance. If the body is exposed to continued stress without the ability to cope, we risk a condition known as **burnout**.

Burnout is an 'exhaustive psychophysiological response to repeated unsuccessful efforts to meet the demands of training stress' (Cox, 1994).

The term 'psychophysiological' is used to indicate that burnout not only affects our physical ability to perform but also our mental function as well. Symptoms of burnout may include:

- increased heart rate and blood pressure
- increased muscle soreness and chronic muscle fatigue
- frequent colds and upper respiratory tract infections
- decreased body weight
- decreased performance
- decreased libido and appetite
- increased mood disturbance, including decreased self-esteem, and increased perception of mental and physical exhaustion (Dale and Weinberg, 1990; Hackney et al., 1990).

The only way to treat staleness and burnout is to remove yourself from the activity causing the stress, in this case your training. The recovery process can be facilitated using methods that minimize and treat fatigue, such as meditation, massage and other relaxation strategies. Proper sleep and improved nutrition may also be important factors in optimizing recovery. The better the quality of our rest, the faster our recovery. Burnout left untreated generally results in the athlete leaving the activity in question as they become disillusioned and stop enjoying exercise. This is known as **dropout**.

We have to intervene well before a client or athlete becomes stale or approaches burnout through over-training. We achieve this by writing programmes that incorporate adequate quantities of rest and recovery and by changing acute exercise variables on a regular basis, providing new and novel training methods that will stimulate the body to adapt. This can be achieved through the process of **periodization**.

PERIODIZATION THEORY

A periodized programme is generally based on three levels of planning: macrocycles, mesocycles and microcycles. The **macrocycle** describes the overall plan of training, incorporating the client's long-term goals, the **mesocycle** describes short-term goals and is also known as the **training phase**, and the **microcycle** describes weekly plans, including details of the exercises to be performed on a daily basis. **Active rest** is the term we use for periods of reduced or very low-intensity and low-volume exercise used to allow recovery and super-compensation. This is not to be confused with complete rest in which no training is done.

KEY POINTS

Macrocycle	Long-term plan (6 months to a year)
Mesocycle	Mid-term plan (1–2 months), also known as a training phase
Microcycle	Short-term plan (weekly/session description)
Active rest	4–7 days of low-intensity activity unrelated to training

Figure 4.3 shows one example of how the macro-, meso- and microcycles can be organized. This represents a basic structure and there exist many variations dependent on the type of training, the characteristics of the sport being trained for and variations based on what you feel is most beneficial.

The following section gives a more detailed account of the differences between macro-, meso- and microcycles.

4.3 An example of a mesocycle

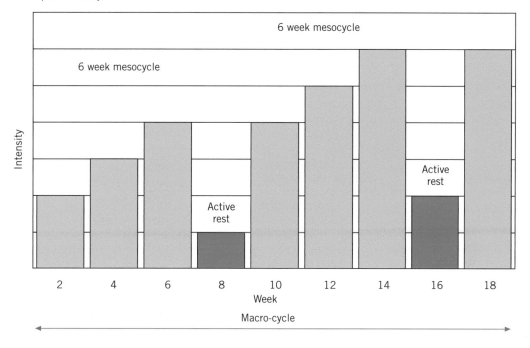

Macrocycle

Figure 4.4 shows an example of a macrocycle in the form of a periodized plan. It describes the structure of a long period of training ranging from up to six months to four years. If we used a classic example of a track runner, a macrocycle might be their full-year running plan, including training during **off-season** when they are training alone, **pre-season** when they start to train with other athletes and **competitive season** when they compete against other athletes (1*). Footballers often talk about pre-season training prior to their competitive season. A macrocycle would contain the dates when the pre-season ends and would have the dates of each of their competitive games or events (2*).

The macrocycle plan would show details of when each mesocycle is due to start and finish (3*). Alongside this you might also include the goals of each training phase. Progress might be monitored during test sessions in which performance at exercises specific to the client or athlete is measured and recorded (5*). For example, for a runner you might test their 60 m sprint, standing jump and bench press on a monthly basis in order to monitor their progress. These would be performed at specific dates in the training schedule. The macrocycle can also contain other information for a client or athlete, such as details of the cardiovascular training to be performed (4*), dietary requirements they may have (7*), skills training if the client is involved in a team sport (6*) and so on. The macrocycle essentially contains all the information the client requires to structure their training throughout their entire season. After each mesocycle they should have achieved the performance parameters specific to their sport and know what their next phase of training involves.

An example of a sheet you could use to structure a client's periodized plan is shown in Figure 4.5. It is essentially down to you and the client as to how much information you put on a macrocycle plan, and the structure of the periodized plan will vary greatly based on the goals and context of the client.

4.4 Example basis of a periodized plan

Dates			
Off-season	Pre-season	Competitive Season	1*
		Competition Dates (Races Matches etc.)	2*
Training Phases Conditioning Hypertrophy Strength Power			3*
Cardiovascular Training Aerobic Endurance Anaerobic Endurance Speed Sport Specific Agility			4*
Test Dates 1 2 3 4 5 6 7 8 9 10 (Exercise to be measured = 60 m sprint time/standing jump/bench press)			5*
Skills Training Ball control Passing Shooting Game Tactics			6*
Nutritional Focus Low carb. (Wt loss) High protein (Hypertrophy) High carb. (performance)			7*

Although periodized plans are particularly pertinent to athletes, they are also essential for normal non-sport performing clients. You may find they might be slightly less detailed or may contain slightly different information.

Mesocycle

The mesocycle describes the particular *phase of training* that the client or athlete is in over a 4–8 week period. After this time the body requires a different training stimulus in order to adapt, and acute exercise variables must be changed to avoid plateau. In Chapter 3 we saw that rep ranges, loads, rest periods etc. will all vary depending on the specific goals we want to achieve. Within each mesocycle the acute exercise variables will be prescribed based on whether the client wants to improve conditioning, build muscle (hypertrophy), strength or power. Throughout each mesocycle the intensity of exercise generally increases to ensure an overload as the client's body adapts. After each mesocycle there is a period of

active recovery (see below) to ensure super-compensation. Exercise variables are cycled systematically in each phase of training. This is discussed in further detail in the next section.

Microcycle

The microcycle covers the 4–7-day cycle of training. It describes precisely on what days we train and what exercises are to be performed in any particular week. Within each microcycle there will be days of increased or reduced intensity with some other days of complete rest to allow recovery. Rest or reduced-intensity exercise will usually follow days of higher-intensity training or competition to allow recovery, as well as preceding competition days to facilitate high levels of performance. The structure of the microcycle will tend to vary depending on the number of times the client is looking to train, how many competitive events they have if they are an athlete or sport performer and how well they recover from exercise. Remember that a muscle will require

4.5 Basis of a periodized plan

Name of client:

Outcome																					
Goals																					
Week	1	2	3	4	5	6	7	8	9	10	11	12	13	14	15	16	17	18	19	20
Date																					
Phase																					
Goals of phase																					

4.6 Example of a periodized plan

Name of client: Joe Bloggs

Outcome Goals	To tone up and lose weight (10kg) ready for a wedding in 20 weeks time To improve cardiovascular fitness for football To improve on test exercises which include multi-stage fitness test, 10 rep max squat and jump height				
Week	1 2 3 4 5 6 7	8 9 10 11 12	13 14 15 16	17 18 19 20	21 22 23 24
Date					
Phase	Conditioning phase	Hypertrophy phase	Strength phase	Power phase	Post season
Goals of phase	Weight to be measured weekly. Waist and bicep circumference to be measured on test days. Client to do 3 sessions in gym per week plus extra walks outside.				
Resistance	12–15 reps, 3–2–1 tempo, 45 secs rest	8–12 reps, 2–1–2 tempo, 1 min rest	4–6 reps	4–6 reps explosive	
	2 sets of 10 exercises	3 sets of 10 exercises	4 sets of 10 exercises	4 sets of 10 exercises	Recovery utilising:
	Complex exercises with high neurological demand	Stable exercises, low neuro demand	Functional exercises	Power (some strength ex.)	Swimming
	Long steady distance work building CV volume	Intervals, 5 min work, 1 min rest	Short intervals	Agility exercises	Yoga
Cardiovascular			1 min work, 1 min rest	Massage	
					Alternative sports
	Reduced snacking on sugary foods, reduced alcohol	Increased protein	Increased water intake	Alter dependant on weight	(e.g. tennis)
Diet	Reduced carbohydrate in evenings	Addition of protein filled snacks			
	Improve flexibility	Improved balance	Improved core strength	Improved power	
Other	Improved posture			Use throwing exercises	
	Improved segmental core stability	Improved gross core stablity			
	Lose 4kg in weight by end of phase	Lose 6kg in weight by end of phase	Lose 8kg in weight by end of phase		
Outcome	Build up to 30 minutes continuous running	Build muscle tone	Improve loads being lifted		
	Master exercise technique				
Test dates	X X X	X	X	X	X
	Consider cardiovascular/resistance training (sets, reps)/nutrition/core/posture/flexibility				

48–72 hours to recover for activity depending on the intensity of exercise, so modes of training and rest have to be structured to allow recovery and super-compensation. Training on consecutive days is acceptable as long as different muscles are worked or different energy systems are challenged.

Figures 4.7–4.9 show examples of microcycles used for various clients in various different situations. They illustrate how rest and changing intensity can be incorporated into different programmes.

4.7 A seven-day cycle of a novice exerciser looking to train the full body three times a week

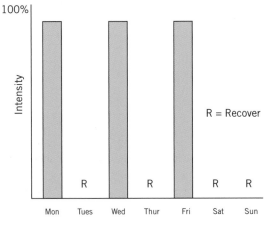

4.8 An intermediate exerciser looking to perform four sessions with an upper body and lower body split

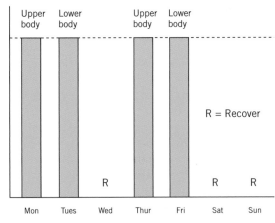

4.9 A footballer with a game on Sunday and training on Wednesday, looking to do three additional cardiovascular workouts

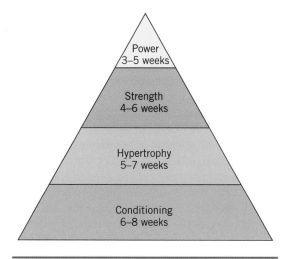

4.10 Periodization of resistance exercise

4.11 Periodization of cardiovascular exercise

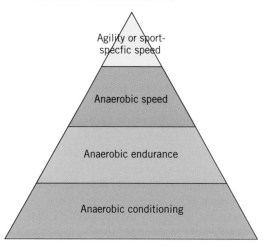

As personal trainers, we must understand the objective of each training phase and how they build logically from one to the next. The acute exercise variables required for each one can be found in Chapter 2, Exercise prescription and programme design.

Conditioning phase

The first phase of training usually involves preparing the body for more intense periods of work and is known as the *conditioning phase*. If we fail to condition ligaments, tendons, bones and muscles using lower-intensity training we may predispose our client to injury when we ask them to perform higher-intensity work during later training phases. If we do not condition the body, the strain of lifting heavy weights during strength and power phases of training may cause damage and injury.

In the conditioning phase athletes often build a base of aerobic conditioning that will support recovery in periods of more intense aerobic or anaerobic training. This is often characterized by *long steady distance (LSD)* aerobic work. This type of training should be used sparingly for anaerobic athletes such as sprinters or ball-sport players because it can detract from their speed and power. For these athletes interval training should be used predominantly to build cardiovascular fitness (see Chapter 5).

CYCLING OF EXERCISE VARIABLES

Exercise variables are systematically cycled to produce optimal results and avoid injury. These exercise variables should be organized so that the benefits build logically from one to the next with increasing intensity. Figure 4.10 gives a visual representation of the order in which training gains should be prescribed, starting with the conditioning phase. The size of each block represents loosely the relative time spent in that training phase. Remember that this is a recommendation but not a fixed rule.

We can also call this a **corrective phase** as we focus on correcting any muscular imbalance, loss of flexibility and postural deviation, and aim to repair injuries. Without doing this we may again predispose our client to injury when exposing them to more intense exercise. Details of how we might go about correcting posture are found in Chapter 9.

In the conditioning phase for novice athletes, the potential for learning new skills is very high. Exercises should be progressed by adding neural demand, increasing the complexity of the exercises. In this way a client's skill will rapidly rise, improving their overall performance.

The conditioning phase is an excellent time to focus on weight loss and reduction of body fat. Calorie intake can be reduced as the intensity of exercise during this phase tends to be lower.

Hypertrophy phase

As described in Chapter 3, muscular hypertrophy is an increase in muscle bulk due to enlargement of the muscle fibres. In this phase we attempt to stimulate muscle growth and increase the size of our muscles. The amount of force a muscle can produce is linked to its cross-sectional area (the size of the area we would have if we took a slice from the middle of the muscle). By increasing muscle size we increase our potential to produce strength and power, reflected in improved performance in later phases of training. The additional muscle mass around the joints and the time taken to condition the muscles to lifting increased loads will also aid in preventing injury.

Long steady distance exercise can be detrimental to hypertrophy and to the development of strength and power. For this reason cardiovascular work should consist of higher-intensity training such as interval training.

To gain muscle we also need sufficient calorie intake, so food consumption may be slightly higher than during a conditioning phase. We should ensure that our clients have an adequate intake of protein and carbohydrates (see Chapter 15 for details).

Strength phase

During this phase the aim is to increase strength or **maximal force production**. Care is needed. The intensities a client experiences when lifting the near-maximal loads required to build strength increase the likelihood of injury. We have to consider seriously whether this type of training is appropriate for any individual without at least a year's training experience or a high level of conditioning.

Conducted correctly, increases in maximal strength will result in increased power. Higher maximal strength should translate into more power production in the power phase.

Power phase

In this phase we start to increase the explosive power of the athlete. Exercises such as Olympic lifting, medicine ball exercises and plyometrics can be introduced at this stage. As with strength training, we have to consider the appropriateness of power training for individuals with little or no training experience.

We see that as we rise up the pyramid shown in Figure 4.11, the intensity of the training increases, as does the potential risk for injury. This is why we should never jump straight into the top of the pyramid and should generally progress from one phase to the next. As intensity increases it is a general rule that the length of the training phase should decrease. The stress on the body is higher when intensity increases, therefore the length of time we expose our clients to this stress should be less and we should ensure that they take more recovery time.

ALTERNATIVE SYSTEMS

There are numerous ways of adapting and altering a periodized plan and there are no hard-and-fast rules other than ensuring that we adhere to the principles of exercise and make sure that our clients take adequate rest. For example, **non-linear periodization** is a method in which each workout within a microcycle is different, challenging different properties of muscle. This can be highly effective as the body is always experiencing a different training stimulus, but we have to ensure that the client has sufficient conditioning to be able to cope with high-intensity workouts that focus on strength or power development.

ACTIVE REST

Active recovery is a period of reduced-intensity exercise and increased rest designed to allow super-compensation and to avoid staleness or burnout. It can be incorporated into the plan at various points:

- following competition days or high-intensity training (one day in duration)
- following each microcycle (one day in duration)
- between mesocycles (3–7 days in duration).

Athletes or competitive sportsmen may have longer periods of active rest before starting their pre-season, known as an off-season (2–3 months in duration).

The mode of exercise is often changed during the active recovery period to provide a mental break from training. Swimming, basketball or other activities may be used as active recovery for a sprinter, for example. Rest can be enhanced through massage, stretching sessions and mental relaxation strategies such as meditation. We normally prevent the client having total rest for periods of longer than 48 hours because performance can drop rapidly. Some activity or light training is always included to ensure that training gains are at least maintained.

PEAKING

The *peak* is the point in time when performance should be at its highest during the macrocycle. For a sprinter this may mean their most important

race of the year, for a footballer their most important game, or for a non-athlete it may mean when they want to be in their best shape, a wedding, for example. A client has to understand that their performance will not be optimal throughout the entire macrocycle and that some phases of training, whilst being an integral part of their long-term training plan, may even result in a fall in performance of their key skill. For example, endurance training within the conditioning phase may initially make a sprinter slower, but the adaptations will support even higher performance when they start speed training in their power phase. We might say the wider the base of the training triangle, the higher the triangle can become.

The key concept is that the client's key skills are at their peak when their performance is most important. For a sprinter their biggest race would coincide with the end of their active recovery following the power phase of training, for example. It is important to design a client's programme in order that they peak at the correct time with sufficient rest and recovery to allow maximal performance.

PERIODIZATION AND CARDIOVASCULAR EXERCISE

Cardiovascular exercise should be periodized along the same sorts of lines as resistance training. Depending on the sport the athlete performs, there can be a wide variation in the types of training employed. Intensity of exercise increases as we climb higher up the pyramid (Figure 4.11). Off-season training will predominantly involve lower-intensity and higher-volume training to increase aerobic endurance. This will progress on to higher-intensity training that will match more closely the requirements of the client's particular sport or activity.

For many clients or athletes these resistance training and cardiovascular training programmes will run side by side. Again, the weight of one to the other will depend on the sport and the goals of the client.

KEY COMPONENTS OF PERIODIZATION SUMMARY

The key components of the periodized plan are that:
- exercise is structured into a long-term macrocycle, including details of each mesocycle
- acute exercise variables are changed from one mesocycle to the next, providing a new stimulus that the body has to adapt to, thereby preventing plateau
- acute exercise variables are systematically cycled from one mesocycle to the next so that training gains build logically from one to the next (i.e. conditioning to hypertrophy to strength to power)
- intensity of exercise is progressed gradually throughout each mesocycle as we see performance gains to ensure overload
- upon starting a new mesocycle, intensity is lowered to allow adaptation to the new training stimulus
- active and complete rest is programmed between each mesocycle to allow super-compensation
- complete rest is programmed after and within each microcycle
- training sessions are structured to allow high- and low-intensity days
- low-intensity sessions or rest precede competition to allow for optimal performance and follow high-intensity sessions or competition to allow for recovery
- muscles need 48–72 hours to recover following intense training.

DESIGNING A PERIODIZED PLAN

The process of putting together a client's periodized plan can be a complex and highly individualized process. We have provided some basic steps.

1. Determine the client's goals: Are they performance or body-shape orientated? If the client competes in a sport, what are the key skills of their sport or activity (endurance, speed, strength, power, balance, skill)? See Chapter 16 for more guidance on effective goal setting and Chapter 8 for sports analysis.
2. If the client is an athlete or sport performer, determine their off-season, pre-season and competitive season start and end dates.
3. Determine when the client needs to peak, or alternatively by when they want to achieve their goals. For a non-sport performer this may tie in with a specific event, such as a holiday or wedding.
4. For an athlete, determine any other competition dates if relevant. Programme for complete or active rest before and after these competitions.
5. Determine any times when there will be planned interruptions to training (holidays etc.).
6. Break down the client's macrocycle into off-, pre-, and competitive season.
7. Break this down again into mesocycles, including details of resistance (conditioning, hypertrophy, strength and power) and cardiovascular (aerobic endurance, anaerobic endurance, anaerobic speed and agility) training.
8. Add periods of active rest between each mesocycle, detailing alternative activities if required (massage, stretching, swimming, alternative sports games, walking, yoga, Pilates etc.).
9. Set SMARTER goals (see Chapter 16) for the end of each mesocycle.
10. Set short-term goals to be achieved throughout each mesocycle.

11. Add test dates when objective performance in key exercises can be measured (weights lifted, distances run, times achieved, weight reached, body fat lost etc.).
12. Design each microcycle: exercises to be done on which days, including days for complete rest.

13. Add details of any other considerations such as nutrition, skills training, psychology sessions. These may require liaison with other health professionals, depending on your own skills and qualifications and the resources available to you.

CHAPTER SUMMARY

Periodization is an essential part of effective exercise prescription and programme. Without it, a client or athlete will invariably fail to maximize the benefits of their training. They will experience plateau in training gains and increase their likelihood of over-training and burnout. Having read this chapter you should understand the importance of rest and recovery from exercise as well as progression to ensure overload. You should understand that whilst exercises have to be specific to meet a client's demands they will also require variation in order to avoid plateau and prevent injury. You have also seen how designing periodized programmes effectively satisfies all these requirements and you should know how to design periodized programmes for your clients.

REFERENCES AND RECOMMENDED READING

1. Bompa, T.O. (1999) *Periodization; Theory and Methodology of Training*, 4th edn. Champaign, IL: Human Kinetics.
2. Cox, R.H. (1994) *Sport Psychology: Concepts and Applications*, 3rd edn. Dubuque, IA: Brown and Benchmark.
3. Dale, J. and Weinberg, R. (1990) Burnout in sport: A review and critique. *Journal of Applied Sport Psychology* 2:67–83.
4. Fleck, S.J. (1999) Periodized strength training: a critical review. *Journal of Strength and Conditioning Research* 16:69–81.
5. Hackney, A.C., Pearman III, S.N., Nowacki, J.M. (1990) Physiological profiles of overtrained and stale athletes: a review. *Journal of Sport Psychology* 2:21–33.
6. Seyle, H. (1956) *The Stress of Life*. New York: McGraw-Hill.
7. Silva, J.M. (1990) An analysis of the training stress syndrome in competitive athletes. *Journal of Applied Sport Psychology* 2:5–20.
8. Wathen, D. (2000) Training variation: periodization. In: Baechle, T.R. and Earle R.W. (eds) *Essentials of Strength Training and Conditioning*, 2nd edn. National Strength and Conditioning Association. Champaign, IL: Human Kinetics.
9. Weinberg, R.S. and Gould, D. (1999) *Foundations of Sport and Exercise Psychology*, 2nd edn. Champaign, IL: Human Kinetics.

5

CARDIOVASCULAR EXERCISE: ENERGY SYSTEMS

THIS CHAPTER CONTAINS

- Energy systems
- Cardiovascular training and performance adaptations
- Alternative training adaptations
- Types of cardiovascular training
- Interval training
- Calculating work intensity
- Cardiovascular training and periodization
- Making cardiovascular exercise fun
- References and recommended reading

Whether it is for reasons of health or for athletic performance, optimizing cardiovascular function is of fundamental importance to all clients. In this chapter we look at the strategies the body has to produce energy for movement and how they rely on the cardiovascular system to provide fuel and oxygen as well as remove waste products such as carbon dioxide and lactic acid. We will consider the different facets of cardiovascular performance, ranging from slow steady distance to high-intensity interval training and discuss how they can be structured into a systematic programme of training for your client.

ENERGY SYSTEMS

Before looking specifically at different forms of aerobic exercise it is first essential to understand some basic physiology of how the body produces the energy for movement. A working knowledge of these energy systems is essential to understand the effect of exercise on the body.

When we eat carbohydrates, proteins and fats, they are digested and broken down to produce sugars that can be used as fuel. Our *energy systems* are the different ways we metabolize this fuel to produce energy in the form of *adenosine triphosphate (ATP)*. ATP is the energy carrier of the body and is essential for a number of processes in the body, including muscular work and growth. ATP consists of adenosine and three phosphates attached together via *high-energy bonds*.

High energy bond

Whenever one of these bonds is broken, *adenosine diphosphate* (ADP) is formed and energy is released as a by-product, along with the remaining phosphate.

– Energy

The body requires a constant supply of ATP with which to produce muscular work. Because

ATP stores are quite limited, energy has to be continually produced by the body to reform ATP from ADP and phosphate. This energy is produced from one of the body's three energy systems:

- the **ATP-CP (creatine phosphate) system** – for immediate energy
- the **anaerobic/lactic system** – for short-term energy
- the **aerobic/oxidative system** – for long-term energy.

Each of these energy systems relies on the cardiovascular system either to provide fuel and oxygen or to remove waste (carbon dioxide and lactic acid). The type of energy system used during exercise is determined primarily by the intensity of the exercise being performed.

The ATP-CP system

ATP is stored in small quantities within muscle for immediate use. As ATP stores are used up they are immediately replaced from breakdown of **creatine phosphate (CP)**. CP is a molecule formed from a single creatine and a single phosphate held together by a **high-energy bond**. It is similar to ATP in that small quantities are stored within muscle and when the high-energy bond breaks, large quantities of energy are released. This energy is used to regenerate ATP. Activities that require a quick and immediate injection of energy rely heavily on the ATP-CP energy system, particularly those activities lasting less than 10 seconds, such as throwing the shot put, short sprints or a final kick in a long distance race. Power training can increase the amount of ATP and CP stored within the muscles (Brooks *et al.*, 1996) and dietary supplements such as creatine are thought to support performance in power events by increasing CP stores.

The anaerobic (lactic) system

Glycolysis refers to the process by which sugar is broken down to produce energy. **Glyco-** refers to sugar and **-lysis** suggests breakdown. Anaerobic

glycolysis is a form of glycolysis that occurs without the need for oxygen. The breakdown of blood glucose via anaerobic glycolysis is the next-quickest method of energy production for ATP re-synthesis. Anaerobic glycolysis is heavily relied upon for activities requiring near-maximal efforts for sustained periods of time lasting beyond 10 seconds. The drawback to this form of energy production is that it is inefficient and produces **lactic acid** and **hydrogen ions** as waste products. Hence the name, 'lactic' system.

Lactic acid produced in muscles is acidic and causes the sensation of pain associated with high-intensity work. It can be buffered (acidity lowered) and removed via the bloodstream to be used as fuel or converted to glucose. This is known as **lactate clearance**. Cardiovascular training can improve lactate clearance, improving anaerobic performance.

As intensity of work increases, the amount of lactic acid produced increases until production exceeds the body's ability to remove it and acidity levels rise. This point is known as the **lactate threshold (LT)** or **anaerobic threshold (AT)**. If these waste products build up in sufficient quantities blood acidity can interfere with muscular contraction and glycolytic reactions, resulting in fatigue after approximately 60–180 seconds. At this point the level of work we can sustain falls and we experience 'hitting the wall'. That burn you feel with intense activities such as weight training is the lactic acid build-up resulting from anaerobic glycolysis. With training we can lower lactate production and increase lactate removal so that we can achieve higher work intensity before the lactate threshold.

Aerobic (oxidative or slow glycolytic) system

For activities of lower intensity and longer duration (over 3 minutes) during which our respiratory system is more readily able to supply oxygen, the body utilizes the **aerobic system**. During this process the waste products of glycolysis are further broken down to produce energy in groups of reactions known as the **Krebs** cycle and the *electron transport chain (ETC)*. Although the aerobic system produces far more energy than anaerobic metabolism, due to the increased number of chemical reactions involved it produces energy at a much slower rate. The aerobic system is limited by the body's ability to supply the muscles with oxygen and then the ability of the muscles to utilize that oxygen. The body's ability to deliver and utilize oxygen is known as the *maximum aerobic power* (*VO₂max*). Cardiovascular training can increase VO_2max and thus improve aerobic performance.

If we work at intensities well below our VO_2max then performance is limited by our stores of glycogen in the blood and liver. As these stores run out we experience fatigue and our performance falls.

Acute exercise variables, primarily *intensity* (how hard), *volume* (how long) and *rest* (recovery between efforts) will determine the predominant energy system stressed during an activity. In essence, during any activity all of the energy systems are utilized to varying degrees. This is known as the *energy spectrum*. Any individual, regardless of their sport, will require all of these three energy systems in varying degrees. Cardiovascular training will induce adaptations that will lead to improved performance in one or all of these energy systems.

CARDIOVASCULAR TRAINING AND PERFORMANCE ADAPTATIONS

In line with the principle of specificity (see Chapter 2), the type of cardiovascular training you perform will dictate the types of adaptations your body will experience. Selecting the appropriate training stimulus for your client is critical.

ATP-CP system training

The ATP-CP system can be trained using exercises at almost maximal intensity lasting less than 10 seconds in duration. Exercises that are commonly used include maximal sprints, speed, agility and quickness drills, Olympic lifting or explosive

exercises such as throws or jumps (see Chapter 8). Exercises have to be followed by almost complete recovery to allow for ATP and CP stores to be replenished. The greater the recovery or rest, the more time is available to replace these vital energy stores.

- 20–30 seconds = 50 per cent recovery of ATP and CP
- 40 seconds = 75 per cent recovery of ATP and CP
- 60 seconds = 85–90 per cent recovery of ATP and CP
- 3 minutes = 100 per cent recovery of ATP and CP.

Training as well as nutritional supplements can increase the amount of ATP and CP stored within skeletal muscle. This type of exercise will develop speed and power.

Anaerobic training

This type of training is designed to increase *maximum anaerobic power*, the amount of work performed using anaerobic pathways. Anaerobic training is performed at high intensities, up to and above the lactate threshold (>70 per cent VO_2max, >80 per cent max heart rate, HR). This intense level of work stimulates lactic acid production. Training adaptations improve the athlete's ability to remove lactic acid (i.e. *lactate clearance*). In this way athletes can increase the level of work they can perform before reaching the lactate threshold. It has been demonstrated that the lactate threshold typically begins at 50–60 per cent maximal oxygen uptake (VO_2max) in untrained subjects and at 70–80 per cent VO_2max in trained subjects (Farrel *et al.*, 1979). Athletes can also be trained to withstand the raised concentrations of lactic acid and hydrogen ions in the blood (Kraemer, 2000); this is known as *lactic tolerance*. High-intensity exercise cannot be maintained for long periods, so we often introduce periods of reduced intensity to allow recovery. This is known as *interval training*. If the goal is to improve lactate clearance, rest periods are typically longer;

if the goal is to improve lactic tolerance, rest periods are shorter to ensure that lactate levels in the muscle remain high. See below for suggestions on time periods for work and rest periods.

Aerobic system training

Training designed to improve aerobic capacity is performed at intensities below the lactate threshold, (<70 per cent VO_2max, <80 per cent max HR) for increased durations (10 minutes to an hour). Because intensity is lower, work rates can be sustained and rest periods, if provided, can be short. Aerobic training is designed to improve cardiovascular function and improve VO_2max.

There is a strong correlation between VO_2max and aerobic endurance performance (Costill, 1970). VO_2max is the ability to deliver and utilize oxygen, and it is increased by aerobic training as a result of various factors, including improved respiratory function (enhanced oxygen exchange in the lungs and improved blood flow through the lungs), improved cardiovascular function (increased cardiac output, increased blood volume, increased haemoglobin concentration, enhanced delivery of blood to muscles and skin), improved muscuoloskeletal function (increased enzymic action, increased capilliarization) and improved storage of fuels such as glycogen and triglycerides (fats).

ALTERNATIVE TRAINING ADAPTATIONS

There numerous other adaptations that improve cardiovascular performance. These can be summarized as improved exercise economy, improved fuel utilization and improved muscle fibre type profile.

Improving exercise economy

The body can be made to be more efficient when it moves. We can improve running mechanics, for example, by improving posture, increasing core stability, increasing flexibility, improving running technique and improving power production by conditioning the elastic qualities of muscles. These factors combine to make the trained athlete a far more efficient running machine, reducing the energy cost of movement and reducing the stress on the cardiovascular system. Details on each of these areas can be found throughout this book.

Fuel utilization

Training can improve our ability to use fat as an energy source during exercise. This means that vital stores of glycogen are spared and endurance performance can be prolonged. The knowledge that the fitter we are, the more fat we can burn has a profound effect on how we train individuals looking to lose weight (see Chapter 6).

Muscle fibre type profile

Muscle fibres are specifically adapted for particular roles, as described in Table 5.1.

The proportion of each type of muscle fibre in each muscle is genetically determined and will determine the type of performance to which an individual is best suited. Training can influence the fibre-type composition of muscle. It has been demonstrated that type IIb fibres can transform into type IIa fibres, thereby improving the endurance of the muscle in question (Kraemer, 2000). In this way muscles can get better adapted to the role we are asking them to perform.

TYPES OF CARDIOVASCULAR TRAINING

There are various types of training format commonly used to improve various aspects of cardiovascular performance. Here we describe four different types.

Long slow distance training

This is high-volume, low-intensity training without rest periods, designed to stress the aerobic

Table 5.1 Characteristics of different muscle fibre types

Type I	Type IIa	Type IIb
Slow twitch	Fast twitch	Fast twitch
Slow contraction speed	Fast contraction speed	Fast contraction speed
Low force production	Fatigue resistant	High force production
Resistant to fatigue		Susceptible to fatigue

system. Long slow distance training is performed at intensities at or below 70 per cent VO_2max (80 per cent maximum HR) or slightly below race speeds for endurance athletes. Distances covered are greater than those used in their event and training sessions typically last 30 minutes to 2 hours. Long slow distance training is typically performed in the conditioning phase of training in a periodized programme. It improves VO_2max, increases utilization of fat during low-intensity work and raises the lactate threshold.

Tempo training

Tempo training involves work at speeds slightly above those of race speeds or slightly above the lactate threshold so that pace can be sustained for a maximum of 3–5 minutes. Work can be performed at steady pace or by using bursts of pace followed by brief periods of rest. Sessions last approximately 20–30 minutes. This type of training is designed to raise the lactate threshold and increase an athlete's **maximal steady rate**, the maximum pace they can maintain below the lactate threshold.

Fartlek

Fartlek (a Swedish term meaning 'speed play') involves spontaneous variation in intensity to challenge all the energy systems of the body, reduce monotony and boredom and is designed to add variation to training. During running, for example, you might randomly add sprints, tempo speed running, breaks to allow recovery, uphill running etc. Fartlek is less structured than interval training (below) and the choices of intensity and duration are made by the athlete during the session. So, for example, if training in a park, you might sprint to one tree, jog to the next hill, and so on. You might even add resistance exercises during runs, such as press-ups or bench dips to add variety.

Interval training

This is a highly structured type of training consisting of periods of increased intensity work broken up by periods of active recovery. The type of interval prescribed in terms of intensity, duration and length of recovery will dictate the adaptations produced. Below we have provided a more in-depth explanation of interval training techniques.

Table 5.2 Interval training – examples

Primary energy system challenged	Exercise intensity (% maximum)	Approximate ratio of work to rest	Approximate length of work interval
ATP-CP	90–100	1:12–1:20	10 seconds or below
Anaerobic	75–90	1:1–1:5	30 seconds to 3 minutes
Aerobic	30–75	2:1–10:1	>3 minutes

INTERVAL TRAINING

Interval training is based on the concept that greater periods of high-intensity work can be performed if we allow intermittent periods of recovery or reduced intensity, known as **active recovery**. Intervals are generally expressed as a ratio of work to rest (e.g. 2:1 to signify 2 minutes work to 1 minute rest). Some recommendations for the types of intervals you could employ for particular training adaptations are listed in Table 5.2.

Intervals effectively mimic how a sports performer might work during their event or sport, in that we have periods of high-intensity work coupled with periods of recovery.

For the non-sports performer interval training is also a highly effective tool. A walk/jog programme is particularly effective for someone who does not have the ability to run for a long period of time. Interval training will allow for an increased degree of calorie expenditure in a reduced time period. This makes it ideal for personal training sessions where we have to provide a challenging workout in a short space of time. Intervals are also more interesting and make the chore of cardiovascular exercise go much faster for those individuals who find motivation hard to come by.

Excess post-exercise oxygen consumption

Following exercise our metabolism stays elevated as our body recovers. Our raised metabolism means that we continue to burn calories at an increased rate following exercise as well as during it. This can be measured by the extra oxygen used by the body during exercise. This is known as excess post-exercise oxygen consumption (EPOC). The higher the intensity of exercise the greater the EPOC. Interval training achieves greater levels of EPOC because the body is able to perform more work at higher intensities than would otherwise be possible. This will appeal to those individuals looking to lose weight as they are trying to burn as many calories as possible.

Alternative interval training designs

Various alternatives are available in terms of the design of an interval training programme. For example:

- **Ascending pyramid:** A stepped increase in intensity or workload. An excellent way to warm up a client.
- **Descending pyramid:** A stepped decrease in intensity or workload. Excellent as a way to cool down a client.
- **Full pyramid:** A combination of the two, a stepped increase in intensity followed by a stepped decrease in intensity.

Circuit training

Circuit training involves moving between two or more exercises (e.g. run–row–run–row, or run–row–bike–crosstrainer). Remember that circuit training utilizing compound resistance exercises such as squats, lunges, dead-lifts, step-ups can be an excellent cardiovascular workout.

CALCULATING WORK INTENSITY

Part of the role of the personal trainer is to alter work intensity to get the client into their **training-sensitive zone**. This zone is determined based on the goals of the client and any requirements of the sports or activities they participate in. The training-sensitive zone is the work intensity most suited to the client based on their goals and present level of conditioning. Our training-sensitive zone with respect to cardiovascular exercise can be defined by target heart rate.

Target heart rate (THR) can be calculated using a variety of methods. The two most common are using a percentage of **maximum heart rate (MHR)** and taking a percentage of MHR reserve using the Karvonen formula.

The **Karvonen formula** is designed to predict **heart rate reserve (HRR)**. HRR takes into account an individual's resting heart rate, an indicator of

CALCULATING TARGET HEART RATE (THR) AS A PERCENTAGE OF MHR

THR = Predicted Maximal × Desired Training
      Heart Rate   Intensity
(predicted Maximal Heart Rate = 220 − age)

Target Heat = [220-age] × Desired Training
Rate (THR)   Intensity

e.g. Our client is 20 years of age and you wish them to work at between 60 and 80% of the maximum HR.

THR = [220-20]   × 60% or 80%
      = 200   × 0.6 or 0.8
      = 120 to 160

fitness, and is thought to be more accurate, especially for individuals with higher levels of cardiovascular conditioning. To use the equation the trainer must know the client's resting heart rate. Heart rate can be measured manually at the radial pulse in the wrist or at the carotid pulse in the neck. Usually we find the pulse, count the number of beats over a 15-second period and multiply by 4 to get an estimated HR over a minute. Alternatively, heart rate monitors can be bought that will measure HR directly and many

CALCULATION HEART RATE RESERVE USING THE KARVONEN FORMULA

Target Heat = [Pred. Max
Rate Range   HR −   × Desired   + Resting
(THRR)   Resting HR]   Training   HR

For example, you have a 20-year-old client with a resting HR of 55 and you want them to work at between 60 and 80 per cent of their MHR:

THRR = [[220-20] − 55]   × 60% or 80% + 55
       = [200-5]   × 0.6 or 0.8   + 55
       = [145 × 0.6 or 0.8] + 55
       = 142 to 171

cardiovascular machines found in gyms often have HR monitors built into them.

The second score is appreciably higher due to the low resting HR of the individual, reflecting a good level of physical fitness.

Using a measurement of HR to determine work intensity has the benefit of being an objective measure of effort. The client cannot lie to you about how hard they are working. There is also an inbuilt progression: as fitness improves, HR for a given workload will reduce. If you increase the workload to maintain the HR at a given level then you should gradually see your client improve their workload over time. Heart rate is often used by distance runners as an extremely effective way of monitoring work rate in varied conditions (wind, rain, temperature etc.). Also remember that if a client's HR increases steadily for a given work intensity over a series of sessions this may indicate over-training or may point to other factors such as illness or some other form of stress (heat, nutritional deficiency such as dehydration etc.).

In some situations the use of target heart rate range may not be suitable. If your equipment is not of sufficient quality there may be inaccuracies in your measurement of HR as the person works, especially if manual estimations are being made. An individual's MHR is affected by genetic variations so an estimation may be inaccurate, leading to ineffective THRR. It may also be that different exercises elicit different HR responses. Prescription drugs can also affect HR responses to exercise and as such should be screened prior to exercise.

An alternative way of measuring exercise intensity is through the **Borg Scale** (see Chapter 10), which measures perceived exertion, or even a combination of the two. I recommend taking measurements using the Borg Scale and matching this to HR. The HR measurements can then be used and we would expect this to correlate with the same perceived rate of exertion.

CARDIOVASCULAR TRAINING AND PERIODIZATION

It is important to understand that athletic performance generally has input from all our energy systems. Most athletes need certain levels of conditioning in each of the energy systems because they all contribute to performance to a certain degree. We might think that athletes who mainly perform sprinting activities do not rely on their aerobic system because it is mainly the anaerobic and ATP-CP energy systems that supply the energy for these activities. This is not the case. The oxidative system has a significant input in activities of higher intensities. After 20–30 seconds the aerobic contribution to energy production increases dramatically, contributing as much as 40–45 per cent (Baechle and Earle, 2000). The aerobic system also plays a vital role during recovery from higher-intensity work such as sprints (Harris *et al.*, 2000). This makes the aerobic system of key importance even to athletes who mainly sprint and recover, such as footballers and rugby players.

We should be careful about the types of training we use to condition the aerobic system of these types of athletes. We have to be extremely cautious about when and how much long slow distance training we expose them to. Studies have demonstrated that combining resistance training and aerobic endurance interferes with strength and power performance (Kraemer, 2000). Simultaneous sprint and aerobic endurance training can actually decrease sprint speed and jump power (Callister *et al.*, 1988). This means that too much long slow distance type training may actually reduce sprint performance. If we are training a footballer, for example, it would be necessary to reduce long slow distance aerobic training during their competitive season, because it might have a detrimental effect on their speed. For speed and power athletes the cardiovascular system should generally be conditioned using high-intensity interval training rather than long steady distance exercise.

Cardiovascular training follows the same principles of progression and variation as resistance training. If we do not change the training stimulus every 4–8 weeks the client will **plateau** (see Chapter 4). This demonstrates the importance of cycling cardiovascular training in a periodized programme so that the athlete's key skills are at their highest when they need to perform their best. Figure 5.1 shows how you might integrate the different types of cardiovascular training into a periodized programme. Obviously there would be variations

5.1 Cardiovascular periodization

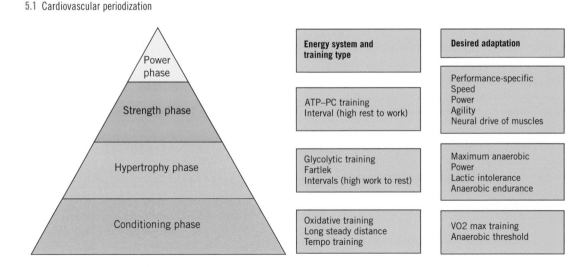

based on the performance demands of the athlete and their sport.

During the conditioning phase athletes generally build an ***aerobic base*** in which they develop maximal aerobic power (VO_2max) that will support anaerobic performance and promote recovery. As the athlete enters a hypertrophy or strength phase, aerobic work can be detrimental to performance, so intensity of work has to increase. As the athlete enters the power phase, intensity is extremely high to match the demands of their resistance training. In this phase cardiovascular work should mimic very closely the demands of their sport. For example, for a footballer this would mean very high-intensity sprints with changes of direction and pace combined with work on power and explosion off the mark.

MAKING CARDIOVASCULAR EXERCISE FUN

We often forget that exercise should be enjoyable. Cardiovascular training in the gym can be dull and uninspiring, which is why people often prefer to play sports rather than join a gym. This does not have to be the case. We can introduce games or other activities in our sessions to keep them fun. Do not be afraid to take clients for a jog outside and introduce circuit-type exercises as you go around. I often use a reaction ball, a rubber ball that is uneven and bounces in different directions, for agility games. If you are qualified in aerobics, do some exercise to music. If you can get a qualification or certification, boxing exercises with pads and mitts can be a fantastic cardiovascular workout. Do not be afraid of suggesting other games or activities to try to add interest to the session. You may find yourself playing a game of squash or badminton with a client if the facilities are at hand. Also remember that a resistance circuit using large muscle groups and compound exercises can also provide an excellent cardiovascular workout if your client prefers resistance work. Do not get stuck in the usual cardiovascular rut of only using the machines that are readily available. It is our job to be slightly more creative.

CASE STUDY: PERIODIZATION FOR A FOOTBALLER

A footballer came to me and asked for a series of programmes to follow specifically for his pre-season training and for when he starts his competitive season. He explained that although his club will look after a lot of his training, he still wanted a cardiovascular programme to follow once a week when he comes into the gym.

I went through the concept of periodization with him and explained the importance of building an endurance base during his pre-season and focusing on speed and agility during his competitive season.

Then I provided some sample sessions to give him ideas:

Early pre-season

1. Warm-up – 5 minutes treadmill starting at a walk and building to a jog
2. Tempo run – 5 minutes at 70–80 per cent max heart rate (RPE* 6–7), followed by 1 minute recovery (RPE 3–4), repeated 5 times
3. Cool-down – 5 minutes, gradually reducing intensity, finishing with a walk
4. Post stretch

Late pre-season

1. Warm-up – 5 minutes treadmill starting at a walk and building to a jog
2. Fartlek – 30 minutes fartlek, randomly changing pace and/or incline to include short sprints and hill climbs

3. Cool-down – 5 minutes, gradually reducing intensity, finishing with a walk
4. Post stretch

Early competitive season

1. Warm-up – 5 minutes treadmill starting at a walk and building to a jog
2. Anaerobic intervals – 1 minute sprints at 85–90 per cent max heart rate (RPE 8–9), followed by 2 minutes recovery (RPE 2–3), repeated 10 times

3. Cool-down – 5 minutes, gradually reducing intensity, finishing with a walk
4. Post stretch

Late competitive season

Speed, agility and power sessions as described in Chapter 8. I recommended against too much steady distance running, especially during his competitive season, due to its detrimental effects on speed.

*See Chapter 10 for details on perceived rate of exertion (RPE).

CHAPTER SUMMARY

Whilst essential for athletic performance, cardiovascular training also has important benefits in terms of preventing and treating chronic disease such as diabetes and coronary heart disease, as well as playing a key role in a weight-loss or maintenance programme. We can see from this that cardiovascular training is vitally important for all clients and should always be introduced into a programme to some degree. Having read this chapter you should be able to design varying cardiovascular programmes and integrate them within a client's periodized programme.

REFERENCES AND RECOMMENDED READING

1. Baechle, T.R., Earle, R.W. (eds) (2000) *Essentials of Strength Training and Conditioning*, 2nd edn. National Strength and Conditioning Association. Champaign, IL: Human Kinetics.
2. Bompa, T. (1999) *Periodization*. Champaign, IL: Human Kinetics.
3. Brooks, G.A., Fahey, T.D. and White, T.P. (1996) *Exercise Physiology: Human Bioenergetics and its Applications*, 2nd edn. Mountain View, CA: Mayfield.
4. Callister, R., Shealy, M.J., Fleck, S.J. and Dudley, G.A. (1988) Performance adaptations to sprint, endurance and both modes of training. *Journal of Applied Sport Science Research* 2:46–51.
5. Costill, D.L. (1970) Metabolic responses during distance running. *Journal of Applied Physiology* 28:251–255.
6. Farrel, P.A., Wilmore, J.H., Coyle, E.F., Billing, J.E. and Costill, D.L. (1979) Plasma lactate accumulation and distance running performance. *Medicine and Science in Sports* 11:338–344.
7. Harris, G.R., Stone, M.H., O'Bryant, H.S., Prouix, C.M. and Johnson, R.L. (2000) Short-term performance effects of high speed, high force, or combined weight training methods. *Journal of Strength and Conditioning Research* 14:14–20.
8. Kraemer, J.W. (2000) Physiological adaptations to anaerobic and aerobic endurance training programs. In: Baechle, T.R. and Earle R.W. (eds) *Essentials of Strength Training and Conditioning*, 2nd edn. National Strength and Conditioning Association. Champaign, IL: Human Kinetics.
9. Kraemer, W.J., Patton, J.F., Gordon, S.E., Harman, E.A., Deschenes, M.R., Reynolds, K., Newton, R.U., Triplett, N.T. and Dziados, J.E. (1985) Compatibility of high-intensity strength and endurance training on hormonal and skeletal muscle adaptations. *Journal of Applied Physiology* 78:976–989.
10. Kraemer, W.J., Noble, B.J., Culver, B.W. and Clark, M.J. (1987) Physiologic responses to heavy resistance exercise with very short rest periods. *International Journal of Sports Medicine* 8:247–252.

6

WEIGHT LOSS: OUR EVER-EXPANDING NATION

THIS CHAPTER CONTAINS

- The energy balance equation
- Basic guidelines for weight loss
- Why low-calorie diets are not recommended
- Dietary recommendations for weight loss
- Exercise and weight loss
- References and recommended reading

Throughout the developed world people are getting more overweight every year. In the US from 1984 to 1994, the proportion of people classified as obese increased from 12 to 20 per cent of men and from 16 to 25 per cent of women (Flegal *et al.*, 1998). This was mainly due to lack of exercise and over-eating. Studies suggest that nearly 15–20 per cent of middle-aged Europeans are obese (Bjorntorp, 1997).

Being overweight can have a cascade of negative health consequences. Links have been demonstrated between obesity and chronic diseases such as heart disease, cancer, hypertension and diabetes (Tuck *et al.*, 1981). Every year in the UK more than 260,000 people die of cardiovascular disease (diseases of the heart and blood vessels) and over 130,000 die of cancer.

It has been estimated that as many 1 in 3 women and 1 in 5 men in the UK are actively trying to lose weight at any given time. In response to this trend the number of fad diets is on the increase. The UK slimming industry is now worth more than a billion pounds a year, driven by the hopes of many to find ways of losing weight. The problem is that although people who take part in

and complete a weight-loss or dieting programme typically lose about 10 per cent of their weight, most of them put the lost weight back on again.

Weight loss will be the main goal of many of your clients if you work in a mainstream health club or gym. This chapter provides advice that you can give regarding simple, scientifically validated techniques for safe and long-lasting weight loss. There will be no mention of fad diets, only a common-sense approach to eating and exercise.

THE ENERGY BALANCE EQUATION

The basic laws of thermodynamics suggest that weight loss is essentially very simple, albeit not easy. If we consume more calories than we need, regardless of what type of calories they are, we will gain weight. These excess calories are inevitably converted to fat and stored. If we use more calories than we consume then these energy reserves are tapped into, fat is metabolized to produce fuel and we lose weight. We can therefore apply this very simple equation to weight loss.

$$\text{Energy storage } (+/-) = \text{Energy consumed} - \text{Energy used}$$

When more calories are going out than coming in we are said to be in **negative energy balance**. Likewise a **positive energy balance** is when the converse is true and we have more calories coming in than going out. If a client's weight is stable then you know that their calorie intake and expenditure are the same. This explains why weight loss is a simple mathematical equation in which we have to either consume less or become more active in order to lose weight. This suggests that the types of calories we eat (carbohydrates, proteins or fats) may not be as important as the number of calories we eat in regard to weight loss.

We use calories in three different ways:

■ After eating, to digest, absorb, transport and store food. We call this the **thermic effect of food (TEF)**.
■ During activity or whenever we move, known as the **thermic effect of physical activity (TEPA)**.
■ To perform all the other functions that the body requires, such as the energy needed to keep us breathing, keep the heart beating, supply the brain with energy to think, as well as the thousands of chemical reactions that occur in the body every second. The amount of calaries needed for this is the **resting metabolic rate (RMR)**. The RMR comprises as much as 75 per cent of total energy usage in the average person.

6.1 Energy balance

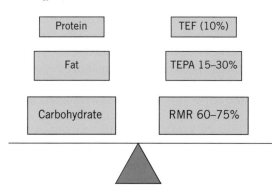

Protein		TEF (10%)
Fat		TEPA 15–30%
Carbohydrate		RMR 60–75%

The set of scales shown in Figure 6.1 represents our energy balance equation, with calories ingested on one side in the form of carbohydrate, protein and fat, and calories being used on the other side. Which way the scales tip dictates whether we gain or lose weight. We can lose weight by increasing calorie expenditure (calories going out) or by decreasing calorie intake.

Calorie expenditure can be increased by:

■ Increasing RMR by developing **fat-free mass (FFM)** (i.e. muscle) through resistance training. Muscle is metabolically active (i.e. it burns calories).
■ Increasing TEPA by raising physical activity levels through activities such as walking, gardening and sport or by exercising in the gym.
■ Increasing TEF by increasing the frequency with which we eat. Every time we consume food or drink our metabolism increases and we burn energy.

These three strategies are discussed in greater depth below.

BASIC GUIDELINES FOR WEIGHT LOSS

If losing weight were as simple as exercising more and eating less we would not have the problems we have with weight-related illness that we see today. Maintaining a healthy diet and exercising can pose great motivational challenges for many individuals. We need to provide more advice on how to overcome these barriers.

As a starting point, make sure your clients understand the following principles when attempting to lose weight:

■ To reduce risk of adverse health and performance consequences, the rate of weight loss should not exceed 0.5–1 kg of body weight per week.
■ The interventions you make should be lifestyle changes that the client agrees they can stick to for the rest of their lives.

- Maintain a healthy balanced diet to ensure consumption of all essential vitamins, minerals, proteins and fats in order to maintain good health and prevent illness.
- Avoid reliance on supplements and fad diets.

It is generally recommended that we should lose a maximum of 0.5–1 kg of body weight per week. There are approximately 7700 calories per kilogram of body fat (Williams, 1995) so exercise levels and diet should be adjusted to create an energy deficit (negative energy balance) of 500–1000 calories per day. It would be possible to start by estimating your client's daily calorie requirements based on weight and estimates of activity levels, then calculate a level of calorie intake to lose weight, but this can be time-consuming and is often inaccurate. It is far easier to alter your client's activity and diet until their weight is at least stable, indicating a balance between consumption and usage of calories. From this point we know we have to make a further 500–1000 calorie deficit in daily calorie balance to produce the desired drop in weight.

As we reduce calorie intake by eating less there is a danger that we fail to take in all the essential nutrients the body needs for good health. This is why diet has to be altered in a way that maximizes nutrient intake to maintain health. Safe and effective ways of achieving this are recommended in this chapter and we should always adhere to the nutritional guidelines for healthy and balanced eating discussed in Chapter 15. Whatever changes we make, the client must be willing and able to adhere to them for the rest of their life, otherwise fluctuations in diet inevitably lead to fluctuations in weight that can be harmful and damaging to the body. Applying the principles of behaviour change found in Chapter 16 is also of key importance.

WHY LOW-CALORIE DIETS ARE NOT RECOMMENDED

Many fad diets recommend a far more radical approach to diet and weight loss. Some recommend very low calorie plans, some recommend removal of entire food groups from the diet. There are several very good reasons why this is not an effective weight control strategy.

Loss of fat-free mass

Sudden reduction in body weight as a result of dieting and aerobic exercise can result in reductions of fat-free mass (FFM) (i.e. muscle). Garrow (2000) demonstrated that with periods of moderate dieting, weight loss is about 75 per cent fat and 25 per cent FFM. During total starvation the loss of FFM rises to 50 per cent. In other words, the faster we lose weight, the greater proportion of the weight that will come from lean tissue (FFM). This loss in FFM (i.e. muscle) has been shown to reduce RMR (Cavallo et al., 1990) because muscle burns calories even at rest. This will make it progressively harder to achieve your 500-calorie negative energy balance. Some authors suggest that a low RMR may be a key factor in contributing to weight regain (Astrup et al., 1999). The loss of muscle mass and a general lack of energy that result from dieting also mean our training suffers and our activity levels may drop. An effective dietary plan factors-in strategies to maintain FFM in order to maintain metabolism.

Starvation mode

The brain perceives drastic negative energy balance as a possible threat to our survival. For all the body knows when we are seriously lacking nutrition, we are on a desert island and need to survive on fat stores for as long as possible. Through control of the thyroid gland the body can lower metabolism in order to conserve energy and avoid further reduction in energy stores during periods of low calorie intake (Cavallo et al., 1990). An underactive thyroid results in a reduction in RMR and a lowering in energy requirements. This again makes it harder for our client to achieve their 500-calorie deficit. The brain also influences our physiological desire to eat by activating hunger centres in the brain. It can also influence perceptions of taste and smell to make food more appealing. The result is a feeling of hunger – an increased desire to eat that makes adherence to a very low-calorie diet very difficult. An effective dietary plan allows gradual loss in weight with periods of weight maintenance to maintain metabolism and alters diet to help relieve sensations of hunger.

Lipoprotein lipase production

Low-calorie diets stimulate the production of the enzyme *lipoprotein lipase*, an enzyme that aids in fat storage. This is the enzyme responsible for storage of dietary fat in *adipocytes* (fat cells). In this way the body becomes hyperefficient at storing fat in response to this long-term negative energy balance. As soon as we come off a strict diet and there is suddenly a surplus of calories (positive energy balance), the body is superadapted to store calories as fat and weight returns. In this way when we diet we are almost training the body to store calories as fat. Exercise, especially intense exercise, trains the body to release calories and give up fat stores. Effective weight-loss programmes improve the body's capacity to use fat rather than store it.

Adherence

The foods we have to eat on a low-calorie diet are often unpalatable and fad diets are usually extreme in nature. These factors combine to make such diets extremely hard to stick to on a long-term basis. An effective dietary plan is one that is tailor-made to suit your food preferences and lifestyle.

Health

As we eat less and less food the chances of us consuming all the essential vitamins, minerals, proteins and fats we need to maintain health gradually decreases to the point where we can easily become ill as our immune system deteriorates. How many times have you dieted and then come down with a cold or some other illness? Some people will even reduce the food they eat drastically but still consume alcohol or some of their favourite foods in the evening when they socialize. Removing food groups on fad diets increases our chances of chronic undernutrition. In situations such as this we cannot predict the negative health consequences. By eating more healthy food in combination with exercise we increase our chances of meeting the body's needs in terms of nutrients such as vitamins and minerals.

These factors combine to make sustained and long-lasting weight loss from a strict low calorie diet very hard to maintain. These diets lower our metabolism, meaning that we require fewer calories than previously and our body becomes geared towards storing fat. In fact, it has been shown that upon losing weight many people find this weight loss hard to maintain for any longer than a year (James and Wyatt, 1999). For this reason drastically reducing calories can hinder the weight-loss process. As we come off the diet weight rapidly returns to previous levels and then beyond initial weight in many cases. This type of weight fluctuation or 'yo-yoing' places strain on the heart and predisposes us to illness. Frequent changes of weight can increase risk of heart disease and can damage our health. It could be said that in using strict very low-calorie diets we are training ourselves to store calories, in essence training ourselves to be fat.

The following guidelines provide advice on how to lose weight effectively and minimize some of the factors we have highlighted above.

DIETARY RECOMMENDATIONS FOR WEIGHT LOSS

The easiest way to impact on energy balance is to reduce calorie intake. Consider that 300–400 calories are burnt during a typical workout. This is the calorie equivalent of drinking three pints of lager. The main aim of dietary interventions for a weight-loss programme is to reduce calorie intake in the hope of creating a negative energy balance. This method of calorie reduction should never compromise the dietary principles for healthy eating found in Chapter 15. In fact, in many instances by simply applying a healthier and balanced diet you do enough to encourage weight loss. If a diet is balanced and varied and weight still remains the same we can then simply reduce portion size to reduce calorie intake. The key to dietary modification for weight loss is to reduce calorie intake whilst maintaining levels of nutrients to ensure good health.

KEY POINT

Eat a balanced diet with contribution from all food groups (carbohydrates, proteins and fats).

Eat a wide variety of foods to ensure recommended daily intake of all nutrients.

Try to emphasize intake of vegetables, salad and fruit.

Emphasize complex forms of carbohydrate, using sugars sparingly.

Try to moderate fat intake, keeping saturate fats to a minimum.

Eat whole foods and freshly prepared food and reduce the amounts of processed food in your diet.

Limit intake of anti-nutrients, those foods with little nutritional value (alcohol, coffee and tea, nicotine, saturated fats).

Consume nutrient-dense options (see Chapter 15).

The major challenges to sustained weight loss and ideal weight maintenance are the same as those we talked about when we discussed the changes the body makes when we enter negative energy balance. Namely:

- a failure to adhere to a dietary plan over an extended period of time
- a fall in resting metabolic rate, causing a reduction in the number of calories required to maintain weight
- an increased desire of the body to consume food, especially highly calorific foods due to sensations of hunger

- a loss of athletic performance, making calorie expenditure fall.

The client's diet should try to combat all these factors. Here are some tips to help you overcome these obstacles.

Adherence

Any changes you make to your client's diet should follow the principles of behaviour change discussed in Chapter 16 to ensure that any changes are long-lasting. Psychological techniques highlighted in this chapter such as self-monitoring (a food diary) and behavioural cues (reminder notes, removing unhealthy foods from the house etc.) should also be used. To aid adherence any dietary changes should take into consideration the client's lifestyle as much as possible. We should try to stick to the client's normal dietary routines as much as possible without compromising their chances of successful weight loss. A diet should also be selected that is palatable to the client, taking account of their tastes and preferences, including advice on healthy foods that they like to eat. An in-depth consultation with the client should include discussion of how, when and what they eat, to learn more about their dietary habits.

Thermic effect of feeding

We can increase energy usage by increasing the ***thermic effect of feeding*** (***TEF***). Every time we eat, our metabolism rises and our calorie expenditure goes up. We can increase calorie expenditure due to the TEF by eating smaller quantities of food frequently throughout the day. The one danger of 'grazing' is that we may lose control of the number of calories we consume, so care must be taken not to eat more than normal.

It should also be noted that all foods and therefore all calories are not equal. The TEF is different for each type of nutrient because different levels of energy are required to metabolize each one. For example, the digestion of protein uses up nearly 10 times as much energy as

Table 6.1 Calculated thermic effect of feeding (TEF) for four types of nutrient showing the relative increase in energy expenditure after eating these types of food

Nutrient	Fat	Carbohydrate	Protein	Alcohol
TEF	0–3%	5–10%	20–30%	10–30%

the digestion of fat. Table 6.1 shows the relative increase in metabolism in terms of TEF values.

In simple terms, this shows that we burn more calories in trying to digest and use proteins as fuel than we do when using fat, which can be broken down very easily and stored. That is why it is important to maximize protein in the diet and minimize fat.

Drinking water

When we drink cold water it takes energy (calories) to heat the water up to a temperature appropriate for the body. It has been estimated that drinking 2 litres of water per day augments energy expenditure by approximately 96 calories (Boschmann et al., 2003). Water is also very important in the way the body metabolizes fat. Dehydration prevents efficient metabolism of fat (Boschmann et al., 2003). Hydration is also very important for cardiovascular performance and therefore TEPA would fall if we exercised while dehydrated. See Chapter 15 for hydration strategies.

Satiety

Hunger is a massive problem for people on a diet. Trying to combat sensations of hunger is very important. Protein is very satiating (see Chapter 15). Someone who has eaten a protein-rich food (meat, fish) will feel fuller than if they had eaten the same number of calories in carbohydrate (bread, rice) or fat (chocolate, nuts). This is one of the reasons why high-protein diets work so well, because people are less likely to overeat. Eating smaller meals with frequent low-fat and high-protein snacks should also help satiety and satisfy feelings of hunger. Fat is very un-satiating. We are very likely to overeat and enter a positive energy balance if we have a diet high in fat (Lawton et al., 1993). Most people can eat

plenty of crisps and nuts without feeling full even though they are very calorific.

In Chapter 15 we also see that the way foods are broken down affects how we digest and store them. By eating meals that are 'slow-release' we should feel fuller for longer, making us less likely to snack. These slow-release foods also balance insulin levels, making us less likely to store calories as fat. See Chapter 15 for more information on glycaemic index and its benefits for weight loss.

We should also eat the majority of our calories earlier in the day and before or after training to aid performance and recovery. Avoid eating large meals, especially meals high in carbohydrate and fat late at night when our activity levels are lower. I try to encourage clients to consider what they are doing in the next three hours. If they are going to be active they can introduce more carbohydrates into their meal, if they are going to be sedentary I recommend they reduce carbohydrates and fats drastically.

EXERCISE AND WEIGHT LOSS

A weight-loss programme is most effective when dietary modification is combined with an exercise programme (Zuti and Golding, 1976). Maintenance of exercise and increased activity can be key in long-term maintenance of ideal weight (Pratley et al., 1994). Exercise has two primary roles within a weight-loss programme:

■ to increase calorie deficit through TEPA
■ to maintain metabolism by maintaining FFM (muscle).

We might also assume that if we can make exercise enjoyable and sociable, the likelihood of that person adhering to their exercise programme is far greater than of them adhering to a strict diet.

Consider the additional health benefits we experience from exercise, such as improved cardiovascular function, improved bone density (think osteoporosis for women), improved psychological well-being and protection from many major diseases (heart disease, cancer, diabetes etc). It is far healthier to attempt to lose weight through exercise compared to severe calorie restriction.

So what types of exercise are most effective for weight loss? If we want to make most immediate impact on our energy balance the exercise that consumes the most calories is cardiovascular exercise. Cardiovascular work is characterized by rhythmic movement of large muscle groups, usually the legs, over long periods of time: cycling or running, for example. The more cardiovascular work we can perform, the more calories our body will consume. In the case of long slow distance training *volume* is the key variable. The more we do, the more calories we will burn. Twenty minutes of moderate work will burn far more calories than 10 minutes' work at a slightly higher intensity, for example.

Imagine a new client who has very little training experience. They may not be used to going to the gym, they do very little exercise at present and want to lose weight. I recommend that the initial goals for these types of client involve increasing *cardiovascular volume*. I usually set an initial target for beginners on a weight-loss programme of building to 120 minutes per week of low-intensity cardiovascular exercise of *preferred exercise intensity* (i.e. they choose how hard they work). This can be achieved in whatever format they like over however many training sessions, using exercises of their choice. In the initial stages I feel it is more valuable to increase volume rather than intensity (how hard they work). Once this target is achieved they will either continue to increase cardiovascular volume if they have the time available; if they do not, I will then ask them to increase exercise intensity. The benefit of this is that it allows them to set realistic goals for themselves, using exercises that they feel comfortable using, and they become accustomed to spending more time in the gym. The lower-intensity work will condition them in preparation for higher-intensity

work in later stages of their training. Just setting a target of 120 minutes of cardiovascular work gives them the freedom to choose when, where and how they achieve their goals, enabling them to fit exercise around their other life commitments.

Although this may be appropriate for a novice client, it has been generally accepted that this is not the most time-efficient way of losing weight through exercise. We have to increase the intensity of exercise for more effective results. Tremblay *et al.* (1994) demonstrated that a group doing **high-intensity interval training (HIIT)** (see Chapter 5) achieved over three times as much fat loss as a group using endurance training, despite expending less than half as many calories. If the calorie level is the key variable, how can this be the case?

Excess post-exercise oxygen consumption (EPOC)

Energy expenditure does not return to normal levels immediately after exercise. The body has to work to recover to a resting state after exercise, repairing muscle damage, removing waste products (lactic acid) and replenishing energy stores. These tasks require energy and therefore metabolism is raised for a period following exercise. This elevated energy expenditure following exercise is called **excess post-exercise oxygen consumption (EPOC)**. The size and duration of this period of raised metabolism are controversial, but they have been shown to be proportional to the intensity and duration of the exercise (Poehlem, 1989). The intensity and duration of exercise engaged in by most non-athletes (40–70 per cent VO_2max for 15–40 minutes) typically result in a return of metabolism to baseline values within 5–40 minutes. This accounts for only a further 21–125 kcal of energy expended beyond that used in the exercise itself (Melby, 1993). By increasing the intensity of the exercise we can increase the level of EPOC. In individuals able to maintain higher-intensity exercise for long periods, the resultant EPOC may be more significant. Fat burnt post-exercise was seen to be 23.8 per cent higher 3 hours after exercise in high-intensity conditions compared with low intensity.

One way to achieve this increased EPOC in unconditioned individuals unable to sustain high-intensity exercise for any length of time is through the use of *interval training* (see Chapter 5). This involves the use of bursts of higher-intensity exercise followed by rest periods to allow recovery and continued work. A walk–jog programme can be very effective for those unable to sustain long periods of running, for example.

The fat-burning zone

It is a common misconception that we burn more fat at lower intensities of work and therefore low-intensity work is good for weight loss. We do see that at lower-intensity exercise greater percentages of fat are burnt compared with carbohydrate. At 65 per cent maximum intensity the greatest percentage of fat is burnt (Romijn *et al.*, 1993). As intensity increases above 65 per cent, the percentage fat oxidation starts to drop off. This might suggest that to burn more fat and lose weight we need to work less hard for longer. Many cardiovascular machines even have fat-burning programmes designed to get you working at this intensity. This is not the case. As we increase intensity of exercise, although percentage fat usage

6.2 Diagram of fat usage, high-intensity to low-intensity

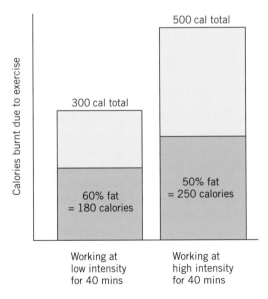

falls relative to other fuels such as sugars, the total amount of calories we consume increases. In fact, because calorie usage increases, the total amount of calories burnt from fat oxidation also increases above those levels seen at a lower intensity of work. This demonstrates that working at higher intensities is more effective for burning fat during your workout (Figure 6.2).

We also know that to have an impact on weight we need to create a negative energy balance by using up more *calories*. For this reason I focus my exercise prescription for weight loss on the number of calories being burnt, not what type of calories are being burnt. We also see above that working at higher intensities also increases EPOC, the total amount of calories burnt after exercise.

Fitness training and weight loss

Improved fitness increases the intensity at which we can work and increases the number of calories we can burn in a given period of time. In this way an individual who trains at high intensities to improve fitness forces the body to adapt to become more efficient at providing their body with energy from fat and carbohydrate. Working at lower intensities and dieting condition the body to conserve fat and carbohydrate. This is one reason why athletes training to get fit are often very lean and toned, and those individuals looking simply to lose weight often have the biggest difficulties in achieving their goals. The best way to increase fitness over a short space of time is through high-intensity interval training.

Removing threshold mentality

We can increase the thermic effect of physical activity (TEPA) in places other than just the gym. Many clients feel that the only time in which they are burning calories is when they are in the gym training and they can watch the calorie counters on the machines. It will help your client's attempts at weight loss if you remove this *threshold mentality* that says that they have to be sweating to be doing worthwhile activity. Playing sports, dancing, walking the dog, gardening are all examples of activities that can burn calories and contribute to weight loss. It has been demonstrated that this type of **lifestyle activity** is as beneficial as structured cardiovascular work as part of a weight-control programme. Westerterp (2001) demonstrated that those individuals performing greater levels of moderate-intensity activities, walking the dog and housework, for example, burnt more calories than those performing more high-intensity activity such as weight training because they spent far more time doing them. These activities may be far easier to maintain and adhere to, as they become part of a client's natural lifestyle far quicker than their gym workout.

Spot reduction

We often see people doing particular exercises to work muscles corresponding to the areas of the body from which they want to lose weight. This is known as **spot reduction**. The classic example is people who do crunches to get a flat 'washboard' stomach. Although increases in muscle mass can change your appearance, it is not possible to select where we will lose fat from and fat certainly does not turn into muscle with resistance exercise. Fat will go from areas predetermined by a combination of genetics, gender and hormone levels. The flat stomach or 'six-pack' will only appear when we reduce subcutaneous (below the skin) fat around the stomach. Crunches will not achieve this because they will not make a significant impact on our energy balance or RMR.

When a client says they want to tone up a certain area, we have to look at what they are actually asking. Are they asking to build muscle size (hypertrophy) to alter their shape? Or do they want to lose weight/fat from that area, making what muscle they have more defined? If it is the latter you would want to prescribe a weight-loss programme over a hypertrophy/muscle-building programme.

Resistance training and weight loss

The arguments for and against resistance training to help with weight loss are quite complex. We

highlighted that exercise can help with a weight-loss programme by either burning calories or by maintaining or increasing resting metabolic rate (RMR). Resistance training is designed to build fat-free mass (i.e. muscle). Resistance training may not burn as many calories but it may be more effective in maintaining or increasing RMR.

Because muscle is metabolically active, we see that 1 kg of muscle can potentially burn between 60 and 100 calories per day, unlike fat, which will only burn 6 calories per kilogram. In theory, if you trained your client to put on 5 kg of muscle, this would equate to 1000 calories burned a day, simply due to the increase in RMR. This would be sufficient to stimulate a 0.5 kg weight loss every week if diet remained the same.

It is important to be aware that there is mixed scientific evidence regarding the effect of resistance training on RMR. Many studies have found no effect of resistance training on RMR. On the other hand, Pratley et al. (1994) observed an 8 per cent increase in RMR during a 16-week period of resistance training in 50- to 60-year-old men, resulting in an increased metabolism of 120 cal/day. Their weight stayed the same but body fat reduced and lean mass increased.

There is significant evidence to suggest that resistance training can be highly effective in a weight-loss programme. In one study 72 overweight individuals participated in an eight-week exercise programme. The participants were placed in two groups. The first group performed 30 minutes of endurance exercise on a stationary cycle. The second group performed only 15 minutes of exercise on the stationary cycle plus an additional 15 minutes of weight-resistant exercises. At the conclusion of the study, the 'endurance only' group lost a total of 1.6 kg, 1.4 kg of which was fat and 0.2 kg was muscle loss (Table 6.2). On the other hand, the 'endurance and weight resistance' group lost 3.6 kg with an actual fat loss of 4.5 kg and an increase of 0.9 kg of lean body weight (Westcott, 1991).

Another study compared a combination of weight training and diet compared with dieting or weight training alone (Ballor et al., 1988). They demonstrated that weight training increased fat

Table 6.2 Difference in weight loss in two groups with and without resistance training

	Endurance training 30 min	Endurance 15 min and weight training 15 min
Weight change (lb)	–3.5	–8
Fat change (lb)	–3	–10
Lean mass change (lb)	–0.5	+2

From Westcott (1991).

Table 6.3 Comparison between a group combining weight training with dieting and groups doing weight training or dieting only

	Control	Diet	Weight training	Weight training and diet
Weight (kg)	–0.38	–4.47	+0.45	–3.89
Fat (kg)	–0.07	–3.56	–0.62	–4.32
Lean mass (kg)	–0.31	–0.91	+1.07	+0.43

loss and maintained fat-free mass. Their results are summarized in Table 6.3.

These studies indicate that resistance training does appear to be very beneficial when used alongside dietary changes and cardiovascular exercise. We have to be very careful in focusing solely on resistance training in order to lose weight. First, muscle weighs more than fat so a client may actually see their weight rise instead of going down. This may be highly detrimental to their motivation unless the visual change in their body shape is highly significant. We see from Chapter 16 that we require a positive energy balance to build muscle effectively. This may mean that they put on additional fat following a purely muscle-building programme. This would again be detrimental to their motivation.

We may question the likelihood that a person looking to lose weight is going to be able to gain 5 kg of muscle in a short space of time, especially if this person is unconditioned. Typically it takes a month to put on 0.5 kg of lean muscle, so the potential for weight loss in the early stages of training is very low.

I would always advise a combination of all three strategies: cardiovascular work, resistance training and dietary modification, if only for the numerous health benefits that exercise offers in addition to achieving desired weight levels. When explaining to my clients why we are doing resistance training in a weight-loss programme I try to explain that weight training will 'stabilize your weight'. In other words, although your weight will go down slower because muscle weighs more than fat, it will also stabilize your weight on the way up by increasing your metabolism, making the impact of a holiday or a relapse from your diet and exercise plan less great. The introduction of exercise also appears to aid in long-term weight maintenance and adherence to a weight-loss programme.

CHAPTER SUMMARY

Although weight loss is simple in theory, it is not always easy in practice. This is why as a nation and in most developed countries we are losing the battle against obesity. After this chapter you should appreciate that a combination of high-intensity cardiovascular exercise, elevated activity levels and appropriate diet is the key to achieving a desired weight goal. Do not underestimate the value of psychological techniques to support adherence to such diet and exercise plans to ensure long-term adherence to a weight-control programme.

REFERENCES AND RECOMMENDED READING

1. American College of Sports Medicine (2001) Position stand. Appropriate intervention strategies for weight loss and prevention of weight gain for adults. *Medicine and Science in Sports and Exercise* 33:2145–2156.

2. Astrup, A., Gøtzsche, P.C., van de Werken, K. *et al.* (1999) Meta-analysis of resting metabolic rate in formerly obese subjects. *American Journal of Clinical Nutrition* 69:1117–1122.

3. Bahr, R. (1992) Excess post-exercise oxygen consumption. *Acta Physiologica Scandinavica* 144:3–70.

4. Ballor, D.L., Katch, V.L., Becque, M.D. and Marks, C.R. (1988) Resistance weight training during caloric restriction enhances lean body weight maintenance. *American Journal of Clinical Nutrition* 47:19–25.

5. Bjorntorp, P. (1997) Obesity. *Lancet* 350:423–426.

6. Boschmann, M., Steiniger J., and Hille, U. *et al.* (2003) Water-induced thermogenesis. *Journal of Clinical Endocrinology and Metabolism* 88:6015–6019.

7. Cavallo, E., Armellini, F., Zamboni, M., Vicentini, R., Milani, M.P. and Bosello, O. (1990) Resting metabolic rate, body composition and thyroid hormones. Short-term effects of very low-calorie diet. *Hormone and Metabolic Research* 22:632–635.

9. Dunn, A.L., Marcus, B.H., Kambert, J.B., Garcia, M.E., Kohl, H.W. and Blair, S.N. (1999) Comparison of lifestyle and structured interventions to increase physical activity and cardiorespiratory fitness. *Journal of the American Medical Association* 281:327–334.

10. Feinman, R.D. and Fine, E.J. (2004) 'A calorie is a calorie' violates the second law of thermodynamics. *Nutrition Journal* 3:9.

11. Flegal, K.M., Carroll, M.D., Kuczmarski, R.J. and Johnson, C.L. (1998) Overweight and obesity in the United States: prevalence and trends, 1960–1994. *International Journal of Obesity and Related Metabolic Disorders* 22:39–47.

12. Garrow, J.S. (2000) *Human Nutrition and Dietetics.* Edinburgh: Churchill Livingstone.

13. Geliebter, A., Maher, M.M., Gerace, L., Gutin, B., Heymsfield, S.B. and Hashim, S.A. (1997) Effects of strength or aerobic training on body composition, resting metabolic rate, and peak oxygen consumption in obese dieting subjects. *American Journal of Clinical Nutrition* 66:557–563.

14. James, O.H. and Wyatt, H.R. (1999) Relapse in obesity treatment: biology or behaviour? *American Journal of Clinical Nutrition* 69:1064–1065.

15. Lawton, C.L., Burley, V.J., Wales, J.K. and Blundell, J.E. (1993) Dietary fat and appetite control in obese subjects: weak effects on satiation and satiety. *International Journal of Obesity* 17:409–416.

16. Melby, C.L. and Hill, J.O. (1999) Exercise, macronutrient balance and body weight regulation. *Sports Science Exchange.* http://wwww.gssiweb.com

17. Melby, C.L., Scholl, C., Edwards, G. and Bullough, R. (1993) Effect of acute resistance exercise on post-exercise energy expenditure and resting metabolic rate. *Journal of Applied Physiology* 75:1847–1853.

18. Poehlem, E.T. (1989) A review: exercise and its influence on resting energy metabolism in man. *Medicine and Science in Sports and Exercise* 21:515–525.

19. Poehlem, E.T., Melby, C.L. and Goran, M.I. (1991) The impact of exercise and diet restriction on daily energy expenditure. *Sport Medicine* 11:78–101.

20. Pratley, R., Nicklas, B., Rubin, M., Miller, J., Smith, A., Smith, M., Hurly, B. and Goldberg, A. (1994) Strength training increases resting metabolic rate and norepinephrine levels in healthy 50–65-year-old men. *Journal of Applied Physiology* 76: 133–137.

21. Romijn, J.A., Coyle, E.F. and Sidossis, L. (1993) Regulation of endogenous fat and carbohydrate metabolism in regulation to

exercise intensity and duration. *American Journal of Physiology* 265: E380–391.

22. Tremblay, A., Simoneau, J.A. and Bouchard, C. (1994) Impact of exercise intensity on body fatness and skeletal muscle metabolism. *Metabolism* 43:814–818.

23. Tuck, M.L., Sowers, J., Dornfeld, L., Kledzik, G. and Maxwell, M. (1981) The effect of weight reduction on blood pressure, plasma rennin activity, and plasma aldosterone levels in obese patients. *New England Journal of Medicine* 304:930–933.

24. US Department of Health and Human Services. Office of the Surgeon General (2001) The Surgeon General's call to action to prevent and decrease overweight and obesity. Rockville, MD: United States Department of Health and Human Services 2001

25. Westcott, W. (1991) Resistance weight training with endurance training improves fat loss. *Fitness Management* November.

26. Westerterp, K.R. (2001) Pattern and intensity of physical activity: keeping moderately active is the best way to boost total daily energy expenditure. *Nature* 410:539.

27. Westerterp, K.R. (2004) Diet-induced thermogenesis, *Nutrition and Metabolism* 1:5.

28. Williams, M.H. (1995) *Nutrition for Fitness and Sport*, 4th edn. Madison, WI: Brown and Benchmark Publishers.

FUNCTIONAL EXERCISE: EXERCISE FOR IMPROVED MOVEMENT

THIS CHAPTER CONTAINS

- Functional training
- Key components of functional movement
- Neuromuscular coordination
- Nervous system control over movement
- Proprioreception
- Neuromuscular coordination and strength
- How we learn to move: motor learning
- Motor programme compatibility
- Control over external forces for stabilization and balance
- Components of functional muscle action
- Exercise prescription for function
- Exercise examples
- References and recommended reading

Functional movements are those we perform on a daily basis or that relate to some aspect of sport performance. ***Functional training*** is a health industry hot topic. Numerous articles are being produced giving the next new 'functional' exercise designed to improve how we move. But what makes one exercise more functional than another? Are typical gym programmes functional? And how do we design a functional workout? In this chapter we will answer these questions. We will explain how the brain's ability to coordinate muscle action is the key behind accurate and powerful movement. We shall see that instead of focusing solely on training muscles in the gym we should also train our brain to improve the quality of our movement.

FUNCTIONAL TRAINING

Whilst many exercises focus on how we look or how well we fit into clothes, functional training is designed to improve the way we move and the way our body performs. Functional exercises are those that ***reproduce and therefore improve everyday movements***, for example walking, lifting, bending and twisting or – if the person is a sport performer – sprinting, kicking, jumping and throwing. Remember in Chapter 2 the principle of specificity that says we get better at what we do.

functional exercises: exercises that reproduce and therefore improve function.

If we look at how people typically train in the gym, their programmes often include a seated leg press, seated chest press, mid row, machine bicep curl, machine tricep press, crunches and dorsal raises. On first impressions we might see no problem with that programme as it stands. But if we consider how we move in everyday life and the skills required to perform sporting activities, the two probably bear little resemblance. If we were to describe a typical gym routine we might use words such as slow, controlled, stable, seated, predictable, isolated. In reality, everyday movements or skills used in sports are none of these things. Take a rugby tackle, for example. A rugby tackle is a highly-skilled, explosive movement requiring all the muscles of the body working together in an unstable, unsupported environment. How we move and how we see people typically train appear to be worlds apart.

A functional exercise performed with good technique under reasonable loads will result in **functional carryover**. This is the degree by which training in an artificial setting, the gym for example, carries over to our performance at daily tasks.

KEY POINT

Functional carryover is likely to increase if our training more closely resembles our day-to-day activities and reproduces key components of natural movement.

The question is, what elements of normal movement in daily life do we have to reproduce to ensure we increase functional carryover?

KEY COMPONENTS OF FUNCTIONAL MOVEMENT

There are some key aspects of how we move that have to be reproduced in our gym training to increase functional carryover. These key aspects of movement include:

- use of skilled movements requiring fine control of muscles by the brain, known as **neuromuscular coordination**
- use of common and **relevant movement patterns** performed by an individual on a daily basis
- control over forces acting on the body (e.g. gravity) to allow **balance** and **stability**
- functional muscle action characterized by varying **speeds of movement** (from static holding positions to explosive movements), **stretch-shortening cycles** and muscles working in **synergy** (together) rather than in isolation.

This chapter will explain in more depth some of this terminology and why these points are so important when we talk about function.

NEUROMUSCULAR COORDINATION

In Chapter 1 we defined the **kinetic chain** as being the sum total of the nerves and muscles used to move bones and joints during movement. It is the brain that initiates and drives movement. It is the brain that sends messages via our nervous system to drive our muscles in order to move the complex system of levers and fulcrums known as our skeleton (see Figure 1.2).

Unfortunately we often fall into the trap of focusing on training only our muscles in the gym and neglect the other aspects of the kinetic chain, such as the brain and skeleton. We must understand that the brain controls movement. Athletic movement is a skill determined by the nervous system's ability to coordinate muscle action. This skill can be called **neuromuscular coordination**.

neuromuscular coordination: the ability of the brain to control muscles to produce movement.

We can train neuromuscular coordination by increasing the **neural demand** of an exercise. In Chapter 2 we highlighted various different ways of increasing neural demand. These included reducing support and stability, increasing the number of planes of motion used during an exercise, decreasing feedback, unilateral loading or combining movements. A functional programme will increase a client's neuromuscular coordination by providing exercises with high neural demand without compromising form or technique.

NERVOUS SYSTEM CONTROL OVER MOVEMENT

Movement is produced both at a conscious level and at a subconscious level using information passed through different types of nerves using different parts of the nervous system. **Spinal** *reflexes* generate involuntary movements that occur without conscious effort. Examples of these basic reflexes include closing the eyes as an object approaches, withdrawal reflexes that involve movement away from harmful stimuli or pain, and stretch reflexes that cause contraction in response to excessive and sudden stretch in muscle. The **brain stem** generates involuntary muscle action with respect to controlling posture and balance, including equilibrium and righting reactions (see Chapter 8). The **motor cortex** within the brain generates conscious, voluntary movement.

Normal movement (function) involves all three of these centres of movement – spinal reflexes, postural reflexes and voluntary movement – at the same time. This does not happen when we exercise in a supported environment such as when using a machine leg press or chest press, for example. The support provided by a seat in a machine exercise means that there is very little need for reflex control of posture and balance. This is one reason why machine exercises are less functional than free-weight exercises. A person using functional resistance training puts their body in an unstable and unsupported environment that requires reflex control of posture and balance along with conscious drive of muscles to push or pull a weight.

KEY POINT

Functional movement occurs in an unstable, unsupported environment that utilizes both involuntary and voluntary muscle action.

Does this mean that working on a Swiss ball or a wobble board makes an exercise automatically more functional? This is a common misconception and has led to many exercises that are designed to make balance more difficult being labelled as being functional. More unbalanced and unstable exercises are not automatically more functional. The level of instability should mimic that seen in everyday life or in the athlete's sporting context. Training on a wobble board may be functional for a surfer but not for someone who is not required to have the same degree of balance. See Chapter 8 for more information on balance training.

PROPRIORECEPTION

For skilled movement we need to have as much information about our surroundings as possible. Our senses provide us with this invaluable information. This information comes from:

- visual input – the eyes
- auditory input – the ears
- vestibular input – inner ear balance
- mechanical receptors – found within muscles, tendons, joints and skin.

Remove any one of these sources of feedback and see how much more difficult movement becomes. Play sport with an ear infection, for example, or with poor lighting, and see how much your skill deteriorates. Try balancing on one leg then close your eyes for another example of how important sensory feedback is.

Information regarding our surroundings and the position of our body in space is passed through **sensory neurons** back to our brains. The sum of this feedback and information is called our **proprioception**, or inner sense (Schmidt, 1991). The quality of this information and the success with which we interpret it are called our **kinaesthetic sense** or sense of movement (Schmidt, 1991). We might also call it our body awareness. Our ability to produce accurate movement relies heavily on our body awareness. By training in a **sensory-rich environment**, one in which we are unstable, unsupported and that takes a high degree of skill to perform the exercise, will improve proprioception.

Exercise that challenges our clients by placing them in a sensory-rich environment (unstable and high-skill) will train their nervous systems to become more efficient and faster, with the ability to process more information. Reflex pathways will also become more effective and proprioception increases. In this way training can improve neuromuscular coordination and our ability to move with high levels of skill.

KEY POINT

By training in an unstable, unsupported environment using high-skilled exercise we can train the nervous system to produce more accurate and powerful movements.

NEUROMUSCULAR COORDINATION AND STRENGTH

People tend to associate the size of a muscle, its cross-sectional area (CSA), with its ability to produce force. This is by no means the whole story. Muscles are made of a large number of muscle fibres. The force produced by a muscle is determined not only by its size but also by how muscle fibres can be recruited together. This is determined by our nervous system.

As we want to generate muscular force to produce movement our brain sends a message through motor neurons to muscle fibres. We might call this our *neurological drive*. The greater our neurological drive, the more muscle fibres we recruit and the greater the force we produce. It is thought that untrained individuals are not able to recruit a proportion of their muscle fibres and therefore are not able to generate the high levels of force available to trained individuals (Jones and Round, 1995; Komi, 1986). The ability to generate increased levels of neurological drive in order to recruit greater numbers of muscle fibres can be increased using high-intensity strength or power training.

KEY POINT

By training the central nervous system to drive the muscular system we can increase muscular force-production independent of muscle size.

Muscles do not work in isolation. When we move, many muscles work together to produce movement and force. This is known as muscle synergy and will be discussed in greater depth below. Another way of describing muscle synergy might be in terms of form or technique. The more effectively our muscles work together in synergy or the better our technique the more force and power we can potentially produce (Clark, 2002). If muscles do not synergize together well we might call this as loss of form or technique. In some cases this may be very subtle and hard to recognize.

KEY POINT

Muscle synergy or exercise form and technique are a large determining factor in the amount of force we can produce during movement.

Below we see how to improve muscle synergy.

HOW WE LEARN TO MOVE: MOTOR LEARNING

The body is required to perform thousands of different movements and thousands of different variations upon those movements. The number of muscles required to perform even the most basic movements is huge. Imagine trying consciously to control each and every muscle required in picking up a pencil from the floor – it simply cannot be done. The brain has to perform much of the muscular coordination required for these movements on a subconscious level. While the brain does not have the capacity to store information about every movement we perform, it does keep templates for basic movements that we perform on a regular basis. These templates have been termed *generalized motor programmes* (Schmidt, 1991).

The brain stores these motor programmes with information about which muscles are required to work at what times to execute a movement. This is known as a *relative timing pattern*. In this way the body can learn different movements without having to store information about each and every variation. It is often said that *the brain knows movements but not muscles*. The better the relative timing pattern of muscle action, the better our form and the more powerful and accurate our movements will be.

A common example of a motor programme we use is putting our car key into the ignition. It is because of a motor programme that we can insert that key so accurately every time. Trying to put the key into the ignition of a different car can be challenging because our old motor programme is not accurate any more. Crossing your arms is another example. Try folding your arm the wrong way and see how strange this feels.

When we learn new skills we have to create new motor programmes. This is known as **motor learning**. Consider when we learn a forehand shot in tennis for the first time. To begin with, our brain has no accurate motor programme for a tennis forehand, so our brain combines components of motor programmes we already have with other information to create the desired movement. This information may be in the form of seeing someone else perform the shot and/or information from a coach. This early motor programme is often inaccurate and the relative timing pattern of muscle action is such that we are not able to produce accurate shots. The shots will lack force and our skill level at this point is low. As we practise we gain experience from our success and failure at getting the ball over the net and receive further feedback from our coach. Our brain uses this information and adjusts the relative timing patterns of muscle action to build slowly a new motor programme. With time, the new motor programme becomes more accurate, the consistency of our play improves and our skill increases.

These ingrained patterns of movement generally take about 300 repetitions to learn. If a client has learned a movement incorrectly it takes roughly 5000 repetitions to relearn that skill and reform a correct motor programme. This highlights the need to instil good technique right from the start and regress any exercise if it is being performed incorrectly.

KEY POINT

Always ensure good technique from the beginning to prevent learning bad habits and incorrect motor programmes.

The better the relative timing pattern of our motor programmes, the better our muscles work together to produce force and the more powerful our movements will be. In some individuals the relative timing pattern is incorrect and form is faulty, with the wrong muscles being used at the wrong time. This causes a loss in stability and a reduction in force production. This type of relative timing error can start to be corrected in the gym by ensuring correct form and technique during weights exercises.

MOTOR PROGRAMME COMPATIBILITY

The basic premise of functional exercise is that it mimics movements that we use in everyday life. In this way we produce useful motor programmes with good relative timing patterns. Key movement patterns used frequently in daily life include the squat, lunge, standing push, standing pull, standing rotation and gait (walking or running). If we can learn motor programmes with good relative timing patterns for these basic movements in the gym this will help us when we move in everyday life. When we lift a heavy weight from the floor we will already have ingrained knowledge of how to perform a squat or dead-lift, and therefore when we lift we use good form that will help prevent injury and enable us to lift more weight.

KEY POINT

During functional training use movement patterns such as the squat, lunge, standing push, standing pull, standing rotation and gait to increase functional carryover.

Ideally it should be possible to analyse how your client has to move in their general daily lives and/or in their sport and then design their training to optimize the motor programmes of most use to them. An elderly person may have difficulty getting in and out of a chair, for example, in which case a good squat motor programme would be of use to them. A boxer who needs a powerful punch will have good use for a pushing motor programme.

If you talk to your client and learn more about their sport or activity you can even start to adapt your exercises to match more closely how he or she moves as they perform. You might start to combine movements, such as a push and rotation for the boxer who wants to improve their punch. The key is to understand that if a boxer has a very good bench press, this does not mean they will naturally have a powerful punch. The two motor programmes are very different, hence the functional carryover will be low. This follows our principle of specificity, described in Chapter 2.

KEY POINT

Strength is developed within the context of specific motor programmes by improving relative timing patterns. Different motor programmes will have limited functional carryover to each other.

Clearly, the first stage of designing a functional programme will be a detailed consultation in which you learn how your client moves in their sport or daily life so that this can be reproduced in their training.

CONTROL OVER EXTERNAL FORCES FOR STABILIZATION AND BALANCE

To be able to move well we need *control over external forces*, *stabilization* and *balance*. These are prerequisites for sound and accurate movement. Without control over external forces, stabilization and balance, the kinetic chain is in no position to perform athletic movement. The major external forces acting continuously on our bodies are *gravity*, *ground reaction force* and *momentum*. The kinetic chain is geared towards coping with these forces in order to maintain posture, stabilization and balance.

Gravity

Gravity applies continual downward pressure through our skeleton. When a body is in a good posture, it is well-balanced, with gravity passing through its centre of balance. Postural muscles have to perform minimal work to hold the body in this well balanced position. Postural reflexes control these muscles to maintain alignment and posture on a subconscious level. In poor posture the joints are not held in good alignment. This compromises function, causing postural muscles to be overworked and predisposing the body to stress and injury. Think about how your back and neck feel after you have been slumped over a computer console for several hours. Any stiffness or pain is due to the overwork of postural muscles that control the position of the head against gravity. Chapter 9 provides a more detailed description of how poor posture effects performance.

KEY POINT

To improve functional movement, it is important to improve posture, to balance the body better under gravity and reduce postural stress.

Ground reaction force

For every force we exert on an object, that object exerts an opposing force of equal magnitude. Every time we land when running or jumping there is an equal force exerted back up our leg. This is known as *ground reaction force (GRF)*. GRF places great strain through the kinetic chain and if it is not controlled the chances of injury are increased.

GRF can be very high:

- during walking GRF = 1–1.5 times body weight
- during running GRF = 2–5 times body weight
- during jumping GRF = 4–11 times body weight (Clark, 2002; National Academy of Sports Medicine, 2002).

Consider the forces exerted on the lower body of a 70 kg man jumping and landing on one leg. As much as 770 kg of force have to be absorbed on that one leg during this exercise. This explains why exercises that involve jumping – plyometrics, for example – place far more stress through the kinetic chain than traditional exercises such as squats and lunges. Shin splints are a common example of an injury caused by overexposure to GRF.

Loss of control over GRF usually manifests as a loss in stabilization. A client should be conditioned to be able to maintain stability against GRF during running. If he or she is losing stability during running (feet are flattening or knees falling in), an alternative low-impact exercise should be selected whilst further conditioning work is performed. Alternatively, more support in the form of orthotics within the shoes can be provided.

Momentum

Momentum is present whenever we are in a state of dynamic posture (i.e. we are moving). Momentum acts to maintain movement in the same direction. Whenever we move our **centre of gravity** outside our base of support we generate momentum that makes our body continue to move in the same direction (see Chapter 8). Skilled manipulation of momentum can be especially useful in sporting situations, as when a rugby player uses momentum to break through a tackle. Momentum, like GRF, has to be *eccentrically* controlled (lengthening of muscle) and *isometrically* stabilized (static contraction of muscle) before we can concentrically accelerate (shortening of muscle) in a different direction. Inability to control momentum can lead to acute injury as forces exceed the ability of muscle and soft tissue to control movement at joints.

KEY POINT

Momentum and ground reaction forces have to be eccentrically controlled and isometrically stabilized before we can concentrically accelerate in a different direction.

Although we have not mentioned other external forces, such as a blow from an opponent in a game of rugby, the three forces described above – gravity, ground reaction force and momentum –

are the primary forces that have to be controlled by the body to achieve *stabilization* and *balance*.

centre of gravity: the point at which all body weight is balanced.

Stabilization

Stabilization involves maintaining good alignment of joints. Muscles and ligaments prevent excessive movement away from neutral, providing stability. *Neutral* is the position of ideal joint alignment at which point the body is well-aligned to cope with external forces such as GRF and gravity, and is ideally positioned to produce force and movement. Imagine when our feet land as we jump, if we do not sufficiently stabilize, our knee might jut in, our back may go into excessive arch or our ankle may twist. Inability to stabilize will result in injury of muscles (strain), ligaments (strain), cartilage and even bone (fracture). Neutral posture is discussed in greater detail in Chapter 9.

Balance

Keeping balance involves controlling the body's centre of gravity so that it always remains within the base of support (see Chapter 8). As soon as the centre of gravity falls out of the base of support, momentum is generated. At this point we have to move our base of support using reflex reactions in order to retain balance.

The use of machine exercises such as the leg press or bicep curl minimizes external forces such as momentum and GRF. During exercise on fixed resistance machines we relate to gravity in an unnatural way: we are often lying down or, at best, seated with weight that does not pull downwards but is altered through a series of cables and pulleys. The support provided by the machine means that there is no need for stabilization or balance. Clearly, exercise using resistance machines has little carryover into functional activities. By working in an unsupported, unstable environment we ensure the body has to work to maintain stability and balance. A client can be taught the importance of posture along with natural control of balance by introducing exercises in which they interact with gravity in a natural way, i.e. by standing, if that is what the person does predominantly, and by using free weights. Stepping exercises, such as lunges or gait cycle (walking, running, jumping), can be used to teach a client to cope with GRFs.

KEY POINTS

To increase functional carryover:
- challenge your client's ability to maintain balance and stability by reducing support, but only to the point where form can be maintained
- get your client to interact with gravity in a natural way (i.e. standing athletes should perform predominantly standing exercises and resistance should be mainly provided by free weights)
- ensure your client is conditioned to cope with GRF by using compound lower body exercises from standing and by introducing stepping, jumping or bounding exercises (see Chapter 8).

COMPONENTS OF FUNCTIONAL MUSCLE ACTION

In the sections above we have seen how the nervous system drives movement. We will now clarify how the muscular system works during functional movement and how this differs greatly from what we tend to see people doing in gyms.

Muscles work very differently in real life compared with how we train them in the gym. The speeds with which the muscles work, the directions of muscle action, the different roles in producing movement and how they generate force differ significantly from the slow controlled movements performed using resistance machines.

The key components of functional muscle action covered in this section are:

- muscular synergy
- use of the full muscle action spectrum

- use of tri-planar movement
- stretch-shortening cycles.

By making the exercises we prescribe adhere to these principles we should increase functional carryover.

Muscular synergy

Movement is generated by a complex coordination of many different muscles, known as *muscular synergy*. The degree to which we produce force during functional movement is dictated by how well we coordinate these different muscles (Clark, 2001). Each muscle involved in a movement will have a different function depending on the type of movement, the position we start in, and the speed and force with which the movement is performed. If we take hip extension during running, for example, there are many muscles that extend the hip and push us forwards. The *prime mover* or *agonist* is the name for the muscle or muscles chiefly responsible for developing force. These are then assisted by other muscles known as *synergists*. There is a plethora of muscles that position the hip so that the force produced by our muscles translates into movement in the direction we want; these are called *neutralizers*. Many more muscles again stabilize other joints so that postural alignment can be correctly maintained and we have a solid base from which to move; these are called *stabilizers*. At the same time muscles on the opposite sides of joints, *antagonists*, have to relax to allow fluid smooth movement.

Table 7.1 gives an examples of the various roles of muscles during hip extension.

Although we talk about isolation exercises that focus on one muscle, this is not actually the case. Even in isolation exercises, many muscles work in synergy to produce movement. In reality we can isolate a movement at one joint but not a muscle.

The function of each muscle will often vary depending on the movement. How a muscle performs its particular function and how well it synergizes with the other muscles have a great influence on the accuracy and power of our

Table 7.1 Types of muscle action during movement

Possible muscle action during movement:		For example, during hip extension
Prime mover (agonist)	The main force-producing muscle in a movement	Gluteus maximus
Antagonist	The opposing muscle group required to relax to allow optimal force-production and movement from agonist	Iliopsoas
Synergists	Muscles that assist the prime mover in creating movement	Hamstrings and some adductors
Stabilizer	Muscle providing solid base on which movement can be produced	Deep abdominal stabilizers (TVA*)
Neutraliser	Muscle acting to limit unwanted movement	Hip adductors and abductors

*TVA, transverse abdominis, a deep abdominal stabilizer described in Chapter 13.

movements. This is why training has to be performed using movements the same as or similar to those that we intend to improve. Only by improving muscle synergy can we improve performance and increase functional carryover. This is achieved by ensuring motor programme compatibility as explained above.

KEY POINT

Improve muscle synergy by training using exercises with motor programmes and relative timing patterns similar to those movements we perform on a daily basis.

Machine exercises reduce the degree of muscle synergy required to move, reducing stabilizing and neutralizing muscle action by providing support and fixing movement in one direction. This again explains why training using resistance machines has less carryover to functional activities. Exercises that require balance, stabilization and coordination generally require increased levels of muscular synergy. Compound exercises that require movement at a number of joints also encourage muscle synergy.

KEY POINT

Training in an unsupported environment using compound exercises increases and improves muscle synergy.

Muscle action spectrum

During functional movements, particularly during the gait cycle (walking or running), due to GRF, muscles have to work *eccentrically* to control external force, *isometrically* to stabilize joints before muscles can contract *concentrically* to push us forwards.

- eccentric muscle action = muscle lengthening
- isometric muscle action = maintenance of length
- concentric muscle action = muscle shortening.

Due to the large loads experienced when our feet hit the ground during the gait cycle, there is an emphasis on eccentric and isometric muscle action to absorb and then stabilize momentum and GRF. This is contrary to normal resistance training that tends to focus on concentric muscle action as we lift weights. A more functional programme would therefore place greater emphasis on these other phases of muscular work. Conditioning phases of training might emphasize eccentric and isometric phases using tempos such as 3–2–1 or 4–2–2 rather than the usual 1–0–1 that we normally see in the gym. Hypertrophy and strength phases of training may use greater eccentric loads (see negative reps in Chapter 3). We might also include some power training to teach correct stabilization of force when we land from a jump (described in Chapter 8).

KEY POINT

Functional training emphasizes eccentric muscle action, i.e. controlled muscle lengthening under heavy load, followed by isometric stabilization of movement before we concentrically contract muscles.

Tri-planar movement

During typical resistance training programmes, resistance machines are used that isolate movement in one plane of motion at any one time, predominantly the sagittal plane if we consider the chest press, mid row, leg extension, leg press and crunches, for example. During functional movement there is generally a complex interaction of all three planes of movement. During everyday life we bend, twist and turn in any number of different directions. We seamlessly combine movement in all three planes of motion, sagittal, frontal and transverse (see Chapter 1). This is known as **tri-planar movement**. Our training should progress towards tri-planar movement as our skill levels increase, going from exercises that use one, then two and even three planes of movement at the same time. For example, try performing a dumbbell shoulder press, then add a side step (frontal plane movement; Figure 7.1) and then a rotation (transverse plane movement; Figure 7.2) to increase the difficulty and neural demand of the exercise.

7.1a Starting position, shoulder press with side step

7.1b Finish position, shoulder press with side step

7.2 Shoulder press and side step with rotation

During the gait cycle in particular the joints use tri-planar movement to help absorb external forces. As the foot lands, the body moves in all three planes to absorb GRF. The foot flattens (eversion as the medial arch reduces) and externally rotates. We see flexion, adduction and internal rotation at the ankle, knees and hips, in a movement called pronation. The joints are prevented from extremes of motion, also known as **overpronation**, by powerful eccentric muscle action. As the foot pushes off, the opposite occurs, with the ankle plantar flexing and the ankle, knees and hips going into extension, abduction and external rotation, in a movement know as **supination**. During this time the muscles work concentrically to drive the body forwards. Overpronation is the failure to stabilize the lower body from GRF and can be the cause of a variety of different injuries from shin splints to back pain.

Stretch-shortening cycles and counter movements

When we land during running, GRF is eccentrically absorbed as the muscle lengthens. Due to the elastic properties of muscles and tendons, some of the force absorbed can be immediately re-used to propel the body forwards. Described in greater detail in Chapter 8, this is known as **plyometric muscle action**. Because of this effect, pronation is known as the **loading phase** and the subsequent supination of the gait cycle as the **unloading phase**. The whole process from start to finish is known as a **stretch-shortening cycle**. Plyometric muscle action aids power production during functional movements. Functional training in athletes should introduce exercises that use stretch-shortening cycles (plyometric exercises) to improve power production. These exercises can be found in Chapter 8.

Counter movements involve eccentric muscle action prior to concentric movement in order to increase power production. A simple example of a counter movement is the dip in the legs seen before a jump. This type of counter movement is seen throughout the athletic world. Whenever an

7.3 Jonny Wilkinson kicking a rugby ball

7.4 Tennis serve

7.5 Overhead medicine ball throw

athlete wants to generate large amounts of force they tend to incorporate a counter movement in which the origin and insertion of the muscle they are about to use move further apart. Consider the kicking action, for example. A footballer or rugby player will reach back, lengthening through the entire body, the hips, abdominals and chest, thereby eccentrically loading these muscles before concentrically driving their leg through the ball (Figure 7.3).

As with stretch-shortening cycles, this eccentric loading increases subsequent force production. To increase functional carryover in athletes it is important to use exercises that incorporate counter movements to load muscles eccentrically in order to increase concentric muscle activation (see power training in Chapter 8).

In Figure 7.5 we show an overhead medicine ball throw in which the person will use a counter movement to pre-load the lat, and the abdominal muscles prior to throwing the ball.

EXERCISE PRESCRIPTION FOR FUNCTION

Throughout this chapter we have given tips on how to increase functional carryover. In summary, in an exercise programme designed to increase functional carryover it is important to:

- increase neuromuscular coordination by increasing the neural demand of exercises using the guidelines found in Chapter 1
- train in an unstable, unsupported environment so that we:
  - improve neuromuscular coordination
  - utilize conscious and unconscious muscle action
  - challenge proprioception

Table 7.2 Comparison of fixed resistance and functional training: summary

Resistance machine training	Functional training
Low neural demand	High neural demand
Single/fixed plane of motion	Tri-planar motion
Single joint involvement	Multiple joint involvement
Training without respect for gravity	Training in relation to gravity
Externally stabilized	Internally stabilised
Large base of support	Reduced base of support
Limited requirement for balance reactions	Large requirement for balance reactions
Predominantly concentric muscle action	Sequential eccentric, isometric and concentric work
Push and return exercise	Load and unload exercise
No plyometric muscle action	Large plyometric muscle involvement
Prime mover dominant	Emphasis on muscular synergy

- enhance muscle synergy
- improve balance
- challenge stability

■ ensure the client maintains correct form and technique so that no faulty movement patterns are learnt
■ introduce high-intensity training in conditioned athletes to increase neurological drive of muscles
■ use movements relevant to the individual to improve useful motor programmes and improve relative timing patterns.

This can be achieved by:

■ using primal movement patterns such as the squat, lunge, standing push, standing pull, standing rotation and gait
■ identifying and emphasizing the client's key primal movement patterns
■ adapting exercises to correspond with how your client has to move in their sport and general daily lives
■ making sure your client interacts with gravity in a natural way (i.e. standing athletes should perform predominantly standing exercises)
■ conditioning a client to be able to cope with GRF
■ ensuring functional muscle action by:
  - introducing exercises using more than one plane of motion
  - emphasizing eccentric and isometric phases
  - using stretch-shortening cycles and counter movements.

Table 7.2 demonstrates how fixed resistance training and functional training can differ.

Speed of movement compatibility

The relative timing patterns of muscle actions are likely to be different at different speeds. We need to mimic the speed of movement used by the client during their functional activities in our training. Similar movements performed at different speeds will have far less functional carryover. In the case of power development, exercises performed at slower speeds may even be detrimental to performance. A boxer performing a slow pushing movement in the gym may even reduce the power of their punch. We might question the benefit of doing a lot of punches holding dumbbells, for example.

Energy system compatibility

We should try to challenge the energy systems used in the activities that the athlete performs. It would be unwise to train a tennis player, for example, using predominantly aerobic long slow distance training because most of their sporting activity would be anaerobic, sprinting from one shot to another. Too much of this training may be detrimental to the athlete's speed performance (see Chapter 5).

Loading compatibility

We need to condition the athlete to be able to cope with the demands of their sport in terms of the loads that have to be absorbed, stabilized and produced by their kinetic chain. A rugby prop, for example, has to be able to push massive loads whilst in the scrum. Using light weights with high neural demand for this type of activity will have little functional carryover because the loads used are so dissimilar.

7.6a One-leg deadlift (front position)

7.6b One-leg deadlift (side position)

7.7 One-leg squat

7.8a One-leg squat touchdown (start position)

7.8b One-leg squat touchdown (finish position)

Unilateral and bilateral loading

Eighty-five per cent of the time during running is spent on one leg. If we look at most sporting activities we spend a lot of time on one leg. From this we can see the importance of training not just on two legs, utilizing squats, dead-lifts and split squats (static lunge), but also on one leg. This is known as *unilateral loading*. Exercises we might use would include one-leg deadlifts or one-leg squats, balance reaches and one-leg squat touch-downs. Try to progress from bilateral loading into semi-unilateral, where most of the weight is put through one leg, with some weight through the other leg, the lunge for example, then into unilateral exercises (Figures 7.6–7.8).

EXERCISE EXAMPLES

Table 7.3 shows examples of exercises that I prescribe to improve particular sporting movements.

These exercises should adhere to the principles described above, making them more functional and increasing their functional carryover. Do not forget that we cannot throw our clients immediately into many of these exercises. We still have to progress our clients gradually towards them, using the principles of periodization and programme design. For many clients these very functional movements may not be appropriate due to their lack of skill and conditioning.

Table 7.3 Exercises prescribed for particular sporting movements

Athletic skill	Exercise the athlete was previously doing	More functional Alternative
Tennis forehand	Abdominal crunch	Woodcut
Basketball pass	Bench press	Medicine ball chest pass
Football throw-in	Lat pulldown	Medicine ball overhead throw
Boxer's punch	Bench press	Medicine ball shoulder pass
Volleyball players jump	Squats	Medicine ball power squat

CHAPTER SUMMARY

When designing an exercise programme you have to take into consideration neuromuscular coordination, functional muscle action and requirements for stabilization and balance. This requires that the exercise is in an unsupported, relatively unstable environment in which muscles are forced to work together at both conscious and subconscious, reflex level. For a programme to have true functional carryover we have to adhere to the principle of specificity and consider the requirements of the individual. This involves analysing how the client is required to move in their everyday life and producing exercises with similar relative timing of muscle action and motor programme compatibility. In this way your client will develop strength and skill in the specific motor programmes he or she will use when moving. Often a high degree of flexibility and imagination will be far more useful than simply following rigid guidelines on repetitions, weights and sets in improving functional movement.

REFERENCES AND RECOMMENDED READING

1. Clark, M.A. (2001) *Integrated Training for the New Millennium.* Thousand Oaks, CA: National Academy of Sports Medicine, 2001.
2. Clark M (2002) *Essentials of Integrated Training Part 8: Strength Training.* www.PTonthenet.com
3. Enoka, R.M. (1988) Muscle strength and its development: new perspectives. *Sports Medicine* 6:146–168.
4. Fleck, S.J. and Kraemer, W.J. (1997) *Designing Resistance Training Programs,* 2nd edn. Champaign, IL: Human Kinetics.
5. Jones, D.A. and Round, J.M. (1995) *Skeletal Muscle in Health and Disease: a textbook of muscle physiology.* Manchester: Manchester University Press.
6. Komi, P.V. (1986) How important is neural drive for strength and power development in human skeletal muscle? In: *Biochemistry of Exercise,* 6th edn. Champaign, IL: Human Kinetics.
7. National Academy of Sports Medicine (2002) *Integrated Function of the Kinetic Chain.* Personal Trainer Distance Learning CD-ROM.
8. National Strength and Conditioning Association (2002) Correspondence course.
9. Sale, D.G. (1986) Neural adaptation in strength and power training. In: Jones, N.L., McCartney, N. and McComas, A.J. (eds) *Human Muscle Power.* Champaign, IL: Human Kinetics.
10. Sale, D.G. (1987) Influence of exercise and training on motor unit activation. *Exercise and Sport Science Reviews* 15:95–151.
11. Sale, D.G. (1992) Neural adaptation to strength training. In: Komi, P.V. (ed) *Strength and Power in Sport.* London: Blackwell Scientific, chapter 9A.
12. Schmidt, R.A. (1991) *Motor Learning and Performance.* Champaign, IL: Human Kinetics.

SPORT-SPECIFIC TRAINING: BALANCE, POWER, SPEED AND AGILITY

THIS CHAPTER CONTAINS

- Speed, agility and quickness
- Relationship between strength, power, speed and sports performance
- Training to develop explosive strength/power
- Reactive power: plyometric training

- Speed
- Agility and quickness
- Balance training
- Sport analysis
- References and recommended reading

Most sports require an element of skill combined with physical attributes such as balance, speed, agility, quickness and power. But because the average gym programme is dominated by muscles working at slow contraction speeds and in isolation, these attributes are not significantly enhanced. Many athletes fail to get the most out of their workout by training in this way. The principle of functional carryover as explained in Chapter 7 helps us to understand that our training should mimic the way we want to move in our sport. In this chapter we introduce the principles of coaching sport-specific skills in order to improve carryover into athletic sport performance. We identify the types of training an athlete needs to perform to make them quicker, stronger and more agile.

SPEED, AGILITY AND QUICKNESS

Speed, agility and quickness are three important attributes in athletic performance. **Speed** is maximal velocity independent of acceleration, and is very important for athletes sprinting over 60 metres in straight lines. **Quickness** is the ability to accelerate or the time taken to reach maximal speed, and is very important in distances less than 60 metres. **Agility** is a combination of acceleration and deceleration, combined with an ability to change direction. Agility and quickness may be of more importance to athletes participating in ball sports such as football, rugby, tennis or squash, in which they are reacting to the movement of a ball or an opponent. These athletes vary rarely have to sprint distances over 20 metres.

There are a number of physical factors underpinning speed, agility and quickness. These include maximal strength, explosive strength (power), reactive strength (plyometric power), quality of movement (skill) and balance.

RELATIONSHIP BETWEEN STRENGTH, POWER, SPEED AND SPORT PERFORMANCE

Many athletes make the mistake of training for sports by focusing solely on developing **maximal strength** in the gym. Maximal strength training involves increasing peak force production. This is the highest level of force an individual can produce or the heaviest weight they can lift. But because muscles require time to produce high levels of force, maximal strength training is generally performed at slow speeds. We can measure maximal strength using a one rep max test, the most weight you can lift once. The bench press or a squat is typically used, and it is not uncommon for sports teams to have the bench press and squat as a measure of performance for their athletes. Unfortunately this type of performance bears very little relevance to many sporting activities in which movements are performed under maximal speeds.

Increases in strength are specific to the speed at which we train. Train slowly and we become slow. We do not want to produce slow athletes so we must train in a **velocity-specific** manner. Activities in sporting contexts such as jumps, kicks and throws tend to require movements at fast speeds. These types of movement require something known as **power**. Baechle (1994) describes power as 'the rate at which work can be done'. Power is a function of force and speed together and in laboratory conditions is measured as **maximum rate of force development (mRFD)**.

Work = force x distance

$$Power = \frac{work}{time}$$

This means that the faster we can produce force, the more powerful we will be. This is best illustrated by our ability to perform a vertical jump. When we jump, the time from the start of the jump to the time we leave the ground is typically less than 350 m (Hakkinen *et al.*, 1985;

8.1 Graph Hakkinen 1985

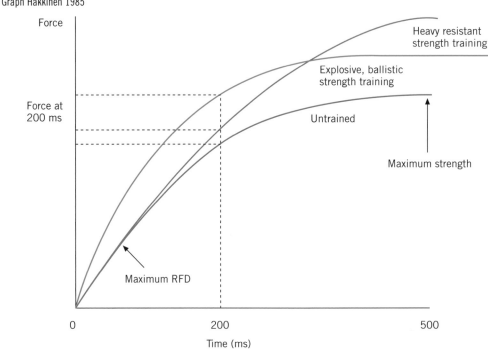

Hakkinen and Komi, 1985). Most of the force-producing potential of the muscle developed through slow maximal strength training cannot be used until way after this time and is therefore of limited use. For this reason maximal strength training does not produce great improvements in functional movements related to sports such as running or jumping (i.e. there is limited functional carryover). In fact, slow exercise may even impair power development if performed alone (Hakkinen and Myllyla, 1990).

Of key importance to our ability to jump high is producing force as quickly as possible. This is known as our maximum rate of force development (mRFD) or power. The graph in Figure 8.1 demonstrates this. It shows the maximal strength (the highest point of the curve), the mRFD (steepness of the curve) and the force developed at 200 m in three subjects, one who is strength-trained, one trained using activities focused at developing power and a third who is untrained.

We see that although maximal force is higher in the strength-trained group there is no increase in mRFD. The highest force at 200 m was in the power-trained subject because of his much higher mRFD. In reality, the greatest benefits in jumping ability and speed are produced from a combination of both maximal strength and power training (Adams *et al.*, 1992). An increased maximum rate of force development will support and provide the foundation for subsequent power training in a periodized programme.

TRAINING TO DEVELOP EXPLOSIVE STRENGTH/POWER

To develop power, explosive movements, usually some sorts of jumps or throws are used, in which a weight is moved as quickly as possible. Several training methods are popular for increasing power. These include Olympic lifting, throwing exercises using medicine balls, and weighted jumping.

Olympic lifting

Olympic lifting can be simply described as jumping with weight. The weight – usually loaded onto a bar, but dumbbells or other tools can be used – is lifted from the ground and explosively driven upwards to enable the athlete to dip under the bar and 'catch' the weight. Power cleans and snatches are examples of Olympic lifts.

8.2a Medicine ball power squat (start position)

8.2b Medicine ball power squat (finish position)

Power clean   8.3 Clean start   8.4 Clean midway shrug   8.5 Clean catch (starting position)   8.6 Clean catch (finishing position)

8.3

8.4

8.5

8.6

- Stand over the barbell with the balls of the feet positioned under the bar slightly wider apart than hip width.
- Squat down and grip the bar with an overhand grip slightly wider than shoulder width.
- Position the shoulders over the bar with spine in neutral. Useful cues are to drop the hips and lift the chest.
- Pull the bar up off the floor by extending the hips and knees keeping the spine in the same position. As the bar reaches the knees, vigorously raise the shoulders while keeping the barbell close to the thighs.

- As the bar reaches midway up the thigh, jump explosively upwards, extending the body and driving the hips forwards.
- Shrug the shoulders and pull the barbell upward with the arms, allowing the elbows to flex out to the sides.
- Keeping the bar close to the body, aggressively pull the body under the bar, rotating the elbows around the bar.
- Catch the bar on the shoulders while moving into a squat position before standing up.

Snatch

8.7 Snatch start   8.8 Snatch high pull   8.9 Snatch catch   8.10 Snatch finish

8.7

8.8

8.9

8.10

- Stand over the barbell with the balls of the feet positioned under the bar, hip width or slightly wider than hip width apart. Squat down and grip the bar with a wide overhand grip.
- Position the shoulders over the bar with the back in neutral.
- Pull the bar up off the floor by extending the hips and knees. As the bar reaches the knees, the back maintains the same angle to the floor as in the starting position. When the barbell passes the knees, vigorously raise the shoulders while keeping the bar as close to the legs as possible.

- When the bar reaches the mid-thigh, jump explosively upwards, extending the body and pushing the hips forwards.
- Shrug the shoulders and pull the barbell upwards, with the arms allowing the elbows to pull up to the sides, keeping them over the bar as long as possible.
- Aggressively pull the body under the bar.
- Catch the bar at arms' length while moving into the squat position. Catch the barbell, locking out arms in the squat position.
- Squat up into standing position with barbell overhead.

Power training should be performed with workloads of approximately 30 per cent of your maximum squat weights. Because of the risk of injury involved with power training, ensure that you are coached on Olympic lifting prior to attempting these lifts and ensure good levels of prior conditioning. The power clean and the snatch are demonstrated in Figures 8.3–8.10 as two examples of Olympic lifts. Realise there are many variations on these two exercises.

Medicine ball training

Accelerating a weight as quickly as possible develops power. The disadvantage of Olympic lifting is that at some stage the weight has to decelerate, so that the lift can be completed and the weight is caught. The advantage of medicine balls is that they can be released and thrown, removing the need for any deceleration of weight. Ideally a partner is required so that balls can be thrown to each other, but medicine balls can also be thrown against walls when required. Here are some example exercises in which a medicine ball can be added.

- *Power squat:* This is ideal for developing lower body power. Any athlete who has to run or jump or push explosively will benefit from this exercise. Simply jump, throwing a ball into the air, starting using a counter movement into a dipped position.
- *Twisting throw:* This is used for force development in the transverse plane and is ideal for athletes who have to throw, hit or rotate explosively. From standing, turn and throw the medicine ball to a partner by twisting through the waist in a similar way to a rugby pass. (Figure 8.11)
- *Overhead throw:* This is used for athletes who have to hit or throw overhead (e.g. volleyball serve, tennis serve, football throw-in). Starting from a standing position, throw the ball overhead as if performing a football throw in. (Figure 8.12)

8.11a Medicine ball twisting throw (start position)

8.11b Medicine ball twisting throw (finish position)

8.12a Medicine ball overhead throw (start position)

8.12b Medicine ball overhead throw (finish position)

■ *Chest pass:* This is used to develop power when pushing a weight forwards. Athletes who require this skill include basketball players, boxers or rugby players when they hand-off a tackle. Throw the medicine ball to a partner as if passing a basketball. (Figure 8.13)

8.13a Medicine ball chest pass (start position)

8.13b Medicine ball chest pass (finish position)

■ *Weighted jumps:* As with the power squat using the medicine ball, we can add resistance to an explosive jump by having a barbell on the shoulders. The weight recommended is light to enable the athlete to accelerate the weight. I generally recommend a weight 30 per cent of your squat, one rep max.

Acute exercise variables with power training

Power training has to be performed under extremely high intensities in order to achieve the speed of movement required. For this reason repetitions are low (1–6) and rest is high (3 minutes or more). If an athlete performs power training when tired, their mRFD falls and they will only develop strength at slower speeds, which may even be detrimental to power development. If you train slowly you will move slowly. Slow power training also increases the chances of injury, as stabilization and posture deteriorate.

Post-activation potentiation

Doing a high-intensity strength exercise immediately followed by a power exercise can increase levels of power production (Baker, 1996). The strength exercise activates type II muscle fibres (see Chapter 3), allowing them to be more readily used to produce power, and trains the athlete to use increased levels of neural drive. Exercises of similar movement patterns should be combined: a squat followed by a jump squat, or a lunge followed by a jumping lunge, for example.

REACTIVE POWER: PLYOMETRIC TRAINING

Reactive power describes the additional force generated using a pre-stretch or counter movement. Whenever we perform an eccentric (lengthening) movement under load, energy is stored within the elastic components of muscle (primarily within tendons). When this eccentric movement is immediately followed by a concentric (shortening) contraction, this stored energy is released and contributes towards subsequent force production. This is called **plyometric** force production. These counter movements add force to explosive movements such as jumps, throws or kicks. It is easy to experience the effect: try to jump as far as you can, starting in a dipped position; try this again but this time move into the dip before jumping. You should jump further the second time around, due to plyometric force production. In one study there was found to be a 18–20 per cent difference in vertical jump height when a counter movement (eccentric contraction) was added, compared with a static crouch (Bosco *et al.*, 1982). The comparison between jump height with and without a counter movement can be a useful indication of the plyometric ability of an athlete.

There is a second major reason why a counter movement causes additional force production. When we perform a counter movement we take the muscles into a sudden stretch. As we shall see in Chapter 11, a rapid eccentric contraction activates a **stretch reflex** within the muscle. This is the sudden reflexive contraction of muscle that serves as a protective mechanism against damage-inducing excessive stretch (Gollhofer and Kyrolainen, 1991). This reflexive force production also contributes to concentric power production following eccentric loading. The greater and quicker the eccentric loading, the greater the subsequent force production. If a counter movement is preceded by a drop from height (drop jump), the jump height is even greater.

Reactive power production is most commonly seen during running, where each step involves an **eccentric phase**, as the foot lands and force has to be eccentrically controlled. This is followed by an isometric stabilization of weight and, as quickly as possible, an explosive **concentric phase** as the foot pushes off and propels the body forwards (see Chapter 7). The time between the eccentric and concentric phases is known as the **amortization phase**. These three phases constitute what is known as the **stretch-shortening cycle**. The longer the amortization phase, the more energy is lost and the less powerful and less efficient the athlete will be through stretch-shortening cycles.

Plyometric training involves the use of counter movements and jumps. The aim of plyometric training is to:

- condition the elastic properties of connective tissue and muscle to store and release energy produced from eccentric work
- condition the nervous system to increase reflex activation of muscle from stretch reflexes by reacting more quickly to eccentric loading
- increase the speed of muscular recruitment and the level of neural drive of muscles
- reduce the amortization phase of running.

Whilst plyometric training will optimize the force generated from the stretch-shortening cycle, it does not have a great effect on muscular power. That is why it is often coupled with or preceded by traditional power training. Power and plyometric training can be of great use to distance runners, who go through thousands of stretch-shortening cycles. It will improve their running efficiency and therefore their overall performance.

Progression

It is important to remember that the kinetic chain absorbs large forces during plyometric exercise. For this reason progression into plyometric training has to be very slow. Power training exposes the body to massive levels of stress and force. Greatly increased levels of skill, muscular coordination and muscular conditioning are required for the kinetic chain to absorb these

8.14 Correct landing position

forces adequately and perform explosive movements with accuracy and sufficient levels of joint stabilization to avoid injury. If we consider that there may be a force as much as 11 times body weight going through our kinetic chain whenever we land after jumping. A person should be highly-skilled and well-conditioned before embarking on a power phase of training. Plyometric training would not be recommended for anyone without a good level of conditioning or anyone with existing muscle imbalance or postural deviation. An athlete should have completed a conditioning, hypertrophy and strength phase prior to entering into this type of power training (see Chapter 4).

When the athlete is sufficiently conditioned, much of the initial stages of plyometric training will involve perfecting landing technique. The athlete should practise jumping and landing in a stable manner, in which the shoulders remain over the knees and knees aligned over the feet, with the knees in good frontal and sagittal plane alignment (Figure 8.14). At this stage we may introduce a counter movement (a dip in the knees) with the initial jump.

Exercise progressions may involve, for example, ankle hop to stabilization (springing from the toes and landing again), two-footed squat jump to stabilization, a jump over a barrier to stabilization, finishing with a jump down from a box to stabilization, known as a depth jump.

Once the athlete can complete this with good technique, a stretch-shortening cycle can be introduced, in which straight after landing the athlete immediately performs another jump. The aim of this exercise is to decrease the amortization phase, the time between landing and take-off in order to increase the power of the second jump. Fatigue should be avoided and will be recognized by a loss of technique, longer amortization phase and reduced jump height. When these start to occur it is time to rest. Never train for power when fatigued; this will be detrimental to performance and may cause injury.

Exercises can be further progressed onto one leg (skipping, bounding from one leg to another, hopping) and we can add multi-directional movement by hopping or bounding from one side

to another or changing direction. Ensure that at each stage the athlete can sufficiently stabilize to perform the exercise with correct kinetic chain alignment.

After this the specific needs of the athlete and the movements required of them in their sport may be taken more into consideration. If the athlete predominantly jumps from two feet, like a volleyball player or a basketball player, then keep their plyometric jumps on two feet. If they jump from one foot or they are involved in a lot of running and sprinting, progress them onto one-leg work with hopping and bounding.

SPEED

Speed is the maximum velocity that we can reach regardless of acceleration. A 100-metre sprint can be broken down into three phases: an ***acceleration phase*** as the athlete accelerates in the first 0–30 m, followed by a ***maximum velocity phase***, in which maximal speeds can be achieved in the next 30–60 m, and a ***speed maintenance phase***, which is the last 60–100 m in which speed is likely to fall (Jarver, 1995). The implication for sports in which distances of over 30 m are rare is that acceleration may be far more important than speed.

Basic speed is reliant on ***stride frequency***, the number of strides in a given time, and ***stride length***, the distance covered in each stride. If we increase one or both of these our speed will increase. An athlete's stride frequency, or leg turnover speed, is determined by their power production and the biomechanical efficiency of their running technique. Stride length is determined by the anthropometrics of the athlete (their height and leg length), their hip flexibility (primarily in the hip flexors and the hamstrings) and the force production in the extensor muscle groups (quads, hamstrings glutes, calves). Power training and flexibility training can improve these factors.

Running mechanics

Tellez (1984) identified improper technique as a major influence on running speed. Correcting running mechanics and analysis of running style is a highly complex skill. Part of the job of a personal trainer is to look at their client's running mechanics and provide some basic correctional advice for obvious errors in form.

The running action involves three phases:

■ **Supporting phase:** This is the time between when the foot lands and the body's centre of gravity passes forward of it. During this phase there is great eccentric muscle action to control ground reaction forces and prevent drop of centre of gravity as the foot lands (see Chapter 7). If there is a drop in the runner's centre of gravity, i.e. the knee goes into excessive flexion and body weight moves towards the floor, there will be a loss of speed.

CUES FOR EFFICIENT RUNNING MECHANICS.

Head and shoulders

■ Ensure the muscles of the head and neck are relaxed and there is no unwanted tension.
■ Prevent excessive head movement. Keep the head still and looking straight ahead (no watching TVs that aren't ahead of you when on treadmills).

Arms

■ The arms are essential for counteracting rotational movement created by the lower body. Without good arm mechanics the body will rotate and speed will be lost.
■ Ensure a 90-degree angle at the arms; any angle greater than this will increase the lever arm and slow the arm speed.
■ Ensure a full arm movement when sprinting, asking for the palms to come to almost chin height and return to the hip when sprinting (hip to lip).
■ Ask for a fast, powerful arm action; this will allow greater force production in the lower body during maximal sprinting.

(If a client does not believe the importance of the arms during running, tell them to try running with their arms held by their sides.)

Trunk

■ Keep the trunk upright and solid; excessive movement through the core will result in wasted power and reduced speed.
■ Not too much movement in the hips. Excessive movement around the hips may indicate a lack of core stability and weakness of muscles around the hips.

Leg action

■ There should be a light foot contact, with as little time on the ground as possible. If a client runs heavily, this may indicate faulty running mechanics, increased foot contact time (i.e. amortization time) and a drop in the centre of gravity.
■ Foot contact should occur below or very slightly in front of the body on landing. Anything greater will result in greater ground contact time and will result in reduced stride frequency and increased amortization phase.
■ The heel should quickly recover towards the bottom. If the heel is not being picked up quickly or far enough there will be a longer lever arm through the leg, resulting in reduced leg recovery speed and reduced stride velocity.
■ As the foot recovers, the foot should be dorsiflexed (foot and toes pulled upwards) to reduce further the lever arm and increase recovery speed.

- **Driving phase:** This begins at the end of the supporting phase and ends as the foot leaves the ground. The sum of these two phases of running when the foot is in contact with the ground is also known as the amortization phase of the stretch-shortening cycle. A shorter amortization phase results in increased plyometric power and greater subsequent force production. A drop in centre of gravity will cause a lengthening of the amortization phase. Power training and plyometric training will decrease the amount of time an athlete spends in this phase of running and will increase the elastic performance of muscles in the calves and quads in particular.
- **Recovery phase:** This includes the time during which the foot is off the ground and is being brought forwards in preparation for the next supporting phase. The mechanical position of the lower body has great impact on the lever length of the leg and therefore speed of recovery. If the foot is not drawn close to the buttocks as the leg recovers, the recovery of the leg will be slower.

Correct running mechanics have a great impact on stride frequency.

Drills to improve running mechanics

Several different drills can be used to emphasize the coaching points highlighted above.

- **Arm swings:** From a stationary standing position drive the arms from hip to lip (just in front of the shoulder) maintaining a 90-degree angle in the arm and a strong, stable trunk. Ensure that the movement comes from the shoulder and not from the elbow. The 90-degree angle at the elbow should be maintained at all times.
- **Heel kicks:** While jogging, every second step pull the heel powerfully up to the backside. The aim is to encourage a fast heel recovery, creating a shorter lever arm and increased stride frequency.
- **High knees:** While jogging, with every second step drive the knee up parallel to the floor and couple

this with a powerful contralateral (opposite side) arm action. This will encourage a powerful knee drive coupled with a powerful arm drive.
- **Ankle springs:** Perform a skipping action, allowing only the toes to contact the ground. This will encourage minimal heel contact and powerful plyometric force generation through the calves.

Flexibility and running mechanics

The first step in correcting faults in running mechanics will be to identify whether they stem from an imbalance in the kinetic chain or from limitations in joint range of motion. Any restriction of range of motion will greatly affect running mechanics (McFarlane, 1987) (see Chapter 9). Overly tight hip flexors will restrict hip extension as the athlete drives forwards during the driving phase, restricting stride length and reducing power production in the extensor muscles. Tight hamstrings may restrict hip flexion as the athlete drives forwards in the recovery phase, restricting stride length. Muscular imbalance and faulty posture may also show up in other kinetic chain deviations during the gait cycle such as overpronation, bowing of the knees and so on. Overpronation may be caused by tight calves or hips or may simply be genetic. These deviations ultimately mean that the kinetic chain is less able to deal with the external forces caused by running, power production will be less and the chances of injury will increase. See Chapters 9 and 11 for ways to identify and correct these areas of muscle tightness.

Alternative methods for training speed

Alternative methods of increasing running speed include resisted and assisted running. **Resisted running** involves adding resistance to running, for example towing a weight sled, towing a parachute, running uphill or running up stairs. The aim is to increase power production in extensor muscles, glutes, hamstrings and calves predominantly, thereby increasing stride length when the resistance is removed. **Assisted running** or **over-**

speed involves removing resistance to running or increasing running speed in order to encourage increased stride frequency. We could get the athlete to run downhill on a slight (10-degree) gradient or tow them using a cord or cable attached to another sprinter.

Remember that fatigue interferes with speed (Cissik, 2005) and training at submaximal speeds will encourage faulty running mechanics and poor muscle fibre recruitment. If you train slowly, you train yourself to be slow. For this reason always allow optimal recovery when training for speed.

AGILITY AND QUICKNESS

Agility involves multidirectional movement, changes of direction and acceleration in new directions. This can be the key skill in many sports settings, as sports performers rarely have to run distances over 20 metres before they have to recover and change direction. Whilst pure speed can be an asset to an athlete, it is often change of pace and change of direction that set sports performers apart. Consider a rugby back looking to beat a defender or a football player looking to dribble past the last man. In situations such as this, acceleration combined with a disguised change of direction are key elements.

Agility drills

Many tools can be used to cue for foot patterns and changes of direction in order to challenge agility and quickness: ladders, markers, cones, lines and mini-hurdles can all be used to set up to cue movement patterns. For example, in the T-drill the markers are set in a T-shape and the athlete is timed on how fast they can reach each marker, always facing forwards. Different patterns can obviously be used (e.g. W-shape, pentagon etc.). Ladders on the floor can be used to cue for different foot patterns, or we can simply sprint through the ladder. Hurdles can be used to run or jump over. There are many excellent texts recommending a variety of speed and agility drills. The important factor is to improve movement patterns that are relevant for the athlete.

An in-depth consultation with a client should include a discussion regarding how they move in their chosen sport, what types of foot patterns they use, and how their pace and direction have to change within their sport. This can then be mimicked in the drills you design. Skills can be progressed to include more than one movement. At this point we can consider how the sport performer might move in their particular game. For example, a rugby player would make a slow jog up the ladder, then sprint with fast feet through the ladder. As they come out of the ladder they would jink through cones, spinning out of the last cone to accelerate away. This can be repeated several times until they start to fatigue.

During these movement patterns we should continually reinforce correct movement mechanics, fast foot speed, light foot contact, change of pace, acceleration, accurate change of direction and disguise.

Points to remember when training agility and quickness:

- start with simple sequences of movement and progress the complexity through the session
- always get your client to warm-up thoroughly using a dynamic specific warm-up and mobilization routine
- emphasize good running mechanics
- programme for movement patterns specific to those used by the athlete
- emphasize quality over quantity
- never perform routines slowly as this will make the athlete slow
- speed training requires high levels of motivation and concentration because of the intensities required
- introduce equipment that is used in the game to train specific running mechanics (hockey stick, cricket pads etc.).

BALANCE TRAINING

Static balance requires the maintenance of centre of gravity over the body's base of support. The *centre of gravity* is the centre point of a body's

8.15 Diagram of centre of gravity and base support

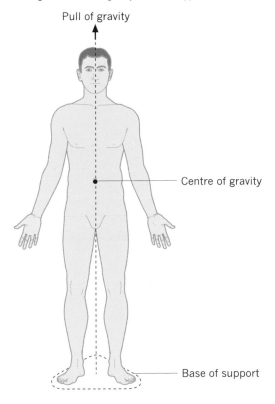

Pull of gravity

Centre of gravity

Base of support

weight, the point at which weight is evenly distributed. The **base of support** is the area around the body's contact points with the ground. When standing, if our centre of gravity falls outside our base of support, gravity creates momentum and movement and we fall. During dynamic stability we are continually moving our centre of gravity outside our base of support and then moving our base of support to regain balance. This is exactly what happens when we walk (Figure 8.15).

Balance requires fine neuromuscular coordination, the nervous control of muscles to respond quickly to changes in body position as it relates to gravity (see Chapter 7). The nervous system has to activate the right muscle, at the right joint, at the right time with the correct amount of force to control centre of gravity and keep it over base of support. The brain requires massive amounts of information about where the body is

in space to be able to achieve this. We have several sources of information regarding the position of the body in space. These sources of information include:

- *Vestibular feedback:* The vestibular system consists of tubes of fluid housed in the inner ear. It provides information about head position and motion with respect to gravity.
- *Visual feedback:* This provides information regarding head position and motion relative to our external environment.
- *Somatosensory feedback:* These are receptors found throughout the body that provide mechanical information. They include:
  - mechanoreceptors within the skin that provide information about contact with things around us;
  - Golgi tendon organs found in musculo-tendinous junctions that monitor tension within or force produced by the muscles;
  - muscle spindles that measure muscle length or change in muscle length (see Chapter 11 for more on Golgi tendon organs and muscle spindles).

This information is essential in order to maintain good balance. To demonstrate to your client the importance of these different forms of feedback, ask them to stand on one leg. Then ask them to perform the same task whilst their head is tilted to decrease vestibular feedback, or with one or both eyes closed, decreasing the quality of visual feedback. The task becomes far more difficult when this is done.

As discussed in Chapter 7, the sum total of this feedback is known as our proprioception, or inner sense. Our **kinaesthetic sense** is our ability to determine our body position in space using this proprioceptive information. The more information we receive and the better we learn to interpret proprioceptive information, the better our kinaesthetic awareness and the better control we have over our movement. Body awareness combined with fine control over muscle recruitment determine the quality of our balance. See Chapter 7 for more on this topic.

Reflex control over balance

Much of the muscle action that helps to maintain our balance is performed at a subconscious level through the reflex activation of muscles. These reflexes can be split into two types:

- *Righting reactions:* These are involved in maintaining head position and drawing the body back into alignment once lost. They are dominant over a fixed surface (e.g. a gymnast on a beam, ice skaters, those in contact sports). To develop righting reactions, challenge balance on a stable surface (e.g. stand your client on one leg).
- *Equilibrium reactions:* These are involved in maintaining control over centre of gravity to keep it over the body's base of support. They are active predominantly when the surface on which you are standing is unstable (e.g. in the case of wind surfer, snow boarder). To train, place your client on an unstable surface (e.g. wobble board or Swiss ball).

In practice, many activities require a combination of both types of reflex. For example, when taking a train journey if someone knocks into you as the train is stationary, righting reflexes work to bring you back to upright, but as the train starts to pull away, equilibrium reactions work to keep your balance.

Factors contributing to good balance

Several factors other than quality of proprioceptive feedback, neuromuscular coordination and body awareness also affect balance.

- *Improved core stability:* Control over the centre of the body, the core, is important in maintaining good balance. A fully-functioning core will make the challenge of maintaining balance far easier.
- *Good posture:* As posture gets worse and the kinetic chain deviates from the ideal position, the quality of proprioceptive information decreases and control over balance becomes harder.

Balance and exercise prescription

By destabilizing the body and adding proprioceptive challenge we can increase the balance challenge of an exercise. This can be achieved in a variety of ways. We can reduce the base of support by bringing the feet together or lifting one leg. This keeps the client on a stable surface and predominantly challenges righting reactions. We can put our client on an unstable surface, such as a wobble board, Swiss ball or foam pad, for example, to challenge equilibrium reactions. We can reduce proprioceptive feedback (eyes closed, for example) or add to the neural complexity of an exercise by adding unilateral loading or adding planes of movement, for example. This is training in a *proprioceptive-rich environment* and will quickly lead to improvements in neuromuscular coordination and proprioception.

Balance is specific to the task we wish to do. It is always more effective to train balance in the context of a movement relevant to the athlete. Improvements in balance seated may not carry over well to balance in a standing position, for example. Improvements on a stable surface may not carry over to skills on an unstable surface. If we want improvements in balance to have large carryover to a client's daily or sporting activities, we have to consider the context of the sport or activities they are going to perform. We have to ask:

- What movement patterns are they likely to perform?
- Are they going to use predominantly righting or equilibrium reflex reactions?

Then we have to design an exercise routine to reflect these specific needs.

SPORT ANALYSIS

The key to prescribing a sport-specific training programme is to break down the particular sport, determining the different skills required. We have to make conclusions regarding which movement patterns are of particular relevance, which energy systems the client will rely upon, and what their requirements are for stabilization and balance. Once we know this we can start to build a programme designed specifically for the needs of that athlete and their sport.

Analysis of a client's sport takes place predominantly during the consultation process. The better understanding you have of the sport, the better the programme you can provide. Key consultation questions for a client may include the following:

- What sport are they training for?
- What position do they play?
- What is the relative importance of skill and motor control compared with athletic fitness?
- What movements will they predominantly perform and what muscles will they be required to use?
- What planes of motion do they predominantly use – front and back movements (sagittal), side to side (frontal) or turning movements (transverse)?
- What energy systems are of key importance?
  - ATP-CP if they are predominantly working for under 10 seconds.
  - Glycolytic if they are predominantly working for under 3 minutes.
  - Oxidative if they are predominantly working for over 3 minutes.
- What skills are of key importance (endurance, speed, strength, power, balance)?

- Are they predominantly standing, seated or lying in their sport?
- Are they in water when they compete?
- What recovery times are provided?
- What level of balance do they require?
- Do they work in a stable environment (e.g. runner) or an unstable environment (e.g. surfer)?
- Is it a contact sport?
- If it is a contact sport do they have protective equipment that adds to weight of collision?
- If it is, do they predominantly have to push or pull their opponent?
- How long do they have to compete for?
- Do they have time to eat or drink while competing?
- Are they allowed to wear any supports when they play?

These are all questions that will provide plenty of information to you about the requirements of the person's sport and therefore how you should train them. Combine this with questions to the athlete:

- What is your present level of conditioning?
- Do you have any injuries at present?
- Have you had any injuries in the past?

These answers can be combined with information you gather yourself regarding the athlete's fitness, their posture and any muscular imbalance that you may wish to improve upon. After all this you can start to build a picture of how the client's programme will look. You can then build up a periodized programme in which the training builds to the point where the client's key biomotor skills are at their highest when they get to their competitive season (see Chapter 4).

CHAPTER SUMMARY

Following an in-depth sport analysis and a breakdown of the client's key skills and movements, you should now be able to design programmes tailor-made to improve an athlete's sporting performance. The exercises above will have far greater functional carryover for athletes who require speed, power, agility, quickness and balance.

REFERENCES AND RECOMMENDED READING

1. Adams, K., O'Shea, J.P., O'Shea, K.L. and Climsteing, M. (1992) The effect of six weeks of squat, plyometric and squat-plyometric training on power production. *Journal of Applied Sport Science Research* 6:36–41.

2. IL: Human Kinetics.

3. Baechle, T.R., Earle, R.W. (eds) (2000) *Essentials of Strength Training and Conditioning*, 2nd edn. National Strength and Conditioning Association. Champaign, IL: Human Kinetics.

4. Baker, D. (1996) Improving vertical jump performance through general, special, and specific strength training: A brief review. *Journal of Strength and Conditioning Research* 10131–10136.

5. Bird, S. (2002) *Sports Performance Analysis; 100m sprint.* www.PTonthenet.com.

6. Bosco, C., Komi, P.V, Pulli, M. and Montonev, H. (1982) Considerations of the training of elastic potential of skeletal muscle. *Volleyball Technique Journal* 1:75–80.

7. Cissik, J.M. (2005) Means and methods of speed training. *Strength and Conditioning Journal* 27:18–25.

8. Craig, B.W. (2004) What is the scientific basis of speed and agility? *Strength and Conditioning Journal* 26: 13–14.

9. Gollhofer, A. and Kyrolainen, H. (1991) Neuromuscular control of the human leg extensor muscles in jump exercises under various stretch-load conditions. *International Journal of Sports Medicine* 12:34–40.

10. Hakkinen, K. (1989) Neuromuscular and hormonal adaptations during strength and power training. *Journal of Sports Medicine* 29:9–26.

11. Hakkinen, K. and Komi, P.V. (1985) Effect of explosive strength training on electromyographic and force-production characteristics of leg extensor muscles during concentric and various stretch-shortening cycle exercises. *Scandinavian Journal of Sports* 7:65–76.

12. Hakkinen, K. and Myllyla, E. (1990) Acute effects of muscle fatigue and recovery on force production and relaxation in endurance, power, and strength athletes. *Journal of Sports Medicine and Physical Fitness* 30:5–12.

13. Hakkinen, K., Komi, P.V. and Alen, M. (1985) Effect of explosive-type strength training on isometric force- and relaxation-time, electromyographic and muscle fibre characteristics of leg extensor muscles. *Acta Physiologica Scandinavica* 125:587–600.

14. Harris, G.R., Stone, M.H., O'Bryant, H.S., Prouix, C.M. and Johnson, R.L. (2000). Short-term performance effects of high speed, high force, or combined weight training methods. *Journal of Strength and Conditioning Research* 14:14–20.

15. Jarver, J. (1995) *Sprints and Relays: Contemporary Theory, Technique and Training.* Mountain View, CA: Tafnews Press.

16. McFarlane, B. (1987). A look inside the dynamics and biomechanics of speed. *NSCA Journal* 9:35–41.

17. Newton, H. (2002) *Explosive Lifting for Sports.* Champaign, IL: Human Kinetics.

18. Paavolainen, L., Hakkinen, A., Hamalainen, I., Nummela, A. and Rusko, H. (1999) Explosive strength training improves 5-K running time by improving running economy and muscle power. *Journal of Applied Physiology* 86:1527–1533.

19. Tellez, T. (1984). Sprint training – including strength training. *Track and Field Quarterly* 84:9–12.

20. Williams, K.R. and Cavanagh, P.R. (1987) Relationship between distance running mechanics, running economy, and performance. *Journal of Applied Physiology* 63:1236.

9

POSTURE AND THE IMPORTANCE OF MUSCLE BALANCE

If you look at a room full of people you will see that everyone sits, stands and moves in a variety of different ways. We might describe the way a person holds themselves as their *posture*. This is a simplistic definition and different exercise professionals have varying perspectives on what posture is. Posture influences quality of movement, athletic performance and predisposition to injury. In this chapter we identify the key factors contributing to posture and what is meant by 'good posture'. We look at how posture can be assessed and what steps can be taken to start to correct a client's posture so that they move and perform better.

The assessment of posture is a highly complex skill and it is important to understand that a trainer should never make assumptions about a client's posture and should never claim to be able to 'diagnose' medical conditions on the basis of this information. It is extremely important that as personal trainers we refer on anyone with any chronic or acute pain and build a relationship with their physical therapist, GP, physiotherapist or chiropractor in order to move the client forwards.

THE IMPORTANCE OF POSTURE

Why should we pay particular attention to our client's posture? The Chartered Society of Physiotherapy summarizes the importance of posture as follows:

Posture ranks right up at the top of the list when you are talking about good health. It is as important as eating right, exercising, getting a good night's sleep and avoiding potentially harmful substances like alcohol, drugs and tobacco.

If posture is less than ideal there is a range of negative consequences to health and performance.

Increased postural stress

Postural stress is a term used to describe the stress resulting from chronic exposure to poor posture and prolonged static body position, for example sitting for too long with a rounded back. As posture moves away from the ideal, postural stress increases. Have you ever experienced tension in the lower back, neck and shoulders from working too long at a computer? This is an example of postural stress.

The incidence of chronic conditions brought about by poor posture has increased in recent years due to the increasingly sedentary nature of modern living, characterized by long periods of time spent sitting at a desk, in a car or in front of a TV (Schwarzer, 1996). Eighty per cent of people will suffer from back pain at some point in their life (O'Sullivan, 2000), and 35–40 per cent of people will experience an episode of back pain at some point in the next year. Ninety-six per cent of all lower back pain is now known to be a combination of simple mechanical problems involving lack of fitness and muscle strength, faulty posture and faulty repetitive movements (e.g. poor lifting technique). Only four per cent are acute problems such as a slipped disc. This makes posture a massive issue for everyone.

Force production

As we saw in Chapter 2, the ability of muscles to produce force is affected by their length (Jones and Round, 1990), and as the length of muscles is altered by poor posture, with muscles being held in chronically shortened or lengthened positions, this will reduce the ability of muscles to produce force. Poor posture and inflexibility also limit the speed and distance that we can move our bodies. An athlete who has to throw or hit like a golfer or boxer has to generate power by rotating through the hips and trunk. If they are hunched forward and their shoulders are rounded they will struggle to rotate and therefore a great deal of power is lost. You can test this for yourself: in a sitting position try turning as far around as you can; then round your shoulders and try again. See the limits in rotation with poor posture.

Altered proprioreception

The mechanical receptors found within muscles and joints send information back to your central nervous system regarding body position. This is known as proprioreception and was discussed fully in Chapter 7. These receptors assume that the body is in ideal alignment and the lengths of our muscles are normal. If this is not the case and posture is faulty, the result is a reduction in the quality of proprioreceptive information and therefore deterioration in balance, coordination and body awareness.

Quality of movement

Tight muscles reduce the range of motion at joints, affecting our ability to perform functional movements. For example, imagine a person performing a squat. Good flexibility and range of motion are required at the ankle and hips to perform a squat with good form. Poor posture causing tight muscles around these joints will limit range of motion and affect form. We might see knees pulling inwards as the person gets deeper into the squat rather than staying straight in good alignment, or heels lifting or a loss of squat range of motion in a client with poor posture.

Energy cost of movement

Movement requires more effort when our posture is poor. When we run, poor posture will mean that we are biomechanically less efficient, making running harder.

Respiration and breathing

Rounded shoulders and stooped posture will limit the extent by which we can expand the ribcage, limiting how much air we can draw when we breathe heavily. Imagine the effect on cardiovascular performance if we are not able to take as much air into our lungs as normal.

Increased incidence of injury

The incidence of injury is greatly affected by posture (Chek, 2002). The body is aligned in order to disperse and deal with the forces we experience on our bones and joints when we walk, run and jump, forces that can reach as much as eleven times your body weight. For example, the foot is arched to provide cushioning, the knee is aligned to deal with the large forces it has to absorb, and the spine is designed to absorb compressive forces throughout its length. If the body is incorrectly aligned, the feet may flatten, the knees do not track properly and the spine cannot absorb force as effectively. Consequently we cannot absorb force as well and the likelihood of injury increases.

We see from this that good posture is the foundation of quality movement and sport performance. Improving the posture of a client can therefore immediately improve all these factors.

STATIC AND DYNAMIC POSTURE

Posture ultimately refers to the relative alignment of our body and the relationship in space between bones, joints and muscles at any given moment. Before we can assess and correct faulty posture, we must first appreciate the difference between static and dynamic posture. During *static* posture we attempt to maintain the ideal alignment of muscles, bones and joints (the kinetic chain) under adequate stabilization from muscles *without* movement. This may be while we are standing, sitting or maintaining our posture in order to perform a task such as holding a baby, brushing our teeth or pushing in a rugby scrum.

static posture: the position of the kinetic chain without movement.

During *dynamic* posture we attempt to maintain optimal alignment of our kinetic chain within the context of a particular movement. Good alignment allows movement at optimal speed and efficiency with minimal risk of injury.

Dynamic posture requires that we are continuously sensing and responding to changes in our environment, controlling momentum, absorbing external forces and maintaining balance (see Chapter 7). This takes great skill and makes dynamic posture potentially far more challenging than static posture. This is why you may find that although a client's posture appears near perfect when stationary, postural faults and problems become evident when they move.

dynamic posture: the position of the kinetic chain within the context of a particular movement.

FACTORS DETERMINING AN INDIVIDUAL'S POSTURE

Posture is an extremely important and complex predisposition to which there are many different contributing factors.

FACTORS CONTRIBUTING TO POSTURE

- Dynamic balance between muscles
  - Ranges of motion
  - Strength
  - Endurance
- Physical factors
  - Skeletal structure, e.g. bones that have been broken, differing leg lengths
  - Joint mobility
- Environment factors, e.g. sports, occupation, hobbies
- Developmental factors, e.g. activities performed as a child
- Psychological factors
  - Mood
  - Self-confidence
- Nutritional factors, e.g. deficiencies stunting growth
- Injuries or pain that affect movement

9.1 Muscle balancing

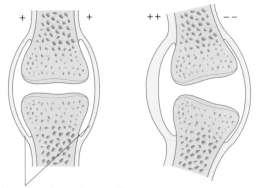

Muscles of equal strength

Note how the joint is pulled concave on the strong side

Through the strengthening and stretching programmes they prescribe for their clients a personal trainer will have great influence over the dynamic relationship between muscles. Joints generally have muscles acting all around them, providing stability and allowing the bones forming the joint to move. The opposing muscles of a joint are known as the *agonist* and *antagonist* muscles; for example, when you flex your arm using the bicep, its antagonist is the triceps. When the agonist and antagonist muscles across a joint have equal relative strength and tightness, the joint is generally held in its ideal alignment, known as *neutral* or *ideal posture*. Neutral posture is a position in which the body is best able to absorb external stress and produce muscular force in order to move. Movement away from neutral will be reflected in a loss of performance, weakness, inability to absorb force and therefore an increased incidence of injury.

In a state of muscle balance the body tends towards neutral. If there is muscle imbalance, greater tension and pull are being applied by one muscle compared to the other. The result will be that the joint will be pulled concave on the side of the stronger muscle, almost like a tug of war in which one side is stronger (Figure 9.1).

When this occurs the joint is pulled away from its ideal alignment, resulting in a loss of function and increased risk of injury as the joint is less able to deal with external stresses. With this in mind

we should always try to achieve balance between muscles across a joint. This is arguably the most important step in achieving good posture.

A resistance-training programme will invariably encourage muscle imbalance. We often have favourite exercises or body parts that we work harder to get the look we want. Imagine the effect we are having on the posture of our upper body if we only work chest or if we only work abs in order to get a six-pack. A personal trainer has to be very careful to design resistance programmes that will encourage muscle balance and maintain range of motion around joints.

CAUSES OF FAULTY POSTURE

We see from the above discussion that muscular imbalance is a major cause of poor posture. Muscle imbalance is often brought about through faulty movement – the inappropriate use of muscles. There are numerous causes of faulty movements. These include:

- Poor form and technique when exercising or moving in everyday life.
- Repetitive movements, e.g. always carrying a bag on one shoulder.
- Pattern overload, i.e. performing too many sets and reps of the same exercise week-in, week-out or repeating the same movement.
- Inappropriate use of momentum to lift a weight when resistance training.
- Training with a limited range of motion.
- Lifting too heavy, causing cheat mechanisms (described in Chapter 10) like reduced range of motion or reliance on momentum.
- Strengthening muscles in isolation (e.g. doing too many crunches from the floor).
- Over-training or training whilst fatigued.
- Poor flexibility leading to limited range of motion.
- Unbalanced training routines.
- Training with an injury.
- Sedentary behaviour (e.g. bed rest or general inactivity).
- Too much time spent in one posture (e.g. sitting for extended periods).

Your role as a personal trainer is to spot your client effectively (see Chapter 10 for an explanation of spotting) to avoid faulty movement, provide balanced workouts or workouts that will positively impact on posture.

IDEAL POSTURE AND GUIDELINES FOR AND ASSESSMENT OF IDEAL POSTURE

Ideal posture very rarely exists; most people have some postural deviations. The following section provides both guidelines for ideal posture as well as tools to help you start to assess objectively a client's posture. We can then make some basic conclusions as to which exercises to avoid and which ones may help move your client towards a position of strength.

FACTORS TO CONSIDER WHEN ASSESSING A CLIENT'S POSTURE

- ■ Symmetry
- ■ Anatomical plumb lines
- ■ Neutral spine
- ■ Pelvic tilt
- ■ Flexibility
- ■ Quality of movement

Assessment of symmetry

A person with ideal posture should be almost symmetrical from one side to the other, with a balance in muscle mass and joint position. Assessment of symmetry is the first step in assessing muscle imbalance. Whilst looking at your client from the front and back you can assess any obvious differences from one side to the other. You can use common landmarks on either side of the body to see if they are symmetrical.

- ■ Are common landmarks level with each other? (ears, shoulders, hips, hands hanging down).
- ■ Is there greater muscle mass on one side compared to the other?
- ■ Are there scars, bruising, inflammation or swelling on one side?
- ■ Are one or both of the feet turned out or pointing in?

If we identify imbalance from one side to the other we can start to build a mental picture of what might be causing postural imbalance. The muscles that are shorter as a result of faulty posture are likely to be tight and strong and may potentially be the cause of the faulty posture. For example, if one shoulder is higher the muscles in the neck and shoulder on that side may be short and tight.

Anatomical plumb lines

An anatomical plumb-line is a line drawn through the body with which we can compare the position of certain landmarks that we would expect to be in line if the client had ideal static posture (Figure 9.2). If we draw a vertical line up through the body, the line should pass from the ankle bone (malleoli), slightly behind the patellar, through the greater trochanter (the prominent bone on the side of leg), through the hip joint, through the acromion process (the shoulder bone) and through

9.2 Frontal plane plumb line

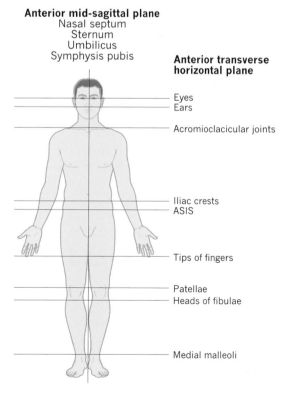

Anterior mid-sagittal plane
Nasal septum
Sternum
Umbilicus
Symphysis pubis

Anterior transverse horizontal plane

Eyes
Ears

Acromioclacicular joints

Iliac crests
ASIS

Tips of fingers

Patellae
Heads of fibulae

Medial malleoli

9.3 Structure of the spine with a plumb line

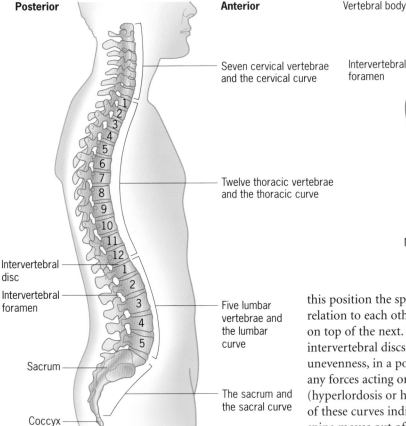

Posterior　　　　　　**Anterior**

Seven cervical vertebrae and the cervical curve

Twelve thoracic vertebrae and the thoracic curve

Intervertebral disc

Intervertebral foramen

Five lumbar vertebrae and the lumbar curve

Sacrum

The sacrum and the sacral curve

Coccyx

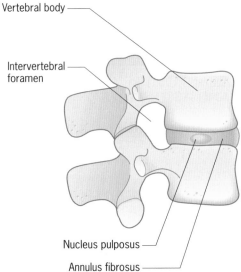

Vertebral body

Intervertebral foramen

Nucleus pulposus

Annulus fibrosus

the ear lobe. Always start by looking at the foot and work upwards, because the foot is the anchored point and all deviations will occur from that point.

Deviations of these landmarks from this line indicate postural imbalance.

Neutral spine

The spine should also be balanced in relation to this line, passing through the lumber and thoracic vertebrae as shown in Figure 9.3. The spine should appear as a smooth S-shape with a concave arch (arch inwards) or *lordosis* in the lower section of the spine (lumber spine), a convex curve (arch outwards) or *kyphosis* in the middle section of the spine (thoracic spine) and a concave lordosis at the neck (cervical spine).

This is described as neutral spinal alignment. In

this position the spinal vertebrae lie in perfect relation to each other with each vertebra balanced on top of the next. When this happens the intervertebral discs are doughnut-shaped with no unevenness, in a position ideally suited to absorb any forces acting on them. Any increased curves (hyperlordosis or hyperkyphosis) or any flattening of these curves indicates postural imbalance. If the spine moves out of neutral one of the discs is pressed into a wedge shape and the compressive forces exerted on that disc increase. Continued stress placed on a disc may damage the outer lining of that disc causing a rupture, commonly known as a slipped disc (Figure 9.4).

9.4 a) Effect of misalignment on intervertebral discs

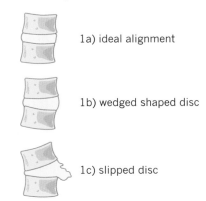

1a) ideal alignment

1b) wedged shaped disc

1c) slipped disc

Neutral posture minimizes wear and tear by reducing forces that would normally result in damage to soft tissue within the back, the intervertebral discs and damage to the vertebra themselves. This position protects the integrity of spinal ligaments, reduces pressure within vertebral discs by equally distributing weight-bearing load throughout the disc. We should therefore check to see how close our client's spine is to neutral during static posture. Clients should always be taught how to lift any significant weight using neutral spine in order to minimize the pressure going through intervertebral discs.

Correct head position

The head should always be considered to be an extension of the spine. The correct anatomical position for the head is with the ears in line with the shoulder, causing the head to balance comfortably on the ribcage. Forward head posture is very common. This is when the head pushes forwards of the shoulders, known as chin jut. The head increases its relative weight as it migrates forwards. This places significantly greater strain on the body, in particular the muscles supporting the head found in the upper back, neck and shoulders (levatae scapulae, upper trapezius etc.). This postural stress can eventually result in chronic pain through the back, neck, shoulders and jaw.

KEY POINT

The forward head position is common in people with a hyperkyphotic posture (a rounded upper back, see below). We can immediately improve thoracic curvature and head posture by asking the client to lift the ribcage. Imagine a piece of string hooking into the chest and pulling straight upwards. Lifting the chest will help reduce a kyphosis in the upper back and draw the head back.

Neutral pelvis

One of the most important factors determining whether your client is in neutral spine is their degree of *pelvic tilt*. The position of the pelvis has

9.5 Finding pelvic alignment

a significant influence on the position of the lumber spine as the two are attached to each other.

It can be quite a challenge to determine whether someone is in neutral pelvis. In men, the hip bone at the back of the body, where the dimple is (posterior superior iliac spine) should be level with or only slightly above the hip bone at the front of the body (the anterior superior iliac spine) (about 1.5 cm above). In women, the posterior superior iliac spine should be slightly higher (2 cm above the anterior) (Figure 9.5).

Pelvic tilt can easily be increased or decreased. *Posterior pelvic tilt* involves rolling the hips back and results in a flattening of the lumber spine. *Anterior pelvic tilt* involves rolling the hips forward, arching the back or increasing the lordosis of the lumbar spine. Neutral for that individual will be in the middle of these two extremes. By asking your client to perform a full anterior tilt, then a full posterior tilt, then asking them to find a mid point between the two should help them to identify their neutral spine. This can be performed lying, on all fours, seated or standing. A useful mental image for your clients is to imagine that the top of their hips forms the top of a bucket. Pouring fluid out of the front would be an anterior pelvic tilt. Pouring water out the back would be a posterior pelvic tilt.

Some clients may not be able to coordinate the muscles that cause pelvic tilt and may not be able to perform these movement. This is often seen in those with lower back pain. For these individuals mastering pelvic tilts will be an important part of rehabilitating the muscles of the lumber spine. A good control of pelvic tilt will be essential in ensuring good dynamic posture. Achieving good flexibility through the hips may be the initial stage of this process as tight muscles, the hamstrings for example, can restrict pelvic movement and place strain on the back.

Shoulder posture

The shoulder (head of the humerus) should be balanced on top of the ribcage in line with the ear. Often in hyperkyphotic individuals the shoulders are forwards (protracted). This can be corrected by lifting the ribcage and by drawing the shoulder blades (scapulae) partially together. This is called *scapular retraction*. A partial scapular retraction (halfway between fully forwards and fully back) puts the shoulder girdle in a neutral position. This is a position of strength and ensures that the shoulder girdle (the scapular and the clavicle) is better aligned under gravity, reducing postural stress.

9.6 Hyperlordotic posture　**9.7** Hyperkyphotic posture　**9.8** Flat back posture

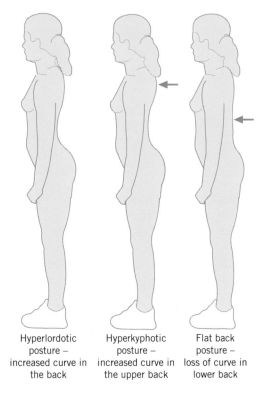

Hyperlordotic
posture –
increased curve in
the back

Hyperkyphotic
posture –
increased curve in
the upper back

Flat back
posture –
loss of curve in
lower back

Ensuring full scapular retraction during pulling movements is essential for working muscles such as the rhomboids through full range of motion. Failure to perform full scapular retraction during pulling movements will encourage a forward (protracted) shoulder position, causing rounded shoulders. Achieving full scapular retraction is an important step in helping hyperkyphotic clients improve their posture.

By correcting pelvic tilt and ensuring neutral spine along with correct head and shoulder posture we place the client into a static position of strength.

COMMON POSTURAL SYNDROMES

Very few people have perfect posture. Many people share similar patterns of postural distortion or 'postural syndromes'. The information below details what each of these postural syndromes looks like, why each posture occurs and what injuries are classically associated with them. We have included lists of muscles which are typically strong and short and muscles that are long and weak with each posture. It is often the tight muscles that pull us into incorrect alignment.

Hyperlordosis

Also known as 'lower crossed syndrome', hyperlordosis is characterized by an increased lumbar lordosis, anterior pelvic tilt with possible hyperextension of the knees. It is commonly caused by weak abdominal muscles, increased abdominal weight, pregnancy or too much time spent sitting, causing tight hip flexors. Lower back pain, hamstring strains and groin strains often occur as a result of the hyperlordotic posture. Think of this as the 'Donald Duck' posture (Figure 9.6).

Short/tight muscles
- Iliopsoas
- Rectus femoris
- Adductors
- Latissimus dorsi
- Erector spinae

Long/weak muscles
- Gluteus maximus
- Biceps femoris
- Gluteus medius
- Transverse abdominis
- Obliques

Hyperkyphosis

Also known as 'upper crossed syndrome', hyperkyphosis is characterized by increased kyphoisis of the thoracic spine, rounded shoulders with external rotation and abduction of the scapulae and forward head posture ('chin jut') (Figure 9.7). Commonly caused by too much time in a slumped posture (driving, working at a computer etc.), this posture can give rise to headaches and shoulder injuries due to reduced shoulder mobility. Injuries such as these are common in athletes performing high-repetition overhead activities, such as tennis players and swimmers.

Short/tight muscles	Long/weak muscles
■ Upper trapezius	■ Deep cervical neck flexors
■ Levator scapulae	
■ Sternocleidomastoid	■ Rhomboids
■ Latissimus dorsi	■ Mid and lower trapezius
■ Pectoralis major and minor	
	■ Thoracic extensors
■ Upper abdominal muscles	

Overpronation syndrome

This is characterized by flattening of the feet and rolling-in of the knees, externally rotated feet (feet pointing out) especially during gait and during the overhead squat. It is commonly the cause of ankle and knee injuries.

Short/tight muscles	Long/weak muscles
■ Gastrocnemius	■ Anterior tibialis
■ Soleus	■ Posterior tibialis
■ Peroneals	■ Vastus medialis
■ Adductors	■ Gluteus medius and maximus
■ Iliotibial band	
■ Iliopsoas	■ Hip external rotators
■ Rectus femoris	

Flat back

This is characterized by a decreased curvature in the lumbar spine, decreased lumbo-sacral angle and posterior pelvic tilt (Figure 9.8). It commonly gives rise to back pain and is often coupled with hyperkyphosis.

9.9 Scoliosis

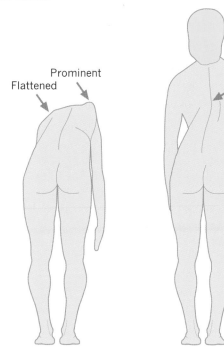

Prominent

Flattened

Scoliosis

Short/tight muscles	Long/weak muscles
■ Biceps femoris	■ Iliopsoas
■ Gluteus maximus	■ Erector spinae
■ Rectus abdominis	

Sway back

This is characterized by an increased thoracic kyphosis; the thoracic spine is also 'swayed back' with the thoracic curve being seen to be backward of the hips. There may also be posterior pelvic tilt and hip joint extension. Think of the 'Pink Panther'. It is very easy to mistake sway back for a hyperlordosis because the back can appear arched. It is therefore very important to check the degree of pelvic tilt to confirm your conclusions. Back pain is a common result of a sway back posture.

Short/tight muscles	Long/weak muscles
■ Rectus abdominis	■ Iliopsoas
■ Biceps femoris	■ Thoracic extensors
■ Tensor fascia latae	

Scoliosis

This is characterized by lateral curvature of the spine in either a C-shape or an S-shape (Figure 9.9). There could be a variety of causes, including leg-length discrepancy, unequal loading on the spine caused by lifting or moving repetitively just on one side (e.g. carrying a baby on one hip, always carrying a bag on one side, playing a one-sided sport), disease or skeletal structural imbalance. Back pain is a common result of a scoliosis.

Short/tight muscles	Long/weak muscles
■ Muscles on the concave side of any lateral curves	■ Muscles on the convex side of the curves

So far we have been talking about assessment of static posture, without movement. Far more challenging can be assessment of postural imbalance during dynamic posture.

Dynamic assessment of posture

Functional movements such as the squat, lunge, dead lift and gait (walking/running) require a good range of motion at certain joints. If range of motion is limited due to muscle imbalance or tight muscles, form, technique and range of motion may be poor during these exercises.

Table 9.1 gives examples of exercises and the joints at which good range of motion is required to perform them. Tightness in muscles affecting these joints may cause the loss of form or technique indicated. These are simply examples and this is not a guaranteed formula and certainly not an exhaustive list. The key is to appreciate that

Table 9.1 Properties of some exercises in terms of range of motion

Exercise	Joints requiring good range of motion	Possible limiting muscles	Deviation
Squat	Hips	Hamstrings	Loss of range of motion Lumbar spine rounds Weight shift
	Knees	Quads	Increased hip flexion Loss of knee flexion
	Ankles	Gastrocnemius and soleus	Loss of knee flexion Increased hip flexion (lean forwards) Heels lift Feet turn out Overpronation
Lunge	Hips	Hip flexors (quads or iliopsoas)	Hip flexion (lean forwards) Hip rotation
Deadlift (20-degree knee bend)	Hips	Hamstrings	Loss of range of motion in hip flexion Lumbar spine rounds
Gait/running	Hips	Hip flexors (quads and iliopsoas)	Loss of hip extension Loss of stride length
	Ankles	Gastrocnemius and soleus	Feet point out Heel flicks out Overpronation

most loss of form or technique will be due to loss of range of motion at a joint or muscular imbalance. We can analyse muscle length using the techniques below to understand more about what muscles are affecting a movement. To be able to assess and make conclusions about deviations in posture when a client moves we really need a good understanding of muscles acting around all the joints involved in the movement.

An overhead squat (see Figure 9.10) is an excellent movement for analysing faults in posture and loss of range of motion (ROM). Many muscles acting at the ankle, hip, and shoulder are put into extremes of ROM. Note how anyone with a kyphotic posture and/or tightness in the latissimus dorsi muscles will struggle to maintain their arms over their head without feeling strain into the lower back. This is because the lats internally rotate and extend the shoulder and anteriorly tilt the hips, making the back arch as they are put on stretch.

Comparative flexibility assessment

If one of the major factors determining posture is muscular balance across joints, assessing the relative flexibility of muscles may reveal a great deal about the causes of postural deviation. A simple assessment of the range of motion will indicate tight muscles, areas of imbalance around joints and lack of symmetry in one side of the body compared to the other. These factors may be directly causing the faults in posture that we identified above.

9.10 Overhead squat

Here we provide methods of assessing range of motion at a joint indicating levels of flexibility in individual or groups of muscles. The type of joint action, the main muscles potentially stretched and the range of motion required at the joint for functional movement are all shown.

These tests can be performed *actively* – the client moving themselves into the stretch to indicate functional range of motion – or *passively*, in which the personal trainer takes the client into a stretched position. When testing passive range of motion the joint should be taken until bind, the point at which increased tension is felt. It is important to ensure that movement in the joint being tested is isolated and there is no movement in any other joints that may mean we get a false reading similar to when we stretch.

Angles can be assessed using a **goniometer**. This is a special tool designed for measuring joint angles. Alternatively, with practice, we can make reasonable estimations about joint angles or we can perform a comparative assessment comparing one side of the body with the other.

Ankle dorsiflexion

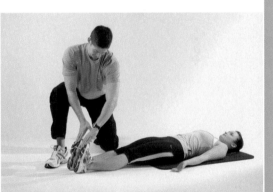

- Normal range of motion (degrees): 20
- Muscles on stretch: Gastrocnemius
- With client lying supine with legs flat, draw both feet back into dorsiflexion. Note any imbalance between the two sides or any significant loss of range.

Straight leg hip flexion

- Normal range of motion (degrees): 80
- Primary muscle on stretch: Hamstrings
- With client lying client supine with both legs flat, take one leg back until the point of tension. Note any imbalance between the two sides or any significant loss of range.

Hip abduction

- Normal range of motion (degrees): 45
- Primary muscles on stretch: Hip adductors (adductor longus, magnus and brevis)
- With client lying supine, abduct one leg at a time as far as possible, ensuring the rest of the body remains neutral and the opposite leg is fixed. Note any imbalance between the two sides or any significant loss of range.

Bent leg hip flexion

- Normal range of motion (degrees): Double leg 110, single leg 125
- Primary muscle on stretch: Gluteus maximus
- With client lying supine, draw knees into chest, back remaining in neutral. First perform both legs together (110 degrees normal), then single leg with the other leg remaining on the ground (125 degrees normal). Note any imbalance between the two or any significant loss of range.

Hip adduction

- Normal range of motion (degrees): 30
- Primary muscles on stretch: Hip abductors (Gluteus min and med)
- With client lying supine, raise the opposite leg to that being tested and support with the knee at 90 degrees. Draw the other knee across the body as far as possible, ensuring the rest of the body remains neutral. Note any imbalance between the two or any significant loss of range.

Knee flexion

- Normal range of motion (degrees): 135 (or heel to backside)
- Primary muscles on stretch: Quadriceps
- With client lying prone, draw the heel to the bottom, ensuring the rest of the body remains neutral. Normal range would allow for the heel to touch the buttocks. Note any imbalance between the two sides or any significant loss of range.

Hip external rotation

- Normal range of motion (degrees): 45
- Primary muscles on stretch: Hip internal rotators
- With client lying supine, bring one knee up above the hips and allow the foot to drop to a right angle. Keeping the knee still, draw the foot across the body. Note any imbalance between the two sides or any significant loss of range.

Hip internal rotation

- Normal range of motion (degrees): 45
- Primary muscles on stretch: Hip external rotators (piriformis)
- With client lying supine, bring one knee up above the hip and bend the knee to right angles. Keeping knee above the hips, draw the foot outwards. Note any imbalance between the two sides or any significant loss of range.

Hip extension

- Normal range of motion (degrees): 30
- Primary muscles on stretch: Hip flexors (iliopsoas, rectus femoris)
- From prone, bend the knee to 90 degrees and lift the knee off the floor to assess ease of motion, ensuring the rest of the body remains neutral. Note any imbalance between the two sides or any significant loss of range.

Movement through the spine

These movements assess range of motion through the spine, bending sideways, twisting and extending backwards.

Side flexion

- Starting from a standing position, hands by sides, the client should side-bend, reaching their hand towards and past the knee, being careful to prevent any rotation in the spine. Note any imbalance between the two sides or any significant loss of range.

Rotation

- Ask the client to rotate whilst seated, holding the arms across the chest. Note any imbalance between the two sides or any significant loss of range.

McKenzie push-up: spine extension

- The client lies prone with hands next to shoulders. Ask the client to straighten the arms, leaving the hips on the ground. An inability to straighten the arms whilst keeping the hips on the ground would indicate a loss of extension through the spine.

Alternative muscle length tests

There are a number of other tests that will help indicate muscular tightness and loss of range of motion at joints.

Arm elevation test: chest and lats

- With the client lying supine, take the arms straight above the head, holding the arms straight by the wrists.
- Shake the arms, encouraging the client to relax them completely.
- When they are relaxed, let the arms go. If the client has good range of motion around the shoulder joint the arms will drop straight to the floor, resting by the ears. Tightness in the latissimus dorsi would pull the arms down by the side. Tightness in the chest would cause the elbows to hover off the ground.

Thomas test: long and short hip flexors

- Ask the client to lie back on a high bench, pulling one knee into their chest and letting the other hang over the edge of the bench. The thigh should drop to parallel with or below the level of the bench, and the lower leg should point vertically towards the floor.
- A thigh not dropping to the bench would indicate tightness in the short hip flexors (iliopsoas) and a lower leg lifted would indicate tightness in the long hip flexors (rectus femoris) or quads.

Using the techniques detailed above we should be able to build a good picture of the client's posture and the factors causing that posture, especially the influence of potentially short, tight muscles. This information will form the basis of your exercise prescription for your client.

STEPS IN THE CORRECTION OF POSTURE

1. Identification of contributing factors to misalignment

You must identify any major factors that contribute to the client's posture in their everyday life. For example, are they sitting incorrectly, are they performing any repetitive movements that may be contributing to their misalignment? Understanding the root cause of their posture and taking this into consideration is an important step that is often neglected. Without taking these factors into consideration the client will simply repeat these behaviours to the detriment of their posture. Prescribing changes in the client's lifestyle will help to reduce postural stress (e.g. improving sitting posture), limit repetitive movements (e.g. kicking with both feet in football) and limit one-sided loading patterns (e.g. carrying a bag on both shoulders rather than just one).

2. Improved body awareness

Throughout your sessions you should be teaching your clients about their posture as they exercise. Unfortunately they will only be in the gym for a certain number of hours per week and will need to be taught to be aware of their movement outside the gym where they will be spending the majority of their time. Providing small cues for them to use every day and increasing their body awareness outside the gym will be invaluable in helping their posture. Teach them what it feels like to stand and move in good posture. Examples of these cues may be 'lift your chest and gently pull your shoulders back gently while you walk or sit' for a hyperkyphotic individual or 'slightly tilt your pelvis posteriorly when standing to flatten the back slightly' for a hyperlordotic individual. Visual cues, such as reminder notes or sticky labels can be used at a client's workstation or in their car to remind them to take care of their posture.

3. Muscle balancing: stretching to allow adequate range of motion

Through flexibility training we can start to restore balance between agonist and antagonistic muscle groups, thereby drawing joints back towards ideal alignment. The aim of our gym programmes will be to stretch short tight muscles that are restricting range of motion and negatively affecting posture.

4. Muscle balancing: strengthening to achieve balance

Once full range of motion is achieved, the balancing programme can be enhanced with resistance exercises to strengthen weak muscles in the kinetic chain. This will not only increase the balance between agonists and antagonists across a joint but will also provide stability and strength around those joints.

5. Improved core stability and strength

A progressive core-stability programme will enhance posture by strengthening deep abdominal muscles. These muscles will help draw the spine into correct alignment and provide support for a successful strength and flexibility routine. A core-stability programme can generally be used alongside all of the interventions detailed above.

Once your client has good postural alignment we must then ensure that their training is balanced (equal training of both agonist and antagonistic muscles of a joint) and their body is sufficiently conditioned to deal with any daily stresses it is likely to be put under.

Many of the factors affecting posture cannot be influenced by the personal trainer. Joint-capsule dysfunction, damage, disease and structural faults in the skeleton (e.g. leg-length discrepancy) are examples of problems affecting posture that must be referred to a qualified medical professional.

CASE STUDY: POSTURE FOR AN IMPROVED GOLF SWING

A golfer came to me and explained that he wanted to improve the power of his swing. As with all clients I assessed his posture. One factor was clear: as I looked at him sideways-on, drawing an imaginary plumb line through his spine, his upper spine was excessively curved, his head was well forward and his shoulders were rounded – the classic hyperkyphotic posture.

I explained to the golfer about his posture without using too many technical terms and in a way that was sensitive to his feelings. We are not saying he has a clinical condition, it is just that with slight changes in his posture his range of motion may improve, as will his golf swing. By bringing him more upright, we can improve

how far he can rotate and therefore how much power he can potentially produce in his swing.

To get the point across I laid a bar across his shoulder while he was seated, and asked him to rotate as far as he could. I then pulled him into an improved posture and asked him to see if he could rotate further.

I explained that improvements in his posture may even make him less susceptible to injury. At this point he told me that he has had shoulder problems in the past when he played tennis and does suffer from some dull back pain. By lifting his chest and tucking his chin in we identified a slightly better postural position. I explained that I wanted him to practise this posture as much as possible and even suggested he used this posture when he addressed the ball before his swing. I recommended that he did this in the driving range first as it can drastically alter the way he moves and therefore alter his swing pattern. His game may get worse before it gets better.

After performing an arm elevation test I noticed he was very tight in the chest and lats. I prescribed a stretching routine that involves mobilizing the neck, shoulders and spine (see Chapter 11 for details) and stretching the chest (pec major and minor), neck (traps and sternocleiodomastoid), lats and upper abdominals. I explained that doing these prior to his golf may help his swing by giving him more freedom of movement.

I then provided some strengthening exercises for his rhomboids, mid and lower traps (a mid row for example) and thoracic extensors (prone cobra). He could do these either in the gym or at home using a resistance band that I provided.

To help strengthen his core I also provided some TVA and lower abdominal exercises (see Chapter 13). To help him develop his golf swing I also gave him a woodcut movement as a functional exercise. These exercises are to be done a minimum of three times per week.

An example programme would be as follows:

1. General warm-up – 5 minutes' brisk walk on the treadmill (cardiovascular exercises may be added for health and fitness benefits)
2. Mobilize neck, shoulders and spine
3. Woodcut (this exercise has been put first due to its complexity and compound nature)
4. Mid row
5. Prone cobra (see picture above)
6. Heel tap
7. Pelvic tilts
8. Cool down – 5 minutes' walk
9. Stretches

CHAPTER SUMMARY

Following this chapter you should have a good understanding of the importance of posture and its effect on movement and performance. You should be able to assess posture objectively, making basic assumptions about possible muscle imbalances that may be contributing towards postural deviation. You should hopefully be aware of strategies to improve a client's posture. Always remember that personal trainers are not physiotherapists and any recommendations made should be given with this understanding between you and your client. Anyone with chronic pain should be referred to the appropriate medical profession. Your role as a personal trainer will be to build a good referral list from which you can recommend respected professionals with whom you can work to help the client.

REFERENCES AND RECOMMENDED READING

1. Chek, Paul (accessed 2002) *Scientific Back Training*. Correspondence Course. www.chekinstitute.com

2. Donkin, S.W. (1986) *Sitting on the Job*. Boston: Houghton Mifflin.

3. Jones, D.A. and Round, J.M. (1990) *Skeletal Muscle in Health and Disease*. Manchester: Manchester University Press.

4. McGill, S. (2002) *Low Back Disorders: Evidence-based Prevention and Rehabilitation*. Champaign, IL: Human Kinetics.

5. O'Sullivan, P. (2000) Lumbar segmental 'instability': clinical presentation and specific stabilising exercise management. *Manual Therapy* 5:2–12

6. Richardson, C., Jull, G., Hodges, P. and Hides, J. (1999) *Therapeutic Exercise for Spinal Segmental Stabilization in Low Back Pain – Scientific Basis and Clinical Approach*. Edinburgh: Churchill Livingstone.

7. Saunders, H.D. (1985) *Evaluation, Treatment and Prevention of Musculoskeletal Disorders*. Minneapolis, MN: Viking Press.

8. Schwartzer, A. (1996) How to investigate the patient with low back pain. *Modern Medicine of Australia* 108–112.

9. Spring, H., Illi, U., Kunz, H.R. and Rothlin, K., Sneider W. (1991) *Stretching and Strengthening Exercises*. Stuttgart: Thieme Medical Publishers.

SPOTTING AND TOUCH TRAINING

Spotting is a term commonly used in the gym. If someone asks for a 'spot', it generally means they want you to watch them whilst they lift a weight and assist if they struggle midway through a repetition. For a personal trainer spotting has to mean far more. Effective spotting is a complex and skilled science in which the trainer has to monitor and provide feedback on every aspect of the client's performance to ensure that they are training as effectively as possible. In this chapter we will learn how to spot our clients to ensure that they exercise with good form and technique using the correct acute training variables. We will also demonstrate how to perform *touch training*, using touch to position the client, indicate range of motion or stimulate muscles to produce greater force.

SPOTTING FUNDAMENTALS

When we are spotting we are essentially looking to see, or 'spot', any problems with our client's exercise. We are watching them for three main reasons:

- to ensure the correct and safe execution of an exercise to prevent acute (sudden) or chronic (slow-onset) injury
- to maximize results
- to convey professionalism to those watching.

To achieve these three aims we can start by broadly applying the following list of spotting guidelines.

Positive body language

A personal trainer should be active, attentive and motivated. They should be totally focused on their client without distraction. There are so many factors to consider to ensure safe and effective exercise that there are no excuses for the personal trainer not to be paying attention. There is no worse sight than a personal trainer talking to someone else, watching TV or reading their clipboard when their client is lifting a weight. Folded arms, leaning on equipment, openly yawning are examples of negative body language that reflect poorly on your professionalism.

Safety first

If the client is lifting a weight that is potentially dangerous and their levels of exertion are high, you should always spot this weight. This means being ready to help the client lift if they reach the point of failure and form deteriorates. Ideally you should be in a position to take the weight fully if needed. Your safety is, of course, important too, so your body position needs to be such that you can lift with good technique if this happens. Only move away from this position if the client is comfortable or there is no danger present.

Get the big picture

Whilst the majority of your time should be spent close to your client so that you can get hands-on and spot the weight in case the person fails during a set, move away for short periods so that you can observe the big picture. Seeing your client from a distance may allow you to see faults in technique that you may miss up close. This should only be done if you are sure the client is comfortable with the weight and not close to failure (RPE 4–5 – see below for a description of rating of perceived exertion).

Spot in three planes of motion

When observing a client perform an exercise, you should be looking for any loss of form or technique that may result in injury. Some deviations whilst apparent from the front or behind may be missed if you are only spotting from the side (if one shoulder is higher than the other, for example). Therefore it is crucial that you *move around your client* and observe them from several different angles and positions, taking into account each plane of motion. Make sure that you spot from directly in front, directly to the sides and directly behind your client to assess their technique and body position.

Use mirrors

A mirror is a great tool for a trainer because it allows you to monitor more than one plane of motion from the same spotting position (i.e. you can see your client from the side and the front at the same time). Clients can also monitor their own body position, gaining valuable feedback regarding their performance and quality of movement.

Use your hands

As well as appearing more professional, **touch training** can be a great tool to provide physical feedback to your client. Amongst other things you can set range of motion, change your client's body position, and cue which muscles you want them to use. This can be achieved all in a fraction of the time it takes to explain what you want. Your sessions should be hands-on whilst remaining discreet and in tune with client's sensitivities. Touch training is covered in greater depth later in this chapter.

Check core muscle activation

We should always be looking for correct abdominal/core muscle activation during exercise. We see from Chapter 13 that this is characterized by the stomach being pulled in, 'hollowed', rather than pushing out or 'doming'. If the client is wearing a baggy t-shirt and this cannot be seen, we should use our hands to check whether core muscles (see Transverse abdominis) are working correctly. Place your fingertips on the stomach, ideally across the navel, and feel whether the stomach is pulled in or pushing out.

Keep at your client's eye level

When talking to your client try to stay at eye level. This will improve the quality of your communication and your body language. Standing over your client not only looks unprofessional but may also intimidate them.

Use the 90–90 position

If the client is sitting or lying you should generally try to use the 90–90 position. This is where one foot and one knee are on the ground, making two

90-degree angles at the knees. If standing is not appropriate, this is an alternative posture that provides a stable base of support from which you can help a client with a weight if necessary. The 90–90 position also appears far more professional than if you are on two knees, sitting or lying when you spot a client.

If you follow these points you will find that you are either moving around your client, using verbal cues to improve technique, or are up close, using your hands to guide your client and spot a potentially dangerous weight. If your body language is good, the overall effect will be of someone working very hard to make the client have the best experience exercising they possibly can. This will be evident to both the client and to anyone watching the session. The rest of the chapter provides more in-depth information about fulfilling the three main aims of spotting that we identified above.

ENSURING SAFETY

Your first role as the personal trainer whilst spotting is to ensure the safety of the client. Interventions to ensure safety include:

- ensuring the client exercises with correct form and technique
- ensuring the client maintains correct posture and alignment
- preventing the client working past the point of failure
- ensuring the client recruits core stabilizers (see Chapter 13).

Checking correct exercise form and technique

As an instructor you should be familiar with the correct technique associated with most common weights exercises. Some of these have been included in Chapter 3 and should be cross-referenced with the postural checks in Chapter 9. An understanding of exercise execution is essential

10.1 Results of faulty movement

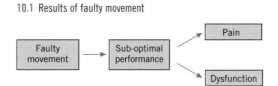

and a trainer must always build on their bank of exercises to keep their programmes fresh and their clients interested. You have to ensure that throughout your client's workout they use good technique and maintain correct form. The use of incorrect technique has been shown to produce faulty recruitment patterns, alter posture and place the body under a mechanical disadvantage that increases stress and leads to injury. Whilst errors in form may not cause immediate damage or pain (acute injury), faulty training can cause micro-damage that accumulates over extended periods of time, causing chronic injury or repetitive strain (Figure 10.1).

Some individuals have poor body awareness and may not understand the drawbacks of faulty movement. For these individuals it is necessary to educate them about the benefits of good technique and quality movement and provide them with additional feedback regarding their form. If the client is unable to maintain good form or technique, you must stop the client and *regress* the exercise before allowing them to continue.

progression: manipulating acute exercise variables to increase the challenge of an exercise.

regression: manipulating acute exercise variables to decrease the challenge of an exercise.

Kinetic chain checks

Posture within the context of a particular exercise should be continually assessed based on the guidelines covered in Chapter 9. In that chapter there is a more detailed explanation of the landmarks and anatomical plumb lines used to assess posture. This is simply a brief summary of some of the main postural checks you should make when spotting a client.

Ensure the client:

- is breathing correctly
- is maintaining neutral head position with the head acting as a natural extension of the spine
- has partial scapular retraction, unless the exercise requires scapular movement
- has a neutral spine, unless spinal flexion or extension is part of the exercise
- has activated muscles stabilizing the core (i.e. stomach drawn in or braced; see Chapter 13)
- has neutral hip position
- has a neutral knee position
- has a neutral foot position
- is maintaining loose joints at the knees and elbows when weight-bearing.

(Note that these are general guidelines and may not apply with certain exercises.)

These checks are made continually from various angles so that you can observe deviations in either the sagittal (e.g. increased lumbar curve), frontal (e.g. one hip higher than the other) or transverse planes (e.g. spine twisting). This may seem overwhelming but, as you practise, the process becomes automatic and semi-conscious.

Recognizing the point of failure

Failure is the point at which a repetition of an exercise cannot be completed without the loss of correct form and technique. At this point the prime mover has become fatigued and is unable to produce enough force to complete another repetition. If we continue to try to lift beyond this point other *synergistic* muscles (those that assist the prime mover) increase their involvement in order to complete the repetition. This is a type of faulty movement known as **synergistic dominance**. Chronic exposure to faulty movement is likely to result in injury.

> **failure:** the point at which an individual is unable to complete a repetition without loss of correct form or technique.

'Failure' is not a particularly nice term to use with clients so you may wish to replace it with something slightly more motivating.

Cheat repetitions are those repetitions performed at the end of a set using synergistic muscles to assist a fatigued prime mover as the person becomes fatigued. A cheat repetition may indicate that the client has passed the point of **optimal overload**, at which point the risk of acute injury increases.

Cheat mechanism is a term for the use of synergistic muscles to perform an exercise from the outset of a set. Whilst cheat repetitions are performed out of necessity because of muscular fatigue, cheat mechanisms represent learned movements that the client is using to make the exercise easier in order to lift more weight or because they are carrying some sort of muscular imbalance or injury.

We often see people using cheat mechanisms so that they can lift heavier weights. Examples include:

- using additional body movement (e.g. swinging the back during a bicep barbell curl)
- repositioning of the body to allow mechanical advantage (e.g. arching the back during a shoulder press)
- using a restricted range of motion
- using momentum to take a weight through a sticking point.

These cheat mechanisms can become ingrained patterns of movement, used by the client whenever they have to lift a weight. All are examples of **faulty movement**, which develops weak areas of muscle action, places strain on weaker synergistic muscles and places the body at mechanical disadvantage. When you spot a client, a major goal is to identify and eliminate cheat mechanisms. This often means lowering the weight. It can be a motivational and educational challenge to teach someone that lifting less weight can get them better results.

Spotting the weight near point of failure

There is a risk when lifting a weight, especially if that weight is on or above them, that the client will either reach the point of failure or suffer an acute injury midway through a set, putting them at risk of further injury. At this point you must be ready to provide the client with assistance in the lift. If a client is nearing the point of failure or the exercise is potentially dangerous, you should be ready to take the weight if needed. Under these circumstances you would not move away to get the big picture or move around to check form.

MAXIMIZING RESULTS

Clients are paying you to get faster results than they could get by themselves. After you have selected appropriate exercises and ensured correct technique, how else can you maximize results?

Two primary interventions to maximize results are to ensure correct work intensity and to motivate and provide verbal encouragement.

Ensuring correct work intensity

Intensity is a key variable with regards to achieving results. If the client does not work hard enough there will be insufficient stimulus to achieve overload and no training effect will be stimulated. If intensity is too high then the client may be unable to achieve the sufficient volume (enough repetitions or time under tension) required for maximum results. Alternatively, they may be forced to use cheat mechanisms to achieve the required repetition ranges. *Exercise intensity* has to be continually assessed by the personal trainer.

Methods of monitoring exercise intensity during *resistance training* include:

- rating of perceived exertion
- alternative verbal feedback
- quality of movement indicators.

Table 10.1 A rating of perceived exertion scale

No.	Borg Scale	Instructor cues
0	Nothing	Relaxation
1	Very weak	Very, very easy
2	Weak	Very easy
3	Moderate	Moderately easy
4	Somewhat strong	Somewhat hard
5	Strong	Hard
6		
7	Very strong	Very hard
8		
9		Extremely hard
10	Very, very strong	Point of failure

From Borg (1982).

Rating of perceived exertion (RPE)

RPE is often the most practical method of assessing work intensity during both resistance and cardiovascular training. It involves the client scoring their internal perception of effort (i.e. how hard they feel they are working) out of 10. An example of the scale used for these scores is provided in Table 10.1.

To make the scores more meaningful for both you and your client, explain how each score might relate to their performance. For example:

If you feel as if you cannot perform another rep with good form this would constitute a 10. Likewise if you are working hard but can only complete seven more reps this may constitute a 5 on the RPE scale.

Check RPE regularly throughout your client's work. For example, during a set of 10 repetitions I would expect a trainer to check RPE an average of 2–3 times: once at the start of a set to ensure the weight is appropriate, and twice more to monitor whether the client feels they are nearing the point of failure. Remember, as the client nears the point of failure you must start to spot the weight more closely in case they experience any problems.

Alternative verbal feedback

Although RPE will be the most effective and time-efficient mode of feedback, the client will also provide other information that may indicate that a weight is too challenging or too easy. They may express pain or discomfort, a lack of balance or stability, for example. I often explain to a client that an exercise should be 'challenging', with effort and concentration required to complete the set with good form. A client chatting about what they want for tea tonight as they work may be an indication that the exercise intensity is too low and lacking in neural demand.

Quality of movement indicators

Quality of movement can often be used to indicate if the weight is too challenging. Cheat mechanisms and unwanted body movement, increased tempo, deviations in the kinetic chain alignment may all indicate that an exercise is too challenging or that the client is unable to coordinate the movement. In this case the movement should be regressed or intensity reduced.

Methods of monitoring exercise intensity during *cardiovascular exercise* include:

- monitoring heart rate
- rating of perceived exertion
- talk test
- alternative performance indicators.

Heart rate

Heart rate can be monitored using monitor straps and watches. Monitors can be found on many cardiovascular machines or you can manually palpate a pulse, usually the carotid pulse in the neck or the radial pulse in the wrist. Take a count of beats in 15 seconds and multiply the number by four to get beats per minute. See Chapter 5 for target heart rate ranges.

Rating of perceived exertion (RPE) in cardiovascular exercise

RPE can be used in cardiovascular exercise in a similar way as with resistance training. We can make the scores more meaningful for the client by explaining in more detail what each score feels like physically. For example:

> A 10 would constitute complete exhaustion, a 0 being complete rest. If you feel you are able to work for a further 5 minutes only at this intensity, how you feel now may constitute a 6 on the RPE scale.

The better you explain the meaning of each score with reference to how they feel, the more information the RPE scale will provide you when your client trains. An RPE of 4–7 is thought to correlate approximately with 60–85 per cent of maximum heart rate.

Talk test

Exercising above *lactic threshold* generally means that the client will not be able to talk comfortably, and they may often have to pause for breath. An inability to finish complete sentences generally indicates that the client has reached their lactic threshold and is working at an intensity somewhere near 85 per cent maximum heart rate.

Alternative performance indicators

A client's body language and the quality of their movements also provide important information as to the intensity of work that you have given them. Although facial expressions and how red they are must not be considered reliable sources of performance feedback, they should not be ignored, especially with clients that you know well. If they are chatting about the weekend, for example, this may indicate that an exercise is not sufficiently challenging to warrant concentration.

Intensity can be altered during a set by manipulating the acute exercise variables. Neural demand can be increased by reducing stability (decrease base of support), weight can be added via manual resistance (i.e. the personal trainer adding their body weight), or weight can be lowered through manual assistance (the personal trainer helping to lift the weight), tempo can be slowed to increase time under tension, or range of motion can be altered to remove rest points. These are all strategies you can use to increase intensity midway through a set. If intensity is far too high, load should be lowered and a lighter weight selected. This way overload is achieved in the target repetition range.

Motivating your client

The perceptions of many clients about what they can achieve are often inaccurate. We all tend towards certain comfort zones to avoid failure or because of a fear of injury. It is the aim of the trainer to push the client outside the boundaries of these comfort zones in a safe and effective manner. Pushing someone to do that extra repetition or that last few seconds on the treadmill is an important part of your service and something that most clients will expect. Just remember that this does not take precedence over ensuring the safety of the client.

To keep the client motivated it is important to clarify your expectations for each set from the outset and reward effort and successful performance (see Chapter 16). This form of positive verbal reward will leave a client feeling successful and motivate them to further efforts.

Don't forget that this is not your only role. Many trainers fall into the trap of becoming motivators and rep counters without any other real substance to their spotting.

ADVERTISING TO PROSPECTIVE CLIENTS

If you are looking to expand your client base, you will find that your session is the best advert to prospective clients thinking about investing in your services. People watching your session may not necessarily be able to hear what you are saying to your client; they can only base their decision on how professional you appear and how much your clients are getting from your session.

With this in mind, remember to:

- use positive body language
- smile and engage the client, showing genuine interest
- avoid negative body language (e.g. leaning on machines, appearing distracted, arms folded)
- use your hands (touch training, see below)
- move around the client to spot in all three planes of motion.

Unfortunately it is not enough simply to know about exercise and educate your clients. We have to add value to every session and to every set and rep through effective spotting.

TOUCH TRAINING

Touch training – the use of physical contact to give your client feedback – is an extremely important skill for a personal trainer. The use of your hands to set range of motion, provide proprioceptive feedback and correct faults in body position will save much time and effort in trying to describe or demonstrate what position you are looking for. Touch training can also profoundly impact on the way your client recruits their muscles and may even affect the forces they are able to produce.

Before starting to use touch training it is important to consider the feelings of the client. It is possible that many clients in the early stages of their sessions may be uncomfortable with physical contact, viewing it as inappropriate and an invasion of their personal space. Whilst such occasions will be rare, you must always explain to a new client prior to the session about touch training, its hands-on nature and your reasons for doing it. If the client is still uncomfortable with the contact involved, focus on using verbal cues regarding exercise technique.

Even if the client is comfortable with touch training, use common sense and discretion and remain professional at all times. Whilst a physiotherapist or doctor can palpate gluteal muscles in the backside or pectoral muscles in the chest to identify pain, a personal trainer with an opposite-sex client should be more conservative. Touch training is designed to optimize the quality of their workout and the client should never feel uncomfortable. Only start to use touch training once you have developed a good relationship with the client. If there is no-one else in the room and you are alone with the client you may again reconsider the appropriateness of some touch-training techniques. Never compromise yourself as a trainer.

Touch training can be used to:

- increase proprioceptive feedback regarding body position
- increase muscle fibre recruitment
- improve muscle isolation
- define range of motion of an exercise
- correct body position or technique
- provide the client with information regarding the direction of muscle action.

Palpation (touching) a muscle or body part sends nervous impulses to the brain. These impulses provide valuable information regarding the position of that body part in space (i.e. proprioception). Touch is therefore invaluable for those clients with poor body awareness (Rothenberg, 1995).

10.2 Keeping elbows still during a bicep curl or cable pushdown

10.3 Cupping hands over the deltoids during lateral raise

Figure 10.2 shows an example of touch being used to provide feedback about body position.

Muscle isolation and muscle recruitment

Touch can also increase the client's ability to recruit the muscle being palpated. Some clients may not be able consciously to feel muscles working. By touching a muscle you make the task of isolating that muscle far easier. Stimulation of the skin receptors over muscle by touch increases the recruitment of fast-type muscle fibres that are key in power and strength production. By placing cupped hands or fingertips onto a muscle you may be able to increase the amount of force that muscle is able to produce.

Figure 10.3 shows an example of using touch to help muscle isolation and force generation.

10.4 Defining range of motion during lateral raise

10.5 Defining line of pull of the biceps during a bicep curl

Squat

Range of motion

Touch can be used to define range of motion during certain exercises. This will cut down on time spent explaining where you want the client to move to during an exercise. Imagine trying to explain how high your client should raise their arms during a lateral raise exercise if they have difficulty in relating the position of the hands to the position of the shoulders (Figure 10.4).

- Range of motion is defined at the knee.
- Hands can palpate the stomach to ensure core muscle activation.
- Hand can be used to cue extent of flexion required at the knee.
- Hand can easily be placed at the shoulder to cue partial repetition range of motion.

Lines of muscle action

Fingertips can be placed along a muscle from its origin to its insertion to highlight to the client the direction in which the fibres are working, how the muscle is working, its line of pull and which way they should work if they want to increase activation of that muscle.

An example of using touch to indicate lines of muscle action is shown in Figure 10.5.

Lunge

EXAMPLE-SPOTTING POSITIONS

To highlight some of the positions that can be taken to spot a client we shall illustrate using some classic exercises in which touch training can be used to define range of motion and muscle activation.

- Hand can define range of motion and both legs and the depth of the lunge.
- Hand can be placed at the shoulder to perform partial repetitions.

Chest press

- Hands can define range of motion.
- Hands can be placed on the back to ensure neutral spine.
- Hands can palpate the stomach to endure core activation.

CHAPTER SUMMARY

Spotting is an extremely complex skill that involves combining postural analysis and manipulation of acute exercise variables along with positive body language and an abundance of energy. Get spotting right and your client will experience safe and effective exercise and those watching your session will be struck by your professionalism and client care. Remember that if we were taking a 30-second snapshot of your skills, something that many people may do, the quality of your client's movements and your spotting will be the only differentiating factor between you and the next trainer. Spotting is therefore your most powerful form of advertising and marketing.

REFERENCES AND RECOMMENDED READING

1. Baechle, T.R. and Earle, R.W., eds (2000) *Essentials of Strength Training and Conditioning*, 2nd edn. National Strength and Conditioning Association. Champaign, IL: Human Kinetics.
2. Borg, G. (1982) Psychological bases of perceived exertion. *Medicine Science in Sports and Exercise* 14:377–387.
3. Chek Paul (accessed 2002) *Scientific Back Training*. Correspondence Course. www.chekinstitute.com
4. Rothenberg, O. (1995) *Touch Training for Strength*. Champaign, IL: Human Kinetics.

FLEXIBILITY AND STRETCHING

Flexibility is the range of motion available at one joint or a series of joints. Exercises aimed at improving flexibility are commonly neglected in the typical gym programme. They are often perceived as having little aesthetic benefit and no effect on cardiovascular performance or muscular strength. The scientific community is also undecided as to the benefits of stretching, with much research demonstrating little or no benefit of stretching for reducing the risk of injury or improving performance. For those who believe that stretching is beneficial there is great debate over what types of stretches are most effective and at what stage of a person's workout stretching should be performed. This chapter will summarize this debate and argue why, with effective exercise prescription and exercise selection, stretching and mobilizing can be highly beneficial for injury prevention and sports performance.

Within this chapter we identify a range of flexibility techniques that can be included in your clients' workouts. We cover *assisted stretching*, in which the trainer is actively involved in the stretching process. We also look at some advanced stretching techniques that utilize neurological pathways to relax muscle and aid in the stretching process. These have been grouped under the heading *muscle energy techniques*.

SCIENCE OF FLEXIBILITY TRAINING

Although the benefits of stretching are open for debate we know that stretches:

- increase range of motion at joints through improved extensibility of muscle and connective tissue (Thacker *et al.*, 2004), and
- increase muscular relaxation and reduce muscle tension or tone (Fleck and Kraemer, 1997).

We can understand more about effective stretching by summarizing some of the fundamental science behind how muscles respond to stretch.

Muscles, the dynamic stabilizers

Joints pushed forcefully past their natural range of motion during movement can easily be damaged. Excessive range of motion at joints is prevented statically by ligaments (which attach from bone to bone) and dynamically by muscles. These structures can be damaged if excessive forces such as a blow or a sudden twist or change in direction push them into excessive range of motion. Damage to a muscle is known as a **strain** and damage to a ligament is known as a **sprain**.

Muscles have inbuilt reflex mechanisms to prevent excessive stretch and help them perform their function in dynamically stabilizing joints at the correct times. **Muscle mechanoreceptors** are receptors found within muscle that detect physical changes in muscle such as changes in length and the amount of tension being placed through them. The main muscle receptors are the **muscle spindles** and the **golgi tendon organs**.

- **Muscle spindles:** These are sensory receptors found along the length of muscle fibres. They are sensitive to changes in length and to rate of change of length in muscles. When muscles are stretched too far or too quickly, the spindles cause a reflex contraction in the same muscle. This contraction is called a **stretch reflex**. We see the stretch reflex in action when our doctor taps our knee with a hammer and there is a reactive extension at the knee joint (i.e. the leg jumps up). While the stretch reflex prevents damage it can be a barrier to effective stretching.

- **Golgi tendon organs:** These are located within the **musculo-tendinous junction**. This is the point at which the muscle and the tendon meet and blend into one another. Golgi tendon organs' receptors are sensitive to changes in muscular tension and the rate of change of muscular tension. When they sense excessive tension in muscle they stimulate a reflexive relaxation in order to prevent the muscle damaging itself by creating too much force. This reflex relaxation response to excessive muscular tension is called **autogenic inhibition** or an **inverse stretch reflex**.

Reciprocal inhibition

Reciprocal inhibition is the natural reflex relaxation of a muscle when its opposing muscle group contracts. This occurs during natural movement. As one muscle contracts and shortens, its antagonist (i.e. opposite muscle group) relaxes to allow smooth and fluid movement.

This reflex relaxation can work against us if our posture and muscle balance are poor. If we have a muscle imbalance around a joint in which one muscle group is particularly tight and strong, it can reciprocally start to inhibit its antagonist. This muscle becomes harder to recruit by the nervous system and will not produce as much force (Chaitow, 2001). We refer to such muscle as being **inhibited**. Overly strong, tight muscles are termed **hypertonic**. Tone is the low level of muscle activity present at all times that helps us maintain posture. When we move, the body uses hypertonic muscle in preference to inhibited muscles even at the expense of the quality of our movement. Below we will see how stretching hypertonic muscles can improve the quality of our movement.

KEY POINT

- A short, tight muscle with too much tension (tone) is called hypertonic.
- Hypertonic muscles can inhibit their antagonists (opposing muscles).
- Inhibited muscles are harder to recruit by the nervous system and thus produce less force.
- Hyperonic muscles can also affect quality of movement by limiting range of motion.

KEY POINT

- Spindles: Cause stretch reflex in response to excessive stretch.
- Golgi tendon organs: Produce autogenic inhibition (relaxation) in response to muscular tension.
- Reciprocal inhibition: Is a reduction in power production of an inhibited muscle.

This knowledge can be used to help our stretching and make it more effective.

TYPES OF STRETCHING

In this section we look at the different types of stretches that we can use. First, it is important to understand that there are two types of flexibility:

- active or functional range of motion is range of motion available under muscular contraction (i.e. how far you can take your own leg into a hamstring stretch)
- passive range of motion is range of motion available due to an external force (i.e. range of motion available when an external force pushes you into a hamstring stretch).

Static stretching

Static stretches involve taking a muscle to the point of comfortable tension and holding. Static stretching is generally recognized as the safest form of stretching (Smith, 1994). Bandy and Irion (1994) demonstrated that a static stretch held for 30 seconds and repeated for several repetitions yields best results. Stretches held for this length of time are known as *developmental stretches* because they improve muscle extensibility. Static stretches are effective at increasing muscle length and passive range of motion, making them ideal for correcting posture and muscle imbalance in a carefully prescribed corrective programme.

When performing a static stretch we should move to a point of mild discomfort without pain at a slow speed to avoid stretch reflex. A painful or overly quick stretch may cause an unwanted stretch reflex, which will prevent improvements in muscle length and may potentially tear muscle fibres, even causing injury. Pain or a shaking of the muscle as it is held is a good indication that we have a stretch reflex.

Static stretches cause a relaxation in muscle. We see a reduction in resting tone and a reduced ability of that muscle to produce force (Evtovich *et al.*, 2003; Young and Behm, 2003). For this reason static stretches should not normally be performed prior to an exercise in which that muscle is involved. We should not statically stretch the gluteal muscles prior to performing a squat, for example. Static stretches can be effective at reducing tone in hypertonic muscles.

Active stretching

Active stretching involves moving in and out of a stretch. To perform an active stretch move into a position of stretch, hold for approximately 2–5 seconds, bring yourself back out of the stretch and repeat the process 5–10 times. This type of stretching utilizes natural *reciprocal inhibition* to cause reflex relaxation of the muscle we want to stretch. For example, during a hip flexor stretch when we move into the stretch the glutes are contracting, causing a reflex relaxation in the hip flexors. Because there is a larger element of movement during a dynamic stretch, there is less lasting muscular relaxation, making this stretch more appropriate for use prior to a workout to improve muscle balance and range of motion.

Ballistic

Ballistic stretches involve more powerful movements that utilize momentum to take the joints through a full range of motion and improve range of motion (Anderson and Burke, 1991). The advantage of this type of stretch is that it prepares the muscles physically and neurologically for explosive movements. Ballistic stretches activate fast twitch muscle fibres and prepare neuronal pathways for power production whilst improving range of motion. This makes these types of stretches ideal for preparing for a power or plyometric exercise.

There is an increased risk of damage or injury when performing ballistic stretches so care should always be taken when they are used. It is generally only highly conditioned sports performers that use ballistic stretching and only then if their posture and muscle balance are good. An extended general warm-up to raise muscle temperature is recommended and the client should begin with slow speeds of movement with restricted range of motion and progress into more powerful movements, utilizing a full range of motion. The element of increased risk is why ballistic stretches of the spine in particular are not recommended for the general/unconditioned population (see Figure 11.1 and 11.2).

Functional stretching

Functional stretching involves functional movements, such as overhead squats, lunges, the Romanian deadlift or medicine ball rotations, to take muscles through a full range of motion under minimal loads. A very light set of repetitions of an exercise you are about to perform carried out using full range of motion prior to your main set can also be used as a functional pre-stretch and specific warm-up for an exercise. A functional

stretch will increase range of motion, mobilize joints and prepare the muscular and nervous system for movements similar to those included in your workout (see Chapter 2).

Mobilization

Mobilization is the slow and deliberate movement of a joint through its full range of motion. Neck rolls, arm circling, shoulder shrugs, pelvic tilts and spinal rotations are examples of mobilizing movements. Mobilization is particularly effective for preparing muscles for work either as part of a warm-up or as active recovery. Mobilization increases active range of motion, aids in reducing muscular tension and helps lubricate joints *without* neurologically switching off muscles and making them harder to recruit. Mobilization is useful before and after static stretching because it

Ballistic stretches

11.1 Sagittal plane hip swings – stretching hip flexors and hamstrings

11.2 Frontal plane hip swings – stretching adductors and abductors (glutes)

increases active range of motion, whereas static stretching increases passive range of motion. Mobilizing movements are commonly neglected but should form the bulk of our stretching exercises.

When to stretch

There is still great debate over when the best time is to stretch. What follows is based on the guidelines I use to stretch my clients and the logic behind these strategies.

Post-workout stretch

I generally recommend a post-workout stretch to return worked muscles back to their original length, to reduce the effects of delayed onset muscle soreness (although scientifically unproven as yet, I anecdotally support this benefit) and to promote recovery. Developmental stretching should be performed at this point to improve flexibility and muscle balance.

Pre-workout stretch

There is little evidence promoting any benefit of a full-body static pre-stretch before training (Shrier, 1999; Thacker *et al.*, 2004). Static stretches can reduce our ability to recruit a muscle, thereby reducing force production for up to an hour after stretching (Evetovich *et al.*, 2003; Young and Behn, 2003). Therefore, if we statically stretch the muscles we want to use during an exercise, we will reduce the amount of force they can produce, causing a loss of performance. If the muscle stretched is a prime mover we may encourage *faulty movement* and *synergistic dominance* (see Chapter 10) and if the muscle stretched is a stabilizing muscle we may predispose the client to injury due to lack of stability. ***Static stretches should not performed on muscles we want to use during an exercise for risk of incorrect technique, instability and increased likelihood of injury.***

Static stretches can be performed prior to a lift on antagonistic muscles (i.e. a muscle not used during the exercise). This is especially effective if this muscle is hypertonic, inhibiting muscles that we want to use during an exercise or limiting range of motion. A static stretch will lengthen and relax these muscles, improving quality of movement. For example, it has been shown that a tight (hypertonic) muscle in the lower back can be active during a crunch, causing pain or discomfort in the lower back. These muscles should not be working during this exercise. Stretching these muscles prior to the crunch should reduce their involvement in the movement and reduce discomfort in the lower back. Likewise, muscles in the chest are often hypertonic, inhibiting scapular retractors (rhomboids) and limiting range of motion during pulling movements. A static stretch of the chest muscles will improve our form and technique during pulling exercises (e.g. barbell row).

I would recommend an ***active/functional stretch and mobilization*** for short muscles that are restricting functional range of motion at a joint. This type of stretch will increase range of motion, thereby improving quality of movement without making the muscle harder to recruit. For example, if we have tight calves they may affect our quality of movement while running. An active stretch of the calves may improve squat form without compromising performance.

I would also recommend using ***mobilization*** and ***functional pre-stretching*** prior to exercising as part of a specific warm-up, to prepare muscles, joints and the nervous pathways for work. ***Ballistic*** stretching should be introduced prior to power exercises with highly conditioned athletes, but should be built into slowly with at least 5 minutes of general warm-up to increase muscle temperature and increase the extensibility of the muscle.

Stretching during recovery periods

The time available between sets can be used to stretch using guidelines similar to those for the pre-stretch. This is known as ***active recovery***. Mobilization can be used to maintain range of motion at joints. We can perform static or active stretches on tight antagonistic muscles to improve range of motion and to reduce reciprocal inhibition. Any muscle to be used during the subsequent exercise should not be statically stretched but can be stretched actively or using mobilizing movements.

KEY POINT

- If a tight hypertonic muscle is to be used in an exercise, then active stretch and/or mobilize this muscle.
- If a tight hypertonic muscle is an antagonist and is not needed during an exercise, static stretch this muscle.

CASE STUDY: STRETCH ROUTINE

After postural and muscle assessment, I found this client to have a tight gastrocnemius, tight lower back and tight/hypertonic iliopsoas that was suspected to be inhibiting gluteus maximus activation. This is a common pattern of dysfunction causing overpronation.
I prescribed a brief stretching routine before performing a squat as follows:

1. General warm-up – Walk, progressing to light jog for 5 minutes
2. Pre-stretch – Active stretch hip flexor, active calf stretch, lower back mobilization (supine twist)
3. Specific warm-up – Functional stretch using overhead squat with minimal weight
4. Perform weighted squat
5. Active recovery – Lower back mobilization
6. Perform weighted squat
   Post stretch – Developmental static stretch to hip flexor, calf, lower back, quads

This routine improved the client's squat form and technique and their overall posture and flexibility.

STRETCHING CONSIDERATIONS

There are several factors to take into consideration when stretching.

Relative flexibility

During any movement there will always be a chain of muscles involved both in creating force (agonists within a kinetic chain) and in restricting movement (antagonistic or muscles being stretched). We can call the comparative tightness of this chain of muscles the *relative flexibility*. The body will generally take the path of least resistance. This means that most movement will come from joints that are less restricted by tight muscle. This is why when performing functional movements through full range of motion we often

11.3 a) Tight hamstrings and lower back, flexible upper spine; b) Flexible hamstrings, tight calves; c) Flexible lower back, tight hamstrings

a) Characterised by an increased curve in the upper back and less movement at the pelvis

b) Characterised by increased plantar flexion (pointing) of the toes

c) Characterised by less movement through the pelvis

see deviations in form and technique due to tight muscles as the body takes the path of least resistance. For example, the feet may turn out if the calves are tight during a squat (see Chapter 9).

Take a forward bending movement, for example (Figure 11.3). This movement places the calves, hamstrings, lower and upper spine all on stretch. Their relative flexibility will determine from which area of the body most movement will come. Movement is limited at joints controlled by short, tight muscles. Most movement will come from joints held by looser, longer and weaker muscles.

With this knowledge, a forward bend from a seated position can be a useful movement to judge relative flexibility, as can most functional movements.

Maintaining good alignment and form

If we do not take into account relative flexibility the body will always take the easiest path to remove tension and achieve the desired body position during a stretch. Look at the two hip flexor stretches in Figure 11.4, the first with the back arching. This person has weaker abdominal muscles than hip flexors. The body allows spinal extension before hip flexion, which causes strain in the lower back. In the second example the person has made sure that the back remains in good alignment, ensuring that the hip flexors are stretched without strain through the back. Note how in 11.4a, an example of poor technique,

the hips are titled forwards (anterior tilt) and twisted, causing the back to arch. This gives the impression of a greater stretch but only serves to place strain on the structures of the lower back.

We have to ensure that the origin and insertion of the muscle we want to stretch are taken further apart. This is why it is essential when we stretch a particular muscle that:

- we use correct form and technique
- we isolate short, tight muscle and prevent stretch in weak, long muscles, and
- we ensure that the origin and insertion of the muscle we want to stretch are moving further apart as we move (Figure 11.4b).

When the origin and insertion of the muscle fail to move further apart the stretch should be held. If we fail to do this we only stretch long, weak muscles and fail to stretch short, tight muscles effectively as we allow the body to take the path of least resistance.

Utilizing three planes of motion

Muscles often exert force and generate movement in all three planes of motion (sagittal, transverse and frontal; see Chapter 1) and often influence more than one joint at a time. This is why when we stretch we should incorporate movement in more than one plane of motion and should incorporate movement from all the joints that the muscle influences.

11.4a HF stretches with poor technique

11.4b HF stretches with correct technique

11.5 HF stretch with side bend

If we take a hip flexor stretch, for example, the psoas muscle, as well as causing hip flexion via its attachments to the leg, also attaches to the spine. We can place the psoas on stretch by taking the hip into extension as shown in Figure 11.4b. If we also introduce some side flexion and rotation through the spine we can target different portions of the psoas muscle and take the origin and insertion of the muscle further apart, thus increasing the effectiveness of the stretch (Figure 11.5).

Try performing the same stretch from Figure 11.4b but lift the back foot and rest it on a bench. This should bring the stretch more into the long hip flexors (i.e. the quads). This does not constitute a loss of form because the origin and insertion of the muscle we want to stretch are still moving further apart.

Stretching all fibres of a muscle

Some muscles are very large and exert forces on joints from a variety of different directions. They can develop tension and restrict range of motion in equally as many different directions. To achieve good flexibility we have to stretch the muscle from all these different angles. Consider the pectoralis major, for example. This muscle has its origins along the clavicle and into the sternum (the breast bone). If we were only to stretch with the arm at one angle we would only ever stretch a small proportion of the fibres of this muscle. Therefore we must change the angle of the stretch by altering the position of the arm. If we were to use a Swiss ball stretch for the

chest, when the arm is above shoulder height the sternoclavicular fibres of pectoralis major are stretched; as the arm is lowered the clavicular fibres of pectoralis major are stretched. We should be aware of which fibres are tighter and spend more time stretching these. This means we should perform our chest stretch several times at a variety of different angles to effectively stretch the muscle. The same is true of almost all the muscles in the body. Stretch at a variety of different angles.

Functional flexibility

During functional movements (e.g. as we bend to lift, run, jump etc.) it is important to appreciate that:

- the direction of stretch is specific to the movement performed
- chains of muscles are put on stretch during any movement.

Stretches follow the principle of specificity – range of motion will improve specific to the joint angle and positions in which we stretch. Remember, we cannot isolate muscles but we can isolate joints when we move. A good example of how muscles communicate and interrelate with each other is when we perform a hamstring stretch. When we put the calf on stretch by dorsiflexing the foot we feel the hamstrings stretch to a greater extent.

Remember that we should try to stretch using movements that mimic the ways in which we want

11.6a General stretch

11.6b A stretch for a rugby player

11.6c A stretch for a golfer

to move. Functional stretching using movements such as the squat or Romanian deadlift, or movements that mimic an athlete's sporting activity are much more effective. Figures 11.6a–c give three examples of stretches for the waist, the first normal the next two functional.

ASSISTED STRETCHING

When we physically take a client into positions of stretch, this is called ***assisted stretching*** or partner stretching. These stretches are highly effective for corrective work because the client is generally passive, they can relax and focus on reducing muscular tension and maintaining good posture. Assisted stretching is a great sales tool for the trainer. It appears professional and adds value to your client's workout.

Guidelines for assisted stretching

- ***Consent:*** As with touch training, before you start assisted stretches for the first time, check with your client to make sure they are comfortable with the physical contact involved. Some clients may prefer some simple static stretches. Most clients will understand if you explain what you are trying to achieve and the potential benefits.
- ***Communication:*** This is paramount during assisted stretching, both to find out when a good point of tension has been reached as you take them into a stretch and to determine whether there is any pain or discomfort. You are looking to reach a point of tension that is 'uncomfortable but not painful'. You may wish to use the rating of perceived exertion (RPE) scale for this (see Chapter 10), with a score of 5–6 representing a good stretching point.
- ***Breathing:*** Deep breathing can induce a **relaxation response** in muscle that aids the stretching process. Ask the client to release tension on the out breath to help ease muscle tension and encourage increased stretch.
- ***Towel etiquette:*** During the stretches always try to keep a small hand towel on the contact points between you and your client. It will prevent any loss of grip due to perspiration and will make the assisted stretch look far more professional to both your client and those who might be watching.
- ***Posture:*** You will probably spend a lot of time performing these stretches. Try to ensure that your own posture is correct. Kneel on sponge mats or another hand towel to protect knees, maintain good posture and avoid placing undue stress on yourself.
- ***Sequencing:*** Remember that your stretches should ideally fall into a smooth sequence. You should always have a point of contact with the client, usually the heel, so that the stretches feel flowing. This may not be possible as each stretch routine may be different in response to the client's posture.
- ***Education:*** Always ensure that the client is comfortable with how to stretch by themselves.

With most clients their stretches will be the first thing they miss out, especially if they do not know how to perform them.

- *Check range of motion:* Always ask your client to perform an active stretch (i.e. move as far as they can into the stretch) and use this as an initial starting point for your passive stretch. You can easily damage a client by taking them too far into a stretch beyond their comfortable range of motion.

Hamstring stretch

- With the client lying supine with legs flat, ask them to take the leg to be stretched back as far as they can in order to assess their active range of motion.
- On one knee and one foot (90–90 position), holding the client's heel and with the other hand (using a towel) supporting the leg just below the knee, take the straight, but not locked, leg back until you reach a point of tension.
- Relative flexibility: avoid the hips tilting posteriorly or side to side.

Calf stretch (gastrocnemius)

- With the client lying supine, take hold of their foot, resting the calf on the top of your thigh.
- Supporting the heel with one hand (using a towel), press the ball of the foot back with the other until you reach the point of tension.
- Relative flexibility: avoid the leg bending. This will remove tension from the gastrocnemius muscle.

Short adductor stretch

- With the client lying supine, place yourself on one knee and one leg.
- Place the client's foot onto your outside hip with their leg bent.
- Stabilize their pelvis by pressing down with your inside hand on their flat leg slightly above the knee, and support their bent knee with your outside hand.
- Using body weight and guiding the knee away from their body, lean and press their bent foot forwards until you reach the point of tension in their inner thigh.
- Relative flexibility: avoid the hips tilting side to side.

Gluteal stretch

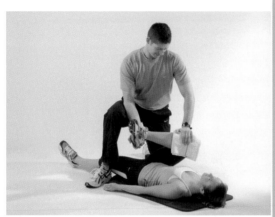

- The client lies supine with the leg not to be stretched laid flat.
- Take a 90–90 position, your foot stabilizing the client's pelvis by supporting on the outside of their thigh.
- Hold their leg bent by the heel with one hand and by the knee with the other hand, holding the leg at 45 degrees to the body.
- Push their leg towards their shoulder opposite, maintaining the 45-degree angle until you reach the point of tension in the gluteal muscle.
- Relative flexibility: avoid the hips lifting or tilting.

Quadriceps stretch

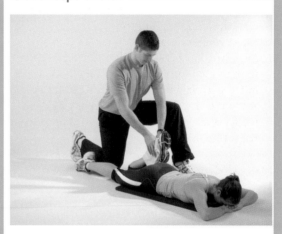

- With the client lying prone, ask them to draw their heel as close to their buttocks as possible.
- In the 90–90 position take their foot closer to their bottom until you reach the point of tension.
- If a stretch is not felt, ask the client to start by posteriorly tilting the pelvis.
- Relative flexibility: avoid the back tilting anteriorly and keep the leg in line with the hip.

Pectoral stretch

- Ask the client to sit upright in a position of comfort to them and place their fingertips on their temples.
- Support their back with your thigh and hip as you kneel behind them in the 90–90 position.
- Using two towels draw the client's elbows back until they feel a stretch into their chest, ensuring the stretch is even on both sides.
- Relative flexibility: avoid the back arching or the head jutting forwards.

Anterior deltoid stretch

- Ask the client to sit upright in a position of comfort to them and place their palms on their lower back.
- Ensuring you are kneeling with a stable base of support, gradually draw the client's elbows together until an even stretch is felt in their shoulders.

Latissimus dorsi

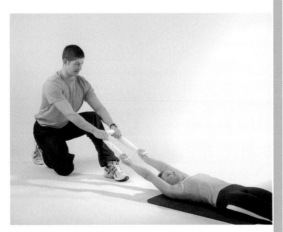

- Ask the client to lie supine and take both ends of the towel in their hands.
- Pull the middle of the towel until the client feels a stretch in the lats.
- Relative flexibility: avoid the back arching upwards.

Assisted rotation

- With the client lying supine, ask them to put one leg straight and place the opposite foot on the top of the opposite knee.
- With one hand stabilizing the shoulder, use the other hand to push the knee on the near side across the body.
- The client should feel a stretch in the obliques and across the lower back in the chest or hips, depending on the relative flexibility imbalance in these muscles.

ADVANCED PARTNER STRETCHING: MUSCLE ENERGY TECHNIQUES

Using our knowledge of the mechanoreceptors important in controlling stretch and range of motion, we can use various techniques to encourage muscles to relax, allowing us to take them to greater levels of stretch. Whist there are different names for these techniques I have grouped them under the heading *muscle energy techniques*.

Post-isometric relaxation

force from trainer   force from client

This technique utilizes ***autogenic inhibition*** to create a state of relaxation in the muscle to be stretched. By contracting the stretched muscle we stimulate Golgi tendon organ receptors, generating a relaxation response, allowing increased stretch in that muscle. To perform post-isometric relaxation:

- Gently take the muscle to be stretched to a point of comfortable resistance.
- Create a barrier against which the client can push to activate the stretched muscle (e.g. if stretching the hamstring, block hip extension).
- Ask the client to contract the agonistic muscle (the hamstring) against your barrier (i.e. try to extend the hip) using only 20 per cent effort for approximately 5–10 seconds.
- Instruct the client to take a deep breath and, as they exhale, release the contraction.
- Ask the client to take another breath and, as they breath out, take the hamstring to the next point of stretch.

Reciprocal inhibition

In reciprocal inhibition a working muscle relaxes its antagonist, which is then stretched. By contracting the antagonist the agonist will naturally relax, allowing greater levels of stretch. To perform reciprocal inhibition:

- Gently take the muscle to be stretched to a point of resistance.
- Create a barrier against which the client can push to activate the antagonistic muscle (e.g. hamstring prior to a quad stretch).
- Instruct the client to contract the antagonistic muscle (hamstring) against your barrier using only 20 per cent effort for approximately 5–10 seconds.
- Ask the client to take a deep breath and, as they exhale, release the contraction.
- Ask the client to take another breath and, as they breathe out, take the hamstring to the next point of resistance.

Note: reciprocal inhibition will also aid stretching if the client initiates the movement and attempts to pull the muscle into a greater level of stretch.

STRETCHING AND INJURY PREVENTION

So does stretching decrease the chances of injury and improve performance? Thacker *et al.* (2004) reviewed 361 articles dating since 1950 and found no significant evidence confirming the benefit of stretching for reducing injury. We have to look carefully at the studies themselves to determine why they found no benefit to stretching.

In Chapter 9 we saw how relative muscle imbalance (an agonist being stronger or tighter than its antagonist) causes movement away from ideal alignment and a deterioration of posture. Poor posture is linked with an increased incidence of injury and chronic pain. We also know that maintaining functional range of motion at joints is required for quality of movement. If range of motion is restricted at certain joints, movements such as a squat or lunge cannot be performed with good form. Poor form or technique has also been linked with increased incidence of injury. It is reasonable to assume that if stretching can reduce muscular tension and therefore impact on muscle balance and posture, we can decrease the incidence of injury.

Accurate muscular assessment can identify imbalance between opposing muscle groups that may be the cause of poor posture and loss of range of motion. Following this assessment we can stretch and mobilize tight, hypertonic (i.e. overactive) muscles in order to restore muscular balance. This should improve posture, decreasing the likelihood of injury. Stretching without this prior muscular assessment is not guaranteed to have the same levels of success. Take 100 people and give them all hamstring stretches and this may impact positively on the posture of only a small percentage of the group. Stretching individuals who already have functional range of motion or stretching that does not promote muscle balance will have little positive impact on performance and may even be detrimental.

Muscles provide stability and support around joints. Stretching an already long and weak muscle can cause **hypermobility**. This is a condition in which there is too much range of motion at a joint, causing loss of stability and support. Stretches that cause hypermobility may increase the incidence of injury. The benefits of stretching are therefore only evident after accurate muscular and postural assessment. Failure to do this may be one explanation for the lack of significant scientific backing for the effectiveness of stretching.

Flexibility and recovery

The post-workout muscle soreness felt 24–72 hours following training is known as **delayed onset muscle soreness (DOMS)**. Symptomatic of DOMS, along with a fall in strength of muscle, is a reduction in range of motion. Although research is far from conclusive it has indicated that stretching may reduce the effect of DOMS. If this is the case, stretching may also play an important part in the recovery process.

CHAPTER SUMMARY

Stretching and mobilizing are an essential part of a client's training both for injury prevention and for athletic performance. I always say to my clients I would much prefer 5 minutes' stretching to 5 minutes' more cardiovascular work at the end of their workout. With care, you can seamlessly run dynamic, active and functional stretches into any workout by filling recovery and rest periods, making the session flow and ebb. Combined with correct musculoskeletal assessment and correct resistance exercise you can build programmes that not only improve basic skills such as strength and power but also improve the quality of your client's movement and reduce the risk of chronic injury.

REFERENCES AND RECOMMENDED READING

1. Anderson B. and Burke, E.R. (1991) Scientific medical and practical aspects of stretching. *Clinics in Sports Medicine* 10:63–87.
2. Bandy, W.D. and Irion, J.M. (1994) The effect of time on static stretch of the flexibility of the hamstring muscle. *Physical Therapy* 74:845–852.
3. Chaitow, L. (2001) *Muscle Energy Techniques*, 2nd edn. Edinburgh: Churchill Livingstone.
4. Evetovich, T.K., Nauman, N.J., Conley, D.S. and Todd, J.B. (2003) Effect of static stretching of the biceps brachii on torque, electromyography, and mechanomyography during concentric isokinetic muscle actions. *Journal of Strength and Conditioning Research* 17:484–488.
5. Fleck, S.J. and Kraemer, W.J. (1997) *Designing Resistance-Training Programs*, 2nd edn. Champaign, IL: Human Kinetics.
6. Gleim, G.W. and McHugh, M.P. (1997) Flexibility and its effects on sports injury and performance. *Sports Medicine* 24:289–299.
7. Herbert, R.D. and Gabriel, M. (2002). Effects of stretching before and after exercising on muscle soreness and risk of injury: Systematic review. *British Medical Journal* 325:468–470.
8. Hines, M. (2004/2005) *Flexibility and Stretching. Flexibility and Injury.* www.PTonthenet.com.
9. Ingraham, S.J. (2003) The role of flexibility in injury prevention and athletic performance. Have we stretched the truth? *Minnesota Medicine* 86:1–12. Online Journal.
10. Laughlin, K. (1998) *Overcome Neck and Back Pain.* New York: Fireside.
11. Norris, C.M. (2002) *The Complete Guide to Stretching.* London: A and C Black.
12. Parkkari, J., Kujala, U.M. and Kannus, P. (2001) Is it possible to prevent sports injuries? *Sports Medicine* 31:985–995.
13. Pope, R.P., Herbert, R.D., Kirwan, J.D. and Graham, B.J. (2000) A randomised trial of pre-exercise stretching for prevention of lower-limb injury. *Medicine and Science in Sports and Exercise* 32:271–277.
14. Shrier, I. (1999) Stretching before exercise does not reduce the risk of local muscle injury: a critical review of the clinical and basic science literature. Clinical Journal of Sport Medicine 9:221–227.
15. Smith, C. (1994) The warm-up procedure: To stretch or not to stretch. *Journal of Orthopaedic and Sports Physical Therapy* 19:12–16.
16. Thacker, S.B., Gilchrist, J., Stroup, D.F. and Kimsey, Jr., C.D. (2004) The impact of stretching on sport injury risk. A systematic review of literature. *Medicine and Science in Sports and Exercise* 36:371–378.
17. Young, W.B. and Behm, D.G. (2003) Effects of running, static stretching and practice jumps on explosive force production and jumping performance. *Journal of Sports Medicine and Physical Fitness* 43:21–27.

12

MANUAL RESISTANCE

THIS CHAPTER CONTAINS

- The benefits of manual resistance
- Things to remember when using manual resistance
- Example exercises
- When not to use manual resistance

Clients benefit from new exercises that stimulate interest and enhance training gains by challenging muscles in new and different ways. *Manual resistance (MR)* is an excellent tool you can use to give a new dimension to your sessions. It involves the use of your own body weight to provide resistance to a client's movement. During an exercise you may use MR to add load and increase exercise intensity by pressing against a bar, dumbbell or even the limbs of the client. Pure MR exercise involves using just your body weight to resist movement. In this chapter we look at the different types of MR we can use that require only your body weight to perform. After this chapter you should have a series of new and interesting exercises that can be used any place and any time.

THE BENEFITS OF MANUAL RESISTANCE

MR is a fantastic tool because the personal trainer is in total control of the exercise. The trainer can manipulate various training variables throughout the set, altering range of motion, resistance and tempo and can focus on concentric, eccentric or

isometric aspects of the muscle action without having to stop midway through a set.

ADVANTAGES AND DISADVANTAGES OF USING MANUAL RESISTANCE

Advantages

- Minimal equipment is required, meaning that MR can be used anywhere.
- It takes very little time and effort to set up.
- It provides an alternative exercise if a machine you require is being used.
- It can easily be used in combination with traditional exercises to form a super-set without having to move around the gym.
- The trainer can easily control the resistance, the tempo and the range of motion.
- The trainer can emphasize concentric, eccentric or isometric phases by altering resistance throughout the exercise.
- Resistance can be altered throughout MR

as the client fatigues, ensuring optimal loading.

■ Rest periods can be eliminated during a set and resistance can be varied throughout a range of motion to remove any sticking points in the action.

■ The trainer can allow the client to move naturally, based on their limb lengths and joint angles in a way they are not able to do under the constraints of resistance-machine exercises.

Disadvantages

■ MR involves considerable contact between client and trainer. You should always ensure that your client is comfortable with this.

■ MR exercises cannot be quantified and therefore progression is almost impossible to measure.

■ MR is physically hard work and tiring for the trainer.

■ It is harder for the trainer to spot an MR exercise. You cannot move around the client, and you cannot use hands-on spotting techniques to check posture, isolate muscles or provide feedback.

■ There is a tendency for the client to compete with the trainer. This should be discouraged as competition may affect quality of performance.

THINGS TO REMEMBER WHEN USING MANUAL RESISTANCE

MR is similar to touch training and assisted stretching in that there needs to be extensive physical contact between client and trainer. This means you have to be careful and always explain to the client what is involved and how they will perform the exercise prior to doing it, just to ensure that they are comfortable and happy to take part. You also need to make sure that both your posture and the posture of your client are appropriate as you would for any exercise.

Other points to note:

■ Because of the lack of resting points within MR exercises there is a tendency to hold the breath. You therefore need to ensure that your client is breathing throughout each repetition.

■ Always ensure you check the rate of perceived exertion so that you know the resistance you are applying is appropriate.

■ Ensure that you always have a solid base of support and are in a stable position to be able to apply sufficient, consistent and safe resistance for your client.

■ Use a towel where possible to avoid direct skin-to-skin contact. This will prevent any slips due to perspiration, keep your client's perspiration off you and will make the exercise appear more professional to your client and those watching.

■ Always check a client's available range of motion prior to applying resistance to ensure that you do not force the client into painful ranges of motion or out of ideal alignment.

EXAMPLE EXERCISES

The kinetic-chain checks and guidelines provided in both the spotting and postural chapters (Chapters 9 and 10) should be applied as well as possible when using MR. If the client is using inappropriate form then you should stop the exercise and give more feedback, or even use an alternative exercise.

Manual-resistance chest press

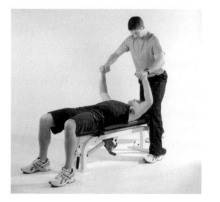

- With the client lying supine on a bench instruct them to put their hands in the air.
- Lock palms with your client, using a towel if appropriate.
- From a standing split stance (one foot in front of the other) apply downward resistance on your client's hands, instructing them to perform a movement pattern identical to that of a dumbbell press (horseshoe shape).
- Ask client to focus on the contraction of the muscles felt in the chest and triceps.

Manual-resistance pec fly

- With the client lying supine on a bench, ask them to place their fingertips on their temples.
- Using towels and from a kneeling 90–90 position, place your hands on the client's elbows.
- Apply resistance as the client draws their elbows towards each other until they reach a horizontal position relative to the shoulders. Increase the resistance in order to ease the elbows back down to a position level with the shoulders.
- Ask the client to focus on the contraction of the muscles felt in the chest.

Manual-resistance tricep extension

- With the client lying supine on a bench, ask them to bring their arms to the horizontal with their palms together.
- Use your arm (the one furthest from them) to provide a guide for their elbow position, directly above their shoulder.
- Using a towel, place your inside hand on their hands.
- As they extend the elbow, apply resistance. Increase the resistance to ease them back into elbow flexion.
- Ask the client to focus on the contraction of the muscles felt in the triceps.

Manual-resistance lateral raise

Lateral raise

- Ask the client to assume a split stance.
- Instruct them to take their arms to their sides with the elbows slightly bent.
- Using towels and from a split stance opposite to that of the client, place your hands on their hands or elbows (your preference).
- Apply resistance as the client raises their arms to horizontal, the same as if they were performing a lat raise; increase the resistance slightly and ease the client's arms back to their sides.
- Tell the client to focus on the contraction of the muscles felt in the deltoids.

Manual-resistance front raise

- Ask the client to assume a split stance.
- Instruct them to put their arms in front of them, making a fist with one hand and placing the other hand on top of it.
- Using a towel and from a split stance opposite to that of the client, place your hands on top of theirs.
- Apply resistance as the client raises their arms in front of them to the horizontal; increase resistance to ease the client's arms back down towards their waist.
- Instruct the client to focus on the contraction of the muscles felt in the front of the shoulders (anterior deltoid).

Front raise

Manual-resistance mid row

- With the client in a seated position, kneel in front of them holding the centre of a hand towel.
- Instruct the client to take the ends of the towel.
- Apply resistance through the towel as the client performs a rowing action.
- Ask the client to focus on feeling work into the lats and the middle of the back, and instruct them to perform complete scapular retraction at the end of the range of motion.

Manual-resistance pull over

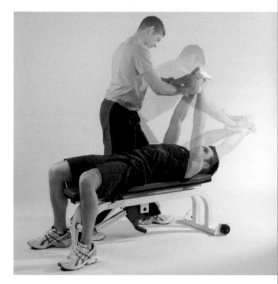

- With the client lying supine on a bench, ask them to put their hands in the air.
- Instruct the client to make a fist with one hand and place the other hand on top of it.
- Check range of motion, keeping the arms straight, taking their arms overhead. The end range of motion is just before the spine goes into extension (the gap between back and bench increases).
- Using a towel and keeping a balanced split stance, place your hands on those of the client.
- Apply resistance as the client takes their arms to their end range of motion and ease resistance off as they force your hands back to horizontal.
- Instruct the client to focus on feeling work into the lat and to use the abdominals to stop the back going into extension (i.e. pulling away from the bench).

Manual-resistance leg extension

- Tell the client to lie flat on their back on the floor with legs bent to right angles.
- Kneeling to the side of the client, ask them to raise the same-side leg into the air.
- Place your far-side hand on the client's far-side knee.
- Instruct the client to lower their raised leg so that the joint rests on your arm.
- Place your other hand slightly above the ankle of the same side leg.
- Apply resistance as the client extends their leg, increase the resistance slightly to ease the knee back into flexion.
- Ask the client to focus on the work into the quadracep.

Manual-resistance leg curl

- Ask the client to lie on their front.
- If this position becomes uncomfortable on the back, consider placing a towel under their stomach, in line with the navel, to help support their spine.)
- Check range of motion by asking the client to draw the heel of one foot as close towards their buttock as possible.
- Using a towel, place your hand onto the client's heel whilst maintaining a kneeling position.
- Apply resistance as the client draws the heel towards the buttock. Increase the resistance to ease the knee back into extension.

Remember that the client is working in both the eccentric and concentric phases of manual resistance. There is never a complete release of tension and the trainer should alter resistance to make each phase equally challenging, regularly checking rate of perceived exertion to ensure that fatigue occurs within the desired rep range.

If a client is struggling to stabilize on the eccentric phases of muscle action or as joints reach the end ranges of motion, it is extremely important to reduce the resistance being applied. Remember that due to length–tension relationships, even though we should be mechanically stronger in the eccentric phase of muscle action, as the muscle reaches the end range of motion we naturally become weaker. Applying large forces at these points increases the likelihood of injury, so ensure you start with minimal resistance and increase it gradually as you become aware of your client's ability.

WHEN NOT TO USE MANUAL RESISTANCE

It is not advisable to use manual resistence when:

- your client is not comfortable with the physical contact involved during MR
- your client is stronger than you are, unless you pre-fatigue the client
- your client gets competitive with you to the point where their form and technique are compromised
- you are fatigued and tired
- your client's form, technique and body awareness are such that more careful spotting would be of greater benefit to them.

CHAPTER SUMMARY

Manual resistance can be applied in a variety of situations, and safety, imagination and effectiveness are the only constraints when devising new MR exercises. Used safely and conscientiously, MR is a fantastic tool to add to your repertoire of exercises. It will provide a whole new way of training for your clients that they will not experience anywhere else.

13

CORE STRENGTH AND STABILITY TRAINING

THIS CHAPTER CONTAINS

- The core defined
- Anatomy of the core
- Mechanisms of core stability through segmental stabilization
- Identifying transverse abdominis activation

- Training transverse abdominis activation
- Abdominal activation under increased loads
- Training gross core stability
- Training core strength
- References and recommended reading

Core training is an important subject that is relevant both for athletes and for those looking to avoid chronic back pain. A personal trainer must have a good understanding of the core and the muscles that contribute towards core stability and core strength. In this chapter we discuss some of the theories of core stability, identify key core muscles and how they work together to create stability. We look at how their function can be assessed and how they can be trained and conditioned. A properly progressed core programme is essential for quality of movement as well as avoidance of injury. Only with an understanding of the mechanism behind core stability can our programme design and exercise prescription be safe and effective. We should be able to identify when a client has good deep abdominal muscle activation and how we can train these core muscles.

THE CORE DEFINED

The core is the centre of the body and is the foundation of all movement. Core muscles that surround the abdominal area are recruited a matter of milliseconds prior to movements of the arms and legs (Richardson *et al.*, 1999). This suggests that all movement originates from the core (Cresswell *et al.*, 1992). Abdominal muscle activation ensures that the centre of the body is stable. This provides a firm foundation from which we can move and produce force. A stable core is essential for transmitting force from the lower to the upper body or vice versa. This is an essential characteristic of functional movements like running, jumping and throwing (Hedrick, 2000). Failure to adequately recruit muscles that support and stabilize the core is associated with many deficits of performance including:

- loss of power and strength (Chek, 2002)

- increased incidence of acute injury (Tyson, 1999)
- increased incidence of chronic lower-back pain (Richardson *et al.*, 1999)
- loss of balance and coordination.

It is important that when we use the term ***core training*** we know exactly which muscles of the body we are using and what structures we are stabilizing. A useful starting point for describing the core to a client would be the centre of the body and the foundation of movement. We can explain that at the centre of the body we find the spine, primarily the lumbar spine, the last five vertebrae in the lower back. Because of their direct attachment to the spine and the large influence that they have on lumbar alignment we can also include the pelvis and hips. Hence we have the term ***lumbo-pelvic hip complex (LPHC)***. The LPHC is useful shorthand when talking about the bones and joints of the core. The muscles of the core can include any muscles acting on these structures.

Core strength is the ability of muscles to produce forceful bending or twisting movements of the trunk. Core strength is of particular importance in functional movements involving rotation such as throwing, kicking or punching. ***Core stability*** involves maintaining ideal static postural alignment of the LPHC against external forces such as gravity, momentum or someone pushing you. Core stability has to be provided both on segmental and gross levels.

Segmental stabilization involves maintaining the optimal position of each vertebra in relation to the others. Without segmental stabilization of the spine there is the risk of inducing wear and tear in the intervertebral discs. ***Gross stabilization*** involves maintaining the natural soft S-shape of the spine. Movement away from neutral increases the stress on the spine, load on the intervertebral discs and reduces the spine's ability to absorb force, thereby increasing the likelihood of injury. (See Chapter 9 for more details on the neutral alignment of the spine.) We can have gross stability without having segmental stability and vice versa but both are extremely important for protecting the spine from damage.

We commonly identify core muscles as those that produce movements of the spine, such as rectus abdominis, external oblique and erector spinae. These are known as ***outer unit*** muscles. Outer unit muscles generally cross over more than one joint. For example, in the spine they cross over many vertebrae. Because of their long levers outer unit muscles are well placed to provide gross core stability and core strength. Less well known are the deeper muscles working together to stabilize the spine, known as the ***inner unit***. These muscles influence the spine over only two or three vertebrae, making them ideally placed to provide ***segmental stabilization***. A good example of an inner unit muscle is ***multifidus*** that is found crossing over vertebrae from the lower back upwards.

Table 13.1 Characteristics of the muscles of the outer and inner units

The outer unit	The 'movers and shakers' Generate dynamic movement around joints Commonly cross more than one joint In the spine produce core strength and gross stabilization Commonly have origins and insertions that pass over many vertebrae
The inner unit	Primary function is stabilization of joints Generally cross over one major joint In the lumbar spine commonly have origins and insertions that pass over only two or three vertebrae Suited for providing segmental stability of the spine

Other major inner unit muscles that contribute towards segmental stability are ***transverse abdominis (TVA)***, the ***pelvic floor***, the ***diaphragm***, and ***internal oblique (IO)***.

gross core stability: the maintenance of neutral spine against external forces.

segmental core stability: maintenance of optimal position of each vertebra in relation to others.

core strength: production of dynamic force, strength or power during bending or twisting movements of the trunk.

The characteristics of the muscles of the outer unit and inner unit are summarized in Table 13.1 on p153.

ANATOMY OF THE CORE

The following is a brief introduction to some major muscles of the core, their functions and attachments. Be aware that this is a simplistic overview of the core muscles and many more exist that influence the spine.

Rectus abdominis

This is the outer unit muscle found at the front of the stomach (Figure 13.1). It forms the characteristic six-pack shape and provides gross core stability and core strength, primarily flexing the spine.

- **Origin:** Pubic symphysis and crest of pubis.
- **Insertion:** Costil cartilages of fifth to seventh ribs and xyphoid process.
- **Function:** Flexes the thoracic (upper portion) and lumbar spine and supports the spine by stabilizing the pelvis (lower portion). Lower portion of rectus abdominus also posteriorly tilts the pelvis.

13.1 Rectus abdominus

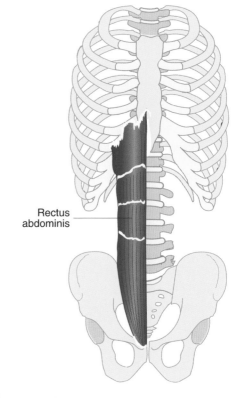

Rectus abdominis

Erector spinae group

The erector spinae comprise of a group of muscles that include the spinalis, longissimus and iliocostalis muscles, which stretch throughout the back of the spine. They provide gross core stability.

- **Attachments:** Sections of these muscles attach from and to the iliac crest and the sacrum, thoraco-lumbar fascia, transverse process of vertebrae throughout the spine and the ribs.
- **Insertions:** Various points throughout the spine.
- **Function:** Bilateral contraction results in spinal extension and unilateral activation results in side-flexion.

External oblique

This is an outer unit muscle that provides core strength (Figure 13.2). It works in conjunction

13.2 External and internal oblique

13.3 Quadratus lumborum and iliopsoas

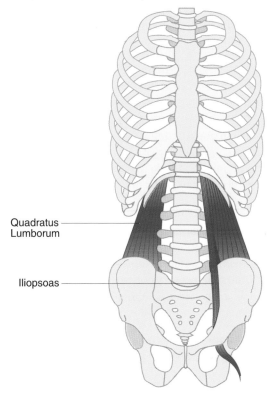

Linea alba

Internal oblique

External oblique

Inguinal ligament

Quadratus Lumborum

Iliopsoas

with the internal oblique during twisting and bending movements. It also works very much like the lower abdominals in causing posterior pelvic tilt and stabilizing the lumbar spine.

- **Origin:** Lower eight ribs.
- **Insertions:** The abdominal aponeurosis forming the linea alba and to the iliac crest.
- **Function:** Contracting unilaterally, it rotates the spine to the opposite side or causes ipsilateral side flexion. Contracting bilaterally flexes the trunk or posteriorly tilts the pelvis or stabilizes the pelvis.

Internal oblique

Inner unit muscle that works in close conjunction with external oblique during side-bending and twisting movements (Figure 13.2). Has attachments to the thoraco-lumbar fascia (see below).

- **Origin:** Lumbar fascia, iliac crest and inguinal ligament.
- **Insertions:** Ribs and linea alba.
- **Function:** Contracting unilaterally, there will be ipsilateral rotation and side flexion. Contracting bilaterally, they will flex the trunk.

Note: In lateral flexion ipsilateral internal and external oblique cooperate to create movement. In right rotation the right internal oblique cooperates with the left external oblique.

Quadratus lomborum

This muscle has dual functions. Medial portions are thought to have an important role in stabilizing the spine, while lateral fibres play a larger role in mobilizing the spine (Figure 13.3).

- **Origin:** Posterior iliac crest.

- **Insertion:** Twelfth rib and transverse processes of the lumbar vertebrae.
- **Function:** Unilateral contraction causes ipsilateral lateral flexion of the trunk, elevates ipsilateral hip. Bilateral contraction extends the lumbar spine. Stabilizes the lumbar spine.

Iliopsoas

This is an outer unit muscle made up of iliacus and psoas major (Figure 13.3). It is thought to have an important role in stabilization due to its direct attachment to the lumbar spine.

Psoas major

- **Origin:** Sides of Thoracic vertabrae number 12 to lumbar vertabrae number 4.
- **Insertion:** Lesser trochanter of femur.
- **Function:** Flexes the thigh, flexes the spine, some side flexion acting unilaterally.

13.4 Transverse abdominus (TVA)

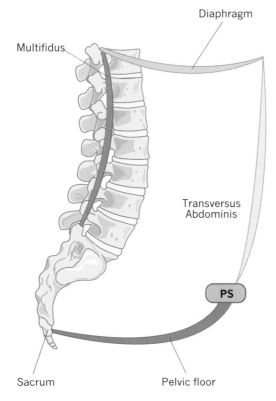

Diaphragm

Multifidus

Transversus Abdominis

PS

Sacrum

Pelvic floor

Iliacus

- **Origin:** Iliac crest, fossa and sacrum.
- **Insertion:** Tendon of psoas major.
- **Function:** Flexes the thigh, flexes the spine, anterior pelvic tilt if unchecked by lower abs.

Transverse abdominis (TVA)

Deep inner unit muscle whose primary role is in stabilization of the lumbar spine. Think of it as an inner corset (Figure 13.4).

- **Origin:** Inner surface of seventh to twelfth ribs, the thoraco-lumbar fascia, iliac crest.
- **Insertion:** Linea alba.
- **Function:** Constricts abdominal contents, increasing intra-abdominal pressure. Can cause traction through the thoraco-lumbar fascia, which causes an extension force on the lumbar spine.

Multifidus

Inner unit muscle that crosses over the vertebrae from the lower back upwards (see Figure 1.7 on p6).

- **Origin:** Sacrum, posterior superior iliac spine, transverse processes of all the vertebrae up to cervical vertabrae number 4.
- **Insertion:** Spinous processes of all vertebrae, crossing between two and four vertebrae at a time.
- **Function:** Segmental stabilization of the vertebrae. Bilateral: extension of the spine; unilateral: rotation to the opposite side.

Diaphragm

The diaphragm is the principal muscle of respiration and forms the floor of the thoracic cavity and the roof of the abdominal cavity (see Figure 1.7 on p6). When it contracts, the diaphragm draws downwards. This decreases thoracic pressure, drawing air in, and increases abdominal pressure, stabilizing the spine.

Pelvic floor

The pelvic floor muscles are shaped like a figure of eight and surround the anus and urethra. Loss of control of the pelvic floor muscles can compromise core stability.

MECHANISMS OF CORE STABILITY THROUGH SEGMENTAL STABILIZATION

We have identified that segmental stability involves maintaining optimal alignment of each vertebra in relation to others, reducing stress on the spine. The main mechanisms of segmental core stability are intra-abdominal pressure and thoraco-lumbar fascia gain.

Intra-abdominal pressure

The transverse abdominis (TVA) is a band of muscle that wraps around the front of the body

almost like a corset. The TVA, thoraco-lumbar fascia (TLF), diaphragm and pelvic-floor musculature (PFM) together form a cylinder around the centre of the body.

All of these muscles contract to create **hoop tension**. The diaphragm pulls downwards, the pelvic floor pulls up and the TVA pulls in, causing the waist to narrow. This hoop tension compresses all the organs and fluid within the abdomen, creating a cylinder of high pressure within which the spine is tightly packed. This pressure in itself creates stability around the lumbar spine (Figure 13.6). Imagine squeezing a tube of toothpaste in the middle with the lid on; the harder you squeeze the tube, the more solid it becomes.

Contraction of the TVA should occur automatically before we lift a weight or any time we move our arms or legs. If you are not sure what this should feel like, imagine pulling your stomach in to put a tight pair of jeans on; this is the TVA muscle working at 100 per cent **maximum**

13.5 Transverse abdominis (TVA) relaxed

13.6 Transverse abdominis (TVA) contracted

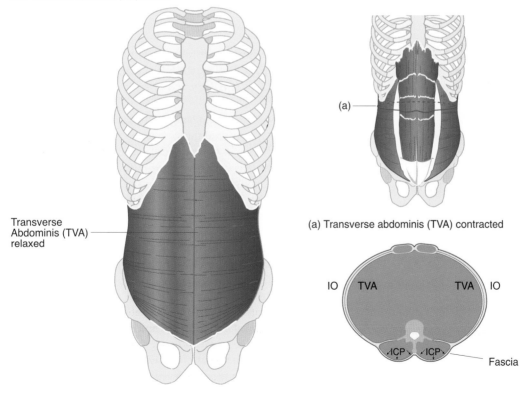

Transverse Abdominis (TVA) relaxed

(a)

(a) Transverse abdominis (TVA) contracted

IO   TVA   TVA   IO

IAP   IAP

Fascia

voluntary contraction (MVC). The TVA usually works at much lower levels than this, at around 30 per cent MVC and it should work at an unconscious level (i.e. it happens without thinking). In many people with back pain this does not happen and they have poor core stability. Retraining the abdominal wall to contract prior to moving is one aim of core stability training.

Thoraco-lumbar fascia (TLF) gain

The TLF is a broad band of connective tissue found on the back of the body. The TLF has attachments to the spine and when it is pulled taut, the orientation of the fibres of the TLF cause the lumbar vertebrae to be pulled into extension (Figure 13.7). Note how muscles attaching into the TLF, including internal oblique and lats, create a pull laterally. Due to the alignment of the fibres diagonally and the attachments of these fibres onto

13.7 Thoraco-lumbar fascia gain

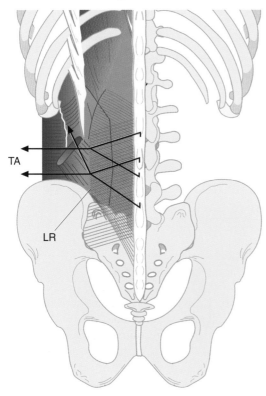

TA

LR

the spine, the TLF can create a slight force in compressive and extension.

This has the effect of stabilizing the lumbar spine, especially during flexion (i.e. forward bending). Muscles that attach into and cause tension through the TLF can therefore play a role in stabilizing the spine during forward bending. These muscles include the TVA, internal oblique and the latissimus dorsi.

IDENTIFYING TRANSVERSE ABDOMINIS ACTIVATION

We can observe a client's tendency to recruit their abdominal wall when they lift. As they lift a weight off the floor (deadlift), watch their stomach; place a hand on the stomach if this cannot be easily observed. A pull inwards would indicate appropriate activation of TVA. If you observe a pushing out of the stomach, this would indicate a failure in the abdominal wall or a failure to recruit TVA. In these individuals we have to retrain the body to recruit inner unit muscles, especially TVA, prior to lifting.

TRAINING TRANSVERSE ABDOMINIS ACTIVATION

With the client lying on the ground, tie a piece of string around the stomach so that it is tight when the stomach is relaxed. Then ask the client to loosen the tension on the string by pulling their stomach in. This is TVA activation and helps to support the spine. Verbal cues for TVA activation may include 'pull navel towards spine', 'pull stomach in' or 'hollow out the stomach'. Be wary of cues that encourage the client to squeeze the rectus muscle, such as 'pull abs tight' or 'strong abs', before they have activated the TVA. As the TVA muscle becomes stronger ask for only a mild TVA contraction. Imagine pulling the stomach in as hard as possible, then halving the effort and then halving that effort again to achieve a 25–30 per cent TVA contraction.

As the stomach is held in, ask the client to perform *thoracic breathing*: breathing only into

13.8a Supine TVA activation

13.8c TVA activation from four-point stance

13.8b Prone TVA activation

13.8d TVA activation from standing

the ribcage with no expansion of the stomach. This can be very challenging for some clients, especially if they are breathless from exercise. The whole process should be practised first in a supine position with legs bent (Figure 13.8a), then prone lying face down (the pull of gravity on the viscera in the stomach increases the challenge to TVA) (Figure 13.8b), then in a four-point stance on knees and hands (Figure 13.8c) and finally from a standing position (Figure 13.8d). Finally, if this can be achieved ask the client to maintain TVA contraction whilst lifting a weight. The aim of all these positions is to be able to draw the stomach

in, narrowing the waist, in order to stabilise the spine by increasing intra-abdominal pressure.

The aim is for the client to be able to maintain a mild TVA contraction whenever they are lifting a weight during their resistance programme. This may start off as a very conscious process with the trainer reminding them if they are 'doming' (pushing out the stomach), but hopefully with practice it becomes more automatic and a natural part of the muscular recruitment pattern. The final aim is for the client automatically to draw in and engage deep abdominal muscles prior to lifting a weight without conscious effort.

Remember that failure to activate TVA and draw the stomach gently in prior to movement represents faulty movement due to poor relative timing of muscle activation (see Chapter 7). This lack of muscle coordination would increase the client's chances of injury during lifting and cause a loss of performance due to loss of stability around the spine.

It is important to note that when a client is not lifting a weight or if they are doing cardiovascular exercise they should be using *abdominal breathing*, in which the stomach pushes forwards and back as the diaphragm moves up and down. Do not ask a client continually to hold their stomach in as this will promote a faulty breathing pattern under normal conditions.

ABDOMINAL ACTIVATION UNDER INCREASED LOADS

The abdominal brace

When greater loads are placed on the spine, increased muscular recruitment is required to stabilize it. TVA recruitment may need to increase in order to raise intra-abdominal pressure and alleviate compressive loads on the spine. Other muscles may also increase their activation to provide stability. McGill proposed the *abdominal brace*, which involves a mild contraction of all the abdominal muscles such as rectus abdominis, external oblique, internal oblique quadratus lomborum and others, to maintain neutral alignment of the spine against external forces.

Valsalva manoeuvre

In preparation for a heavy deadlift or squat, we often find ourselves holding our breath. This indicates that we have an isometric (holding) contraction of the diaphragm in which it is pulled down and then held. This contraction helps decompression of the lumbar vertebrae at the expense of increased blood pressure. This is known as the *Valsalva manoeuvre*. The Valsalva manoeuvre is a natural reaction to increased stress on the spine. It can be used during near-maximal lifts when the spine is under extreme stress, unless there are any coronary risk factors such as elevated blood pressure.

Core muscle activation and lifting

Prior to a near-maximal squat, for example, follow this recruitment pattern. A large breath is taken in that draws the diaphragm down, increasing intra-abdominal pressure. The TVA is contracted, drawing the stomach in further, increasing intra-abdominal pressure. Abdominal muscles are contracted lightly to brace the spine. The breath is held, causing an isometric contraction of the diaphragm on the eccentric phase (downwards for the squat). Air is slowly released through pursed lips as the lift is completed with a concentric phase (pushing the weight back up in the case of the squat). This process ensures optimal stabilization of the spine. Under lighter loads in which the alignment of the spine is not challenged we should simply ensure the client performs thoracic breathing with TVA held contracted.

TRAINING GROSS CORE STABILITY

Once a client can effectively recruit inner unit muscles we can train their ability to maintain gross stability of the spine. Earlier we defined gross stability as the use of outer unit muscles to maintain neutral spine. The first step to improving gross stability of the lumbar spine is to learn to use the *lower abdominal muscles*. These muscles play an extremely important role in maintaining gross stability by maintaining a correct degree of posterior pelvic tilt (see Chapter 9). Pelvic tilt is closely related to the degree of extension or flexion in the spine. If we are anteriorly tilted the spine usually goes into extension, placing stress on the lumbar vertebrae and increasing pressure on the intervertebral discs. Training the lower abdominals to control pelvic tilt and stabilize the lumbar spine is an important first step in providing gross core stability.

Supine leg raises

The supine leg raise is an excellent starting point for training lower abdominal muscles.

- From a supine lying posture with legs bent to 90 degrees, find neutral spine (see Chapter 9 for a description of neutral spine) and activate TVA by drawing navel in.
- Slowly raise one leg to a 90-degree angle so that the knee is stacked over hip, maintaining the angle at the knee.
- Float the knee back into the starting position.
- Perform on alternate legs.
- As the leg is lifted, tension in the hip flexors will pull the back into extension and tilt the hips anteriorly if the lower abs do not contract with equal force.

- Failure to complete the movement successfully can be identified by loss of neutral spine as it is pulled into extension due to anterior pelvic tilt. The client should feel the lower abdominal muscles contracting as they try to control pelvic tilt.

During this exercise the trainer should ensure that the client:

- continues to breathe
- does not develop tension in the shoulders
- does not bring the knee past the hip, allowing the back to flatten
- moves in a slow and controlled manner
- does not over-recruit the abdominal muscles, pressing the back flat into the ground.

The exercise can be progressed by:

- increasing the angle at the knee to lengthen the lever of the leg and increasing the weight on the lower abdominal muscles
- start and finish with both legs in the air at a 90-degree angle
- increase the angle at the knee
- as above but lowering both legs simultaneously.

Plank positions

Whenever the client is prone, gravity will be acting to pull the spine out of neutral and into extension (i.e. the back will arch). Abdominal muscles have to work isometrically to maintain gross core stability and ideal spinal alignment. If at any point the back is pulled into an arch the abdominal muscles are being overloaded and strain is placed on the ligaments and intervertebral discs.

The challenge for the abdominal muscles is to maintain the alignment of the spine against the pull of gravity. This makes plank positions an excellent gross core stability exercise. Start with a

four-point stance on hands and knees, with hands under the shoulders and knees under the hips. This position can be made harder by lifting one hand or one leg off the ground. Progress from here into a traditional plank position (Figure 13.9), starting with knees down and then progressing by taking knees off the floor.

We can add challenge by increasing the distance between the base of support (moving hands further from the feet), reducing the base of support (lift one leg) or decreasing stability (using a wobble board or Swiss ball). The client has to maintain neutral posture of the spine and head. A

13.9 Plank position

light pole can be used to help the client's proprioreceptive sense of correct alignment. Plank exercises should be discontinued when the client is unable to maintain neutral spine and pelvis, causing the lumbar spine to drop down, sending the spine into hyperextension. If the client experiences any pain in the lumber spine, discontinue the exercise. This would indicate increased vertebral disc compression as the spine goes into extension. An increased rounding of the upper back, a hyperkyphosis, may indicate over-recruitment of the upper abdominal.

Try this progression.

- Four-point stance (ensure TVA is activated).
- Lift one hand just 2 cm off the ground.
- Lift one knee 2 cm off the ground.
- Lift and extend one hand and arm to 45 degrees (alternate sides holding for 5 seconds).

- Lift and extend one leg straight behind.
- Arm and knee together.
- Plank from knees.
- Plank from toes.
- Add challenge by lifting one leg.
- Plank from Swiss ball.
- Plank on Swiss ball but add movement by rolling the ball forwards and back or even left to right.

TRAINING CORE STRENGTH

Core strength is the ability of the abdominal muscles to produce dynamic force, moving the spine into flexion, extension, rotation or side flexion. Exercises such as the Swiss ball crunch, dorsal raise, side bend or woodchop are all examples of exercises that would train core strength.

Woodchop pattern

The woodchop is a resisted rotation of the trunk. It can be progressed based on the number of planes of movement used, the degree of integration of movement throughout the full body as well as usual exercise variables such as weight and speed of movement. A horizontal resistance is required from either a pulley system or exercise bands.

Horizontal woodchop without hip rotation

This version of the woodchop generates least stress on the discs of the back, as it does not involve any flexion or extension through the spine. Spinal rotation can be isolated by asking the client to sit or by instructing neutral hips from a standing posture (hips remaining still during movement).

- In a standing posture hold a weight in two hands with the hand furthest away from the weight gripping first (i.e. if you are pulling against a cable to your right side, your left hand grips the cable first and your right hand overlaps this. This is to encourage a pulling rather than a pushing movement).
- Extend the arms so that the weight is held at shoulder height.
- Draw the navel to the spine to activate segmental stabilizers.
- Keeping the hips static, rotate through the trunk.

Horizontal woodchop with hip rotation and weight shift

In the second version the hips are integrated into the movement. Note the pivoting in the foot that reduces the rotational stress on the knee. Weight will start predominantly on the inside foot and then be shifted across to the outside foot as we move the cable outside the body.

Full reverse woodchop pattern with hip movement from standing

As before, but the weight is pulled from a low position and trunk extension is included in the movement. This will place additional strain on trunk extensor (erector spinae).

Full woodchop pattern seated on a Swiss ball

As above, but the weight is pulled from a raised position and trunk flexion is included in the movement. This will place additional work into trunk flexors (rectus abdominus).

Safety factors and considerations: Be aware of a client's medical history and ensure that clients with a history of disc derangement have clearance from their doctor before performing these movements under load.

CASE STUDY: CORE STRENGTH TRAINING

A client had a first session. He complained of back pain and on asking him to tilt his hips forwards and back from a standing position I found he was unable to do this smoothly. Upon lifting a medicine ball from the ground I also saw his stomach push forwards as he lifted. This client obviously had very little control of the muscles around his middle. He was unable to activate his TVA, contributing to pain in his lower back. A remedial core programme would be one step in reconditioning this client.

First, I explained to the client about what TVA is and how it helps support the back, using the inner corset analogy. I explained that using this muscle during lifting may alleviate some of the stress through his spine.

Then I took the client through some basic exercises. First, lying supine with legs bent, I instructed the client to practise abdominal breathing, taking air into the stomach without letting the shoulders rise. The shoulders rising during inhalation would be a faulty breathing pattern, and is common in people with tight neck and shoulders. I then tied a piece of string around his waist and asked him to practise thoracic breathing, pulling the stomach in to loosen the string and then holding this as he

breathed. This should be accomplished supine, prone, on all fours and then from standing.

I then asked him to draw his navel to his spine, being careful not to hold his breath, prior to lifting any weight.

We then went back to a supine lying position and learned to control the lower abdominal muscles by practising pelvic tilts. Again the pelvic tilts could be progressed from supine to all fours, to seated on a Swiss ball and then standing. This movement was also used to mobilize his lower back, alleviating some of his back-pain symptoms.

To improve his gross core stability we practised a supine leg raise. Initially, the client was not able even to lift one leg up without movement coming into the hips and spine, but by practising and moving through the supine leg-raise progressions he soon improved. At this stage we moved to a four-point plank position (hands under shoulder and knees under hips). I also introduced some Swiss ball familiarization and balance exercises before moving the client onto more advanced core-stability and core-strength exercises.

These basic exercises helped to alleviate some of the stress on the client's spine and prepared him for resistance training. Only when a client can engage TVA will I give them weights to lift. Until this point only bodyweight exercises should be used, coupled with work to improve their posture and movement.

CHAPTER SUMMARY

Having read this chapter you should have a good understanding of some of the basic mechanisms behind core stability. You should have a range of progressive exercises with which you can train your clients' core stability and strength. You should also understand that if you see that a client is not activating core muscles (i.e. their stomach does not pull in) when they lift a weight, they may be placing their spine under stress with an elevated risk of damage and injury. For these clients, learning how to control their abdominal wall when they lift weight will be of key importance to improving performance and reducing the risk of injury.

REFERENCES AND RECOMMENDED READING

1. Bogduk, N. and Twomey, L. (1991) *Clinical Anatomy of the Lumbar Spine*, 2nd edn. Edinburgh: Churchill Livingstone, pp. 102–103.
2. Chek Paul (accessed 2002) *Scientific Back Training*. Correspondence Course. www.chekinstitute.com.
3. Comerford, M. and Mottram, S. (2001) Functional stability re-training: principles and strategies for managing mechanical dysfunction. *Manual Therapy* 6:3–14.
4. Cresswell, A., Grundstrom, H. and Thorstensson, A. (1992) Observations on intra-abdominal pressure and patterns of abdominal intra-muscular activity in man. *Acta Physiologica Scandinavica* 144:409–418.
5. Gracovetsky, S. (1997) Linking the spinal engine with the legs: a theory of human gait. In: Vleeming A, Mooney, V., Dorman, T., Snijders, C. and Stoekart, R. (eds) *Movement Stability and Low Back Pain*. Edinburgh: Churchill Livingstone, p. 243.
6. Hedrick, A. (2000) Training the trunk for improved athletic performance. *Strength and Conditioning Journal* 22:50–61.
7. Hodges, P. (1999) Is there a role for the transversus abdominis in lumbo-pelvic stability? Review Article. *Manual Therapy* 4:74–86.
8. Hodges, P.W., Heijnen, I. and Gandevia, S.C. (2001) Postural activity of the diaphragm is reduced in humans when respiratory demand increases. *Journal of Physiology* 537:999–1008.
9. Hodges, P. and Richardson, C. (1996) Inefficient muscular stabilization of the lumbar spine associated with low-back pain: a motor control evaluation of transversus abdominis. *Spine* 21:2640–2650.
10. Lawrence, M. (2003) *The Complete Guide to Core Stability*. London: A and C Black.
11. McGill, S. (2002) *Low-back Disorders – Evidence-based Prevention and Rehabilitation*. Champaign, IL: Human Kinetics.
12. Richardson, C., Jull, G., Hodges, P. and Hides, J. (1999) *Therapeutic Exercise for Spinal Segmental Stabilization in Low-back Pain – Scientific Basis and Clinical Approach*. Edinburgh: Churchill Livingstone.
13. Siff, M. (2003) *Transversus Abdominis Revisited*. www.ptonthenet.com.
14. Tyson, A. (1999) Lumbar stabilization. *Strength and Conditioning Journal* 21:17.
15. Wallden, M.J. (2004) *The Core*, Parts 1 and 2. http://www.PTonthenet.com.
16. Williams, P. (1995) Skeletal muscle (muscle – chapter 7). In: *Gray's Anatomy*, 38th edn. Edinburgh: Churchill Livingstone, pp. 739–764.

14

SCIENCE OF SWISS BALL AND SWISS BALL EXERCISES

THIS CHAPTER CONTAINS

- The science behind the Swiss ball
- Integrating the Swiss ball into your client's workout
- Swiss ball exercises
- Swiss ball stretches
- References and recommended reading

For many years prior to its introduction to the health and fitness industry, the Swiss ball had been used by physicians for the rehabilitation of patients with orthopaedic and neural problems (Franklin, 2000). Only recently has its application been extended into use as a tool for strength and conditioning training. Unfortunately, the Swiss ball is in danger of becoming a fad like any other. It is often overused, badly taught and ultimately misunderstood. This chapter aims to clarify the science behind the Swiss ball in order to appreciate its many benefits and to provide a range of exercises that can immediately be taken away and used with your clients.

THE SCIENCE BEHIND THE SWISS BALL

The challenges posed by the Swiss ball are very different to those presented by resistance machines. In the latter the body is almost totally supported, whereas when we sit or balance on the Swiss ball we immediately reduce our **base of support**, the area between our contact points with

the ground. This makes it much harder to keep our centre of gravity within this base of support and thus to keep our balance (see Chapter 8). The fact that the ball is unstable and moving means that we have to control movement in all three planes of motion, forwards and back, from side to side as well as twisting movements. These factors make for a far more challenging workout with an array of benefits compared with the traditional fixed-resistance machines.

If we take a seated posture on the Swiss ball as an example, we see the following effects and benefits:

- ***Increased abdominal muscle activation and coordination:*** Because of the lack of stability on the Swiss ball all the muscles of the abdominal wall, rectus abdominis, obliques, erector spinae, transverse abdominis etc. all have to coordinate and work together to maintain good posture and to stabilize the spine. Ideally, various levels of pelvic tilt should be used to manipulate the centre of gravity so that it stays over the base of support in order to maintain balance.

- *Increased reflex control of balance and posture:* Movements to maintain posture generally occur on a reflex level without conscious thought (see Chapter 7). These reflexes are trained using the Swiss ball because of the unstable environment we create.
- *Increased proprioreceptive information and feedback:* To maintain balance the body has to be constantly interpreting proprioceptive information regarding its position. The Swiss ball creates what is known as a *sensory-rich environment,* which requires far greater neuromuscular coordination than is normally needed (see Chapter 7).
- *Increased postural muscle activation and coordination:* Increased muscle activation is not isolated to those muscles of the core. Because of the instability inherent in using the Swiss ball, nearly all the muscles involved with maintaining posture have to work harder to control body position (Vera-Gracia *et al.,* 2000).
- *Increased energy expenditure:* The sum total of this increased postural and abdominal muscle activation causes increased energy expenditure along with a fantastic abdominal or core workout.

Compare this to exercise on resistance machines in which movement can only be made in one plane of motion, where there is very little balance challenge and we can only move in one direction, and we see that exercises performed on a Swiss ball are far more challenging and therefore produce far greater gains in performance.

INTEGRATING THE SWISS BALL INTO YOUR CLIENT'S WORKOUT

The Swiss ball is often inappropriately used by trainers to provide their clients with more varied workouts. Whilst we should make a client's workout enjoyable, we must consider carefully at what point Swiss ball training is appropriate for our client. The following factors should be looked at:

- *The ability of your client:* A personal trainer must always ensure that exercises are properly progressed. If an exercise on a ball is overly challenging to the point where form is poor, the exercise should be regressed until the level of skill of the exercise matches that of the client. This may mean providing the client with a greater base of support (widen their stance) or may mean putting them onto a stable surface such as a normal weights bench.
- *The goals of the client:* The Swiss ball increases neural demand (see Chapter 2) by decreasing stability and challenging balance. If the goal of the client is building muscle then a stable environment should be provided so that more weight can be lifted and greater levels of intensity and muscular fatigue can be achieved. For a client with these goals the Swiss ball may even be detrimental to them achieving their goals.
- *The sequencing of exercises:* Remember that the core Swiss ball exercises will fatigue stabilizing muscles. If these muscles are fatigued and then a compound exercise is prescribed, you increase the risk of injury to the client. Time should be given to allow stabilizing muscles to recover and exercises focusing purely on the core should be left till the end of the workout.

Whilst these factors should be considered, the Swiss ball can be integrated into your workout in a variety of different ways. The Swiss ball is an excellent tool for performing body-weight core exercises at the end of the workout (see below). In the conditioning phases of training, free-weight resistance exercises can be progressed from stable surfaces onto the Swiss ball. The Swiss ball can be used during stretching and can be useful for improving balance and for postural education. Postural and balance exercises can be used during periods of active rest as long as postural/stabilizing muscles are not overly fatigued prior to performing compound exercise requiring the core.

GUIDELINES FOR USING SWISS BALLS

- **Ball size:** When the client sits on the ball the femur (thigh) should be either parallel to the ground or up to 10 degrees above parallel. Choose a slightly higher ball for those with lower back pain to ensure that they can maintain neutral spine. A ball that is too small will pull the client into posterior pelvic tilt, thereby increasing pressure through the lumbar spine.
- **Ball condition:** Check there are no scratches or marks on the ball. These structural faults could cause the ball to burst under excessive weight. Only use marked balls for body-weight exercises, if at all.
- **Inflation:** Always ensure that your Swiss ball is well inflated before using it. If you can push to a depth of greater than 1 cm, the ball may need inflating.
- **The work area:** Always check the area for tacks, pins or other sharp objects that could affect the condition of the ball.
- **Sequencing:** Place more complicated exercises before less complex ones, so do weights exercises on the Swiss ball before stable exercises. Core exercises should generally be left till the end of a programme. Do not fatigue a client's stabilizing muscles using balance exercises then ask them to perform an exercise that requires stabilization.

- **Progression:** Always ensure exercises are mastered in a stable environment before progressing onto the ball and regress the exercise if form is unsatisfactory.
- **Explanation:** Always explain the benefits of using the ball to a client before integrating it into their workout.
- **Gain consent:** Always ensure that the client feels happy using the ball before making them perform advanced Swiss ball exercises.
- **Familiarize the client with the ball:** Always start with ball-familiarization exercises (see below) before progressing onto more complicated uses of the Swiss ball.
- **Periodization:** Always be aware that unstable exercises may not be appropriate for those clients looking to build muscle or develop maximal strength. The lack of stability will mean that they will not be able to lift as much weight, which may reduce intensity and muscular fatigue.
- **Core stabilization:** Ensure that the client can activate core muscles such as transverse abdominis (see Chapter 13) prior to using the ball. If they are not able to do so the unpredictable movements of the ball may increase the risk of causing micro-damage to the lumbar spine in particular.

SWISS BALL EXERCISES

Note that all the exercises in this section will challenge the balance of the client and their ability to stabilize the spine. Whilst certain muscles have been identified as being targeted during each exercise, core muscles such as transverse abdominis have to be activated and the stabilizing muscles and other synergistic muscles should also be working, even though they have not been listed here. When coaching each exercise ensure that the navel is drawn towards the spine and ensure that the client is breathing appropriately.

Seated posture

Teaching clients about correct seated posture using the Swiss ball will help to minimize the onset of many postural problems brought about by long periods of time spent sitting down, whether at a desk, in a car or watching TV (see Chapter 9).

- Start by sitting with good alignment and posture (see Chapter 9 for detailed description). Main cues include:
  - align head with ear in line with shoulder
  - maintain the shoulder over the hip
  - shoulder blades drawn partially back and down (partial scapular retraction, see Chapter 9)
  - neutral spine
  - neutral pelvis (half-way between extreme pelvic tilts)
  - navel drawn to spine to activate core
  - feet shoulder-width apart
  - feet pointing between 0 (straight ahead) and 30 degrees ahead.
- From this position practise thoracic breathing with transverse abdominis engaged.
- **Progression:** From this seated posture you can perform any exercise you would perform on a weights bench (shoulder press, lateral raise etc.).

Ball familiarization: pelvic tilts

This exercise is excellent for increasing proprioception and control of the muscles of the lumbo-pelvic hip complex, as well as getting used to the movement and sensation of sitting on a Swiss ball.

- Start from a seated posture (see above).
- Keeping good posture in the rest of the body, pull the pubic bone up to go into posterior pelvic tilt, utilizing lower abdominal muscles.

- Reverse the movement, tipping the pelvis forward to go into anterior pelvic tilt.
- Continue the rolling motion of the pelvis to mobilize the lumbar spine.
- **Safety factors and considerations:** Stay within pain-free ranges of motion if there is any lower-back pain.
- **Progression:** Try 'hiking' hips from side to side again whist keeping the body still. Progress to a figure-of-eight movement.

Ball familiarization: balance training

We can increase balance challenge by reducing the base of support and/or reducing sensory information.

- Reduce base of support:
  – bring the feet together
  – take one foot off the ground
  – balance both feet on top of one or two medicine balls
  – balance one foot on a medicine ball
  – take both feet off the ground.
- Use of the hands:
  – place both hands on the ball
  – put hands straight out to the sides
  – put hands across the chest.

- Use proprioreceptive feedback (see Chapter 8):
  – rotate the head from side to side
  – track a moving object or your own hands
  – close one eye
  – close both eyes
  – tilt the head to the side.
- Weighted challenge:
  – add a weight to be held
  – hold the weight in one hand
  – progressively take the weight away from, then around the body.

Any combination of these progressions can be used to challenge the client adequately.

Bridge position

This position is the starting point for a variety of Swiss ball exercises. It is also the base from which to perform any resistance exercise that may be normally performed on a weights bench (dumbbell or barbell press/fly, pullover, triceps extension etc.).

- **Primary joint action:** Hip extension
- **Target muscles:** Gluteus maximus
- **Secondary muscles:** Hamstrings, extensors of the spine (erector spinae)
- Starting from a seated position, walk the feet out and slowly lie back.
- Continue until the upper back is supported with the head resting against the ball comfortably and in a neutral position (in line with the spine).
- Push hips into the air, finding neutral spine. The trainer should cue the use of the glutes to maintain height in the hips.

- Feet should be stacked under the knees and the shoulders, hips and knees should all remain relatively in line.
- Throughout the exercise the trainer should cue the client to maintain height in the hips through activation of the gluteal muscles.
- **Safety factors and considerations:** Many individuals subconsciously use the hamstrings or lower back extensors in preference to the gluteal muscles to maintain height in the hips. This is evident in some individuals as the knees slightly move towards each other. A trainer may ask a client manually to palpate the gluteal muscles to help increase their recruitment. The trainer can also provide a block on the outside of the knees and ask the client to push against that block to help activate the gluteal muscles.
- **Progression:**
  – bring feet slightly closer together to reduce the base of support
  – lift one leg
  – ask the client to hold a weight and then move this weight around to disturb their centre of balance
  – weights exercises can be performed from bridge position as if the client were lying on a bench.

Prone lateral slide

This exercise is an excellent way of challenging the client's proprioception whilst providing the gluteal muscles and abdominal muscles with additional challenge.

- **Primary joint action:** Hip extension
- **Target muscles:** Gluteus maximus, obliques
- **Secondary muscles:** Back extensors, hamstrings
- Starting from bridge position, take the arms out to the sides, palms up, in order to open out through the shoulders and chest (external rotation at the shoulder joint).

- Slowly walk the feet to one side, then slide the body in the same direction, maintaining neutral spine as you roll over the ball.
- Take the weight more onto one shoulder in preference to the upper back.
- Maintain neutral alignment, keeping hips, shoulders and knees level in the same plane.
- **Progression:** progress by increasing the distance by which you slide across onto the shoulder.

Hip extension from bridge

This is a useful exercise to prepare the client for weighted work in the bridge position. It will familiarize them with the ball and strengthen muscles required to hold a stable bridge position.

- **Primary joint action:** Hip extension
- **Target muscles:** Gluteus maximus
- **Secondary muscles:** Back extensors, hamstrings
- Starting in bridge position, draw navel towards spine.
- Keeping the ball as still as possible, allow hips to drop towards floor.
- Focus on activating the gluteal muscles as you push hips into the air, returning to bridge position.

- **Safety factors and considerations:** If the client feels unsure of their balance, allow them to let their hands drop to the sides so that they can catch themselves if required. Ask the client to ensure that both gluteal muscles are activated by palpating them as above.
- **Progression:**
  - reduce base of support by bringing feet together
  - raise one bent leg in the air
  - extend the leg.

Russian twist

This exercise is beneficial for both mobilizing the spine and strengthening abdominal muscles.

- **Primary joint action:** Trunk rotation
- **Target musculature:** Obliques
- **Secondary muscles:** General core muscles (obliques, rectus abdominis)
- Starting in bridge position, elevate the arms to a 90-degree angle to the body.
- **Execution:** Keeping the hips level and still, rotate the torso to one side taking weight onto the shoulder as the ball rolls away from you.
- Alternate to each side.
- **Safety factors and considerations:** Do not allow twist and torque in the knees.
- **Progression:** The degree of rotation with increasing spinal mobility should represent the progression. Add weight in the form of a medicine ball or even cable to add load. Momentum and speed can be added and a ball can even be caught and thrown from this position.

Plank progressions

Basic exercises to challenge gross stabilization of the lumbar spine (see Chapter 13).

- **Primary joint action:** Static holding position
- **Target musculature:** Gross stabilizers (rectus abdominis, obliques)
- **Secondary muscles:** Segmental stabilizer, posterior and medial deltoid, quadriceps, and hip flexors, all working isometrically to hold the position.
- **Preparation:** (if choosing basic plank position on the ball) Starting from a resting position with knees on the ground and forearms on the

ball, lengthen through the body until you are in neutral position with arms resting on the ball.

- **Execution:** Hold position until you fail to maintain:
  - neutral spine
  - navel to spine
  - abdominal work in preference to the back (i.e. client feels work in base of spine).
- **Safety factors and considerations:** The aim of all these positions is to use the gross stabilizers (rectus abdominis, external obliques) to maintain neutral spine. If the client is unable to do this or if the client feels any strain through

Plank progressions (continued)

the back then you should halt the exercise or reduce the level.

- **Progression:** The variations on these positions are numerous. You should start by ensuring that the client can activate core muscles from lying to a position on all fours. The client can then progress to planks on the floor before using the Swiss ball. The position of the Swiss ball will greatly affect the intensity of the exercise. If the ball is further away the load on the abdominals will be far greater. The plank can also be performed from the hands rather than forearms and we can add challenge by raising one foot off the floor. This progression adds rotational torque through the spine that must be controlled by the client. When performing these exercises on a stability ball, movement can be added to challenge further the client's ability to maintain neutral spine (see rollouts and jack-knife).

Rollouts

The rollout and jack-knife are examples of plank progressions in which movement is used further to challenge maintenance of a neutral spine.

- **Preparation:**
  - position the knees on the ground and with forearms parallel on the stability ball
  - the body should create a box shape with right angles between legs and body and body and arms
  - ensure spine and head are in neutral.
- **Execution:** Extend through the hip and flex through the shoulder at equal speeds until adequate challenge is felt on the abdominal musculature but the client can still maintain neutral spine and no strain is felt on the back.
- **Safety factors and considerations:** If the spine goes into hyperextension a significant strain may be placed on the intervertebral discs in the lumbar spine, so it is important to halt the exercise if the client cannot maintain neutral spine. Ensure that head stays neutral so as not to encourage a forward head posture. Ensure controlled breathing and core activation throughout.
- **Progression:** The position can be performed from feet rather than the knees if the client is able to roll the ball out adequately whilst maintaining neutral spine. The exercise can even be performed with hands on the ball, but this is an extremely advanced exercise.

Prone jack-knife

- **Preparation:** Start in plank position with feet on the ball and hands on the floor.
- **Execution:** Whilst maintaining neutral spine, draw feet underneath you. Return to original plank position.
- **Safety factors and considerations:** As in rollout. Before attempting the jack-knife, the

client must be able to successfully maintain a plank position with hands on the floor and feet on the ball. If they are unable to do this they will obviously not be able to add movement and still maintain correct posture.
- **Progression:** To add additional challenge, take one leg off the ball.

Supine hip extension

- **Primary joint action:** Hip extension
- **Target muscles:** Gluteus maximus
- **Secondary muscles:** Hamstrings, spinal extensors (erector spinae)
- **Preparation:** Lying on back, place heels onto the middle of a stability ball.
- **Execution:** Maintaining neutral, raise hips into the air until the body is straight.
- **Safety factors and considerations:** Many individuals may subconsciously use the hamstrings or lower back extensors in preference to the glutes to maintain height in the hips.

- **Progression:**
  - bring the feet slightly closer together or move the feet slightly further down the ball to reduce the control you have over the ball
  - reduce the base of support by changing the position of the arms, starting with arms at right angles to the body, then arms by side, then arms crossed over body
  - the position can be progressed further by using only one leg.

Swiss ball crunch

- **Primary joint action:** Trunk flexion
- **Target muscles:** Rectus abdominis
- **Secondary muscles:** Obliques
- **Preparation:**
  - walk feet out from seated position and back until the ball is supporting the spine (note: the more the ball is supporting the hips rather than the back, the harder the exercise will become)
  - extend the trunk over the ball and allow the head to fall back
  - place fingertips on temples
  - push the tongue up into the roof of the mouth to help stabilize the neck.
- Execution:
  - rotate the head forwards into a neutral position (maintaining a gap between chin and chest)
  - flex through the trunk, drawing the ribs towards the pelvis.
- **Safety factors and considerations:** If the movement is too large the hip flexors will be recruited. This may place strain on the spine by increasing the pressure on the intervertebral discs. Fatigue in the lower back or neck is common and if strain is felt in either of these areas you should allow the client to rest and then continue with a less intense version of the exercise.
- **Progression:**
  - the more the ball is supporting the hips rather than the back, the harder the exercise will become
  - you can alter the intensity by changing the hand position. Hands across shoulders would be least intense, then fingertips on temples, then hands above head. If further challenge is required, weight may be given to the client to hold. A medicine ball may even be thrown to the client and thrown back.
  - this exercise may be adapted to place additional strain on the obliques by adding a twist into the end range of movement or by starting the exercise from a position off-centre.

SWISS BALL STRETCHES

The Swiss ball is also a useful tool for stretching muscles as well as working them. Here are some examples of how a Swiss ball can be incorporated in a flexibility programme.

Chest stretch

Note: the Swiss ball is an excellent tool for this stretch as it allows you to move the arm up and down to target different areas of the pec-major muscle.

Abdominal stretch

Whilst being an excellent stretch for the abdominals and the spine, be aware that because of the pliable nature of the Swiss ball the stretch may not be as effective as stretching over a hard surface, as stiff areas of the spine may be neglected for more flexible areas of the spine.

Lat stretch

By supination (turning the palm upwards) we can increase the intensity of the stretch.

CHAPTER SUMMARY

Used appropriately, the Swiss ball is an excellent tool that can enhance your sessions and provide a visual tool that may attract clients and draw attention to your sessions. This chapter should hopefully highlight some guidelines for using the Swiss ball, when to use it in your sessions as well as providing a basic selection of exercises to use with your clients.

REFERENCES AND RECOMMENDED READING

1. Carriere, B. (1998) The Swiss ball: Theory, Basic Exercises and Clinical Application. Berlin: Springer.
2. Franklin, B.A. (2000) ACSM Guidelines for Exercise Testing and Prescription. Lippincott, Williams and Wilkins.
3. Posner-Mayer J (1995) Swiss Ball Applications for Orthopaedic and Sports Medicine. Longmont, CO: Ball Dynamics Inc.
4. Vera-Garcia, F.J., Grenier SG, McGill SM (2000) Abdominal muscle response during curl-ups on both stable and labile surfaces. *Physical Therapy* 80: 564.

15

NUTRITION

Sound nutrition is the cornerstone of athletic performance and is a key element of programme design. Manipulation of diet can enhance athletic performance, support a programme of fat loss or muscle gain, improve recovery and prevent injury or illness by supporting the immune system.

It is important to remember that as personal trainers we do not automatically qualify as nutritionists. Unless you have additional qualifications in nutrition you should limit your prescription and advice to the confines of widely recognized and accepted nutritional practice. We should not be prescribing drugs or supplements or advising extreme dietary interventions outside the commonly recognized guidelines. Nor should we be prescribing dietary plans to special populations, for example pregnant women, people with diabetes, those with nutritional deficiencies or severe eating disorders, for example. If individuals request specific advice about such conditions

always refer them to a specifically qualified nutritional practitioner or their GP.

Nevertheless, we can advise people on the basics of sound nutrition. Whilst the principles of basic healthy eating are generally well known, clients often have difficulty in applying healthy-eating principles to their own lives. Used in close conjuncture with the principles of behaviour change discussed in Chapter 16, we may be able to make valuable changes to a client's eating habits. Whilst this chapter is too brief to cover the topic of nutrition comprehensively, it aims to provide some basic dietary guidelines that a personal trainer can pass on to their clients for improved results and performance.

BALANCED NUTRITION

A balanced diet is one in which a wide variety of foods are eaten in moderation to ensure that all the nutritional requirements of the body are met. Many people fail to eat balanced diets. The modern diet tends to be overly high in saturated fats and carbohydrates such as bread and salt. Portion sizes have also been distorted, with over-exposure to media images and fast-food portion sizes. The result is that people often have very little concept of what a balanced meal looks like. We also have an imbalance of when we eat, with many people eating a vast percentage of their calories late in the evening due to work commitments. Whatever the goals of the client, we should promote good health and longevity by encouraging a balanced diet and a healthy eating plan.

The *food plate* is a useful tool in helping clients to understand what moderation and balanced eating are. The food plate simply gives a visual representation of our diet, showing how much of our food should be made up of breads and cereals, meat and fish, vegetables and fruit, dairy and sugars (Figure 15.1).

Following this balanced dietary pattern whilst consuming enough calories to maintain weight should ensure that our dietary intake of the major *macronutrients* (nutrients required in large quantities) is close to those levels recommended by major food organizations. If we also consume a *varied* diet, it should ensure that we consume all the *micronutrients*, such as vitamins and minerals, that our body needs.

---

macronutrient: nutrients required by the body in large quantities (several grams per day), such as carbohydrate, proteins, fats and water.

---

micronutrients: nutrients required by the body in small quantities (less than a gram per day), such as vitamins and minerals.

The aim of this chapter is to look more closely at these macronutrients and see why they are important, how much of each we should consume and how our dietary habits can be adapted to help achieve our goals, whether weight loss, weight gain or improved athletic performance.

Macronutrients are the main constituents of foods. They include *water*, *protein*, *carbohydrate* and *fat*. If any of these macronutrients are in short supply it can quickly cause deterioration in performance. Ensuring adequate intake of dietary macronutrients can enhance performance and in this way food can be a powerful ergogenic aid for those with poor dietary habits.

PROTEIN: THE MUSCLE BUILDER

Protein is essential for structural growth and repair and has an important role in immune system function. A deficiency will therefore hinder muscular development and will leave your client susceptible to illness. Proteins are made up of 20 *amino acids*, eight of which are known as *essential amino acids* because they cannot be synthesized by the body. The essential amino acids have to be ingested on a regular basis. *Complete proteins* contain all eight essential amino acids and include meat, poultry, eggs, dairy, fish and soy foods. These foods are said to have *high biological value*. Other foods containing protein, such as rice, beans,

15.1 Diagram of a food plate

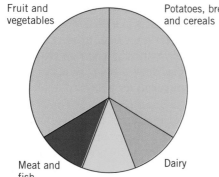

Fruit and vegetables

Potatoes, breads and cereals

Meat and fish

Sugars

Dairy

lentils, nuts and vegetables, are called *incomplete proteins* and are said to have *low biological value*. Because all eight amino acids are not contained in all forms of protein it is important to vary the types of protein in our diet and to consume adequate quantities of complete proteins.

Protein and muscle building

Training increases the amount of protein that we need for growth and repair. Sufficient protein is required to maximize muscle gain as a result of training. Due to its role in muscle growth, body builders are often obsessed with guaranteeing they take on board enough protein. But is this additional protein intake required and is it beneficial?

The recommended intake of protein for the sedentary adult is 0.8 g per kg of body weight per day and there is plenty of research to say this is sufficient to meet even a body builder's requirement for protein. However, there is research backing the argument that we need more protein in order to gain muscle. Recent studies have recommended a range from 1.2 to 1.7 g of protein per kg of body weight (Lemon, 1991; Tarnopolsky, 1992) for those individuals exercising. There is also evidence to suggest that an increased protein intake can actually cause an increase in protein synthesis and therefore development of lean muscle mass (Lemon, 1991). In reality, as people exercise, their calorie intake increases to match their energy requirements and therefore more protein is consumed. This means that clients will tend to get enough protein in their diets without need for supplementation in the form of protein drinks and powders (Clarkson, 1998; Gibala *et al.*, 2000).

Protein and weight loss

As well as being important for building muscle mass, protein can play a useful role for those looking to lose weight. Protein is highly satiating (i.e. it fills you up). This means that if you put a plate of food high in carbohydrate in front of someone for one meal and a plate of food high in protein in front of them for another meal and ask them to eat until they are full, they would eat more calories when eating the carbohydrate meal because the protein meal fills them quickly. This explains the success of many high-protein diets. I recommend using meals and snacks high in protein to control hunger for those people looking to reduce calorie intake in order to lose weight.

FATS

Fat is the primary storage medium for the body's excess calories. Whenever we over-consume calories, wherever they come from, they will be converted into fat and stored in adipose tissue (fat cells). Fat is perfect for this role. It is calorie-dense, containing 9 calories per gram compared with carbohydrate and protein, which only have 4 calories per gram.

Fatty foods are less satiating, meaning that you are more likely to overeat fatty foods because they do not remove feelings of hunger as quickly as protein or carbohydrate. This is why we can easily consume large quantities of crisps or nuts without ever feeling full. Also if we eat too much fat, the calories are more likely to be stored than if we were to eat too much carbohydrate or protein. Because fats are so calorie-dense they can have a negative impact when consumed in our diet, contributing to weight gain. Overconsumption of some fats also stimulates increased levels of cholesterol in the blood (Williams, 1995). For these reasons fats have a bad reputation and are classically associated with weight gain and cardiovascular heart disease.

Many diets try to reduce drastically the amount of fat consumed in order to aid in weight loss. What these diets fail to consider is that certain fats have many important functions. Fat is a major source of fuel for exercise and activity, especially at lower intensities. It insulates our body from cold, helps vitamin storage and transport and is required for the formation of hormones and bile acids (Williams, 1995). The right forms of fat in our diet may actually reduce depression and reduce the risk of certain types of cancer and cardiovascular heart disease. Fats are therefore a vital food group that should be included in our diet. The key is to select foods containing the right types of fat that confer these health benefits.

Fat consists of chains of carbon and hydrogen atoms and can be characterized by the way that these atoms are organized within fat molecules. Fats are either *saturated*, so-called because they are fully saturated with hydrated ions, or *unsaturated*, potentially able to take on board more hydrogen. Unsaturated fats can further be split into *monounsaturated* and *polyunsaturated*. *Saturated fats* tend to be solid at room temperature. It is these fats that have the most negative effect on the body, raising cholesterol levels and increasing the incidence of heart disease. *Hydrogenated fats* are fats that have been heated to high temperatures in a process known as *hydrogenation.* They are just as damaging as saturated fats. Margarine is an example of a hydrogenated fat. *Monounsaturated fats* can actually reduce the risk of cardiovascular disease. These are fats that are liquid at room temperature. Examples include seed oils such as sunflower and linseed oils.

A very low-fat diet is potentially deficient in *essential fatty acids (EFAs)*. The EFAs are like the vitamins of the fat world; they are involved in producing a myriad of important substances in the body, including the structure of every cell membrane within the body. *Omega-3* is an example of an essential fatty acid found mainly in fish oils, seeds and several plant oils (rapeseed, mustard seed, linseed). The best sources of omega-3 fats are found in salmon, sardines and mackerel. Regular fish consumption is associated with reduced risk of coronary heart disease. This is thought to be the reason why a 'Mediterranean-style' diet high in fresh vegetables, olive oils and fish can be extremely healthy.

Your advice as a trainer should be to reduce saturate fats in a client's diet. This may be achieved by:

- altering cooking methods, choosing to grill, steam and bake rather than fry
- not adding fat during cooking
- choosing lean cuts of meat and trimming off visible fat
- keeping dairy product intake moderate
- choosing low-fat options (e.g. skimmed milk, low-fat cheese)
- being aware of hidden fats found in foods such as nuts
- reducing processed foods
- reducing consumption of fat-filled snacks such as crisps, cake and chocolate.

We should also educate clients to understand that not all fats are bad and that certain fats found within fish and seed oils can actually have a positive effect on our risk of coronary heart disease.

WATER AND HYDRATION

The human body comprises up to 75 per cent water. Water is vital as a background solvent in the body, supporting a myriad of chemical reactions. It helps to transport substances around the body and in and out of its cells; it aids in eliminating waste products and helps us to regulate body temperature.

The effect of dehydration

Dehydration has an extremely adverse effect on cell function and can have a massive impact on athletic performance.

During cardiovascular exercise a dehydrated athlete will have a higher heart rate and an increased perception of effort compared with a hydrated athlete doing the same intensity of exercise. They will also produce more lactic acid and burn more energy (Gonzalez *et al.*, 1999). Dehydrate muscle by 3 per cent and it is predicted that we will experience a 10 per cent loss of contractile strength and an 8 per cent loss of speed (Williams, 1995). Even mild dehydration by 2 per cent body mass has the potential to slow physical and mental function (Yoshida *et al.*, 2002). Chronic mild dehydration contributes to general

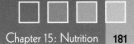

fatigue and lethargy. In fact, dehydration is one of the few things our body cannot adapt to. We simply cannot cope with the demands of not having enough water.

Ensuring adequate hydration

Sedentary adults need about 2 litres/day minimum to maintain hydration. Athletic work is only 30 per cent efficient and the other 70 per cent of energy expanded during exercise is lost as heat. Heat can be extremely damaging to the body; in response to increased body temperature our body starts to sweat so that heat is lost through evaporation of fluid from the skin. For this reason when we calculate the daily water requirements of the body we need to add 1–5 ml of fluid required by the body for every calorie used during training. The maximal sweat rate for a trained athlete is about 2–3 litres per hour. Two litres is equivalent to 2 kg so you can see that it does not take long for a 70 kg distance athlete to lose 2 per cent (1.4 kg) of their body weight in water and start to experience deficits in their performance. Some athletes may lose 5–6 kg of body weight through loss of water over the course of a day's training.

Heat and dehydration can place significant stress on the body. Heat exhaustion through water depletion or heat syncope (loss of blood pressure due to decreased blood volume) is common in distance athletes who do not prepare adequately or take care to remain hydrated. Headache, irritability, chills, pale moist skin, fatigue, dizziness and a rapid weak pulse can all be signs of heat exhaustion.

> **Perhaps the greatest stress ever imposed on the human cardiovascular system (except for severe haemorrhage) is the combination of exercise and hyperthermia (excessive heat). (Rowell, 1986)**

Thirst is generally the worst and last indicator of dehydration. Relying on this as an indication of when to drink may mean you are already dehydrated. Get your clients to drink regularly throughout the day. If their urine is dark this may indicate dehydration. Loss of performance,

lethargy or headaches may all be symptoms of dehydration.

GUIDELINES ON HOW MUCH TO DRINK BEFORE, DURING AND AFTER TRAINING

- Drink approximately 500 ml of fluid 2 hours before exercise to allow for excretion of excess water.
- Drink approximately 1–2 cups 15–30 minutes before exercise.
- If exercise continues over an hour or if the exercise is extremely strenuous, drink 1 cup every 15 minutes during the event, and 1–2 cups afterwards every 15 minutes or so until fluid losses have been replaced.

We can help to prevent dehydration by drinking during exercise, but it is important to be aware that as we can only absorb between 0.8 and 1.2 litres of water per hour, with sweat rates being well above this, long-duration exercise will inevitably cause dehydration.

Rehydration strategies

Rehydration after training is an important part of the recovery process. We should drink fluid in excess of that lost through exercise to account for losses as we urinate (Maughan *et al.*, 1996) and drink approximately 150 per cent of that lost through exercise. By weighing your client before and after exercise you can see how much weight they have lost and get them to drink enough to replace a litre and a half of fluid for every kilogram lost within six hours following exercise.

The human thirst mechanism is highly sensitive to changes in salt concentration in the blood and to changes in blood volume (Hubbard *et al.*, 1990). As we become dehydrated our blood volume decreases and salt concentrations in the blood increase, causing us to feel thirsty. Drinking plain water can prematurely increase blood volume, diluting salt levels in the blood, decreasing our drive to drink and prematurely satiating our thirst. The result is that we may not drink enough fluid to rehydrate ourselves properly. The addition of small quantities of salt in our drink will help maintain our drive to drink by maintaining salt concentrations in the blood, ensuring that we take on board a greater quantity of fluid, sufficient to prevent dehydration (Nose *et al.*, 1988).

Rehydration and hydration strategies are extremely important to athletic performance and care should be taken to ensure that your clients are taking sufficient water on board. Taking on excess water will act like an insurance policy with excess water being excreted by the body.

It is also important for clients to be aware that diuretics (substances that hinder the absorption of water) will cause dehydration. Caffeine in coffee and tea and alcohol will have this effect.

CARBOHYDRATE: BALANCING BLOOD SUGAR FOR ENERGY AND PERFORMANCE

Carbohydrate (CHO) is our primary source of energy and is stored, ready to fuel movement. It is the only fuel that can be used for anaerobic energy production and it is the most efficient fuel for the aerobic metabolism (Williams, 1995). Carbohydrate is able to produce energy for muscle contraction up to three times as rapidly as fat, which explains why when glycogen stores are depleted, endurance performance starts to deteriorate and work levels fall. Fatigue in endurance events is closely linked to the depletion of our energy reserves (glycogen). Numerous studies have demonstrated that if we can elevate our muscle glycogen stores we can increase endurance performance in particular, and carbohydrate intake before, during and after performance can improve endurance performance (Chryssanthopoulos and Williams, 1997). If glycogen stores in the muscles and liver are normal, glucose intake during exercise is not required for those participating in continuous exercise lasting 60–90 minutes, but it is of importance for athletes participating in events

lasting longer than this. Furthermore, carbohydrate is the only source of fuel that can be used by the brain, which explains the rapid drop in mental performance when blood sugar levels start to fall if we skip a meal, for example.

Carbohydrates can be broken down into *simple carbohydrates* or sugars (fruit, table sugar, refined foods) and these can be further subdivided into *monosaccharides* or single sugars (glucose, fructose and galactose) and *disaccharides* or double sugars (maltose, lactose, and sucrose). *Complex carbohydrates* or starches (potatoes, beans, breads, cereals, pasta, rice) are *polysaccharides*, which are molecules made up of three or more glucose molecules. Starches should meet 40–50 per cent of your dietary calorie intake and sugars only 10 per cent. Whether a carbohydrate is complex or simple profoundly affects how fast they are broken down and digested. It also affects their conversion to energy, a topic discussed in more detail below.

As food containing carbohydrate is consumed, the body digests it and breaks it down into sugars, which are then transported into the bloodstream as *glucose*. This glucose may be used for energy by the brain and other parts of the nervous or muscular systems, or it may be converted into *glycogen* and stored in the muscles or the liver. Glycogen that enters muscle is effectively locked in, whereas glycogen stored in the liver can be re-released into the bloodstream as glucose. When we exercise, the stores of glycogen in the liver are used to maintain blood-sugar levels. This is extremely important as glucose is the only source of fuel that can be used by the brain. As soon as blood-sugar levels fall and liver glycogen is depleted, mental and physical function plummets.

Carbohydrate is stored in the liver or the muscles as *glycogen* and there are low levels of carbohydrate found within the blood (Table 15.1).

As with any other sources of calories, if calorie intake from carbohydrate exceeds the requirements of the body, excess carbohydrate is stored as fat. This is why carbohydrate consumed in excess can contribute to weight gain.

Table 15.1 Carbohydrate storage in the human body

	Amount stored in the average human (g)	Calories available from these stores
Liver glycogen	100	400
Muscle glycogen	300	1200
Blood glucose	20	80

Fibre

Dietary fibre is a complex carbohydrate found in plant material that is resistant to digestive enzymes. *Insoluble fibre* passes through our digestive system intact, whereas *soluble fibre* can be broken down in the large intestine. We require 20–50 grams of fibre per day. Fibre in our diet helps prevent bowel cancer, reduces incidence of heart disease and helps in a weight-control programme by slowing digestion and helping satiety. We can increase our intake of fibre by reducing refined carbohydrate, such as white bread, pasta and rice, in our diet and replacing them with less refined versions such as wholemeal or wholegrain breads, brown rice/pasta and vegetables.

---

refined food: Foods that have gone through increased levels of processing, i.e. have been cooked, prepared with added sugars, salt, preservatives, colouring etc.

Ensuring sufficient carbohydrate

Although carbohydrate is not an essential nutrient because the energy it provides can be gained from the metabolism of other energy sources such as protein or fat, it is recommended that carbohydrate provides approximately 40–50 per cent of calorie intake – more if the person is an athlete. Some sources recommend that endurance athletes should increase their intake of carbohydrate so that it represents 70 per cent of total calorie intake. For a 2000-calorie diet, this means that an average individual is recommended to consume approximately 200–300 grams of carbohydrate, and an endurance athlete about 350 grams.

Carbohydrate loading

Carbohydrate loading is the practice of consuming meals high in carbohydrate in the days leading up to an endurance event in order to increase muscular stores of glycogen. Studies have shown that this improves endurance performance. In general, as an athlete approaches an event, they gradually reduce their exercise levels; then, in the three days prior to the event they consume meals high in carbohydrates and take complete rest from exercise. The key is a switch from a normal meal to a very high-carbohydrate meal to increase muscle-glycogen stores known as *carbohydrate super-compensation*. A diet consisting of 8–10 grams of carbohydrate per kg of body weight per day is recommended (Williams, 1995). Carbohydrate loading will only work if the athlete is resting, so it is important to refrain from exercise for three days prior to an event. This method has been shown to increase glycogen stores by as much as 20–40 per cent and has a big effect on endurance performance in events lasting longer than 90 minutes. The effects are reduced if this strategy is used frequently, so it should only be considered for major events or competitions.

Carbohydrate intake prior to performance

Carbohydrate intake has been shown to improve endurance performance in tasks lasting 2 hours or more, delaying fatigue and improving performance (Chryssanthopoulos and Williams, 1997). Consuming a carbohydrate meal (0.5–2 grams of carbohydrate per kg of body weight) 2 hours prior

15.2 Summary guidelines of carbohydrate uptake including water and protein timings and exercise

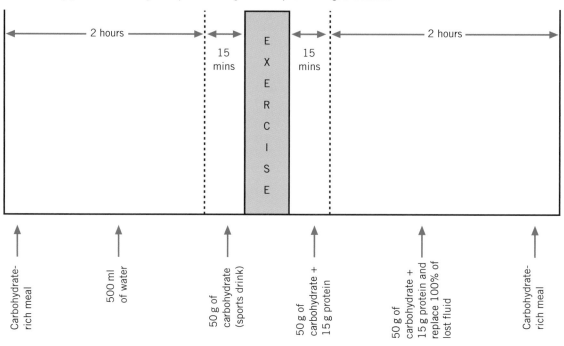

(Ensure adequate hydration)

to training (Wee, 2000) has been shown to raise muscular glycogen by as much as 15 per cent (if the carbohydrate is high-glycaemic index, see below). It is recommended that some protein (25–30 grams max) should be added to this meal in order to help stabilize blood-sugar levels. The meal should also be low in fat to help digestion.

Carbohydrates can be consumed immediately prior to exercise, 10 minutes before the start, for example. Approximately 50 grams of carbohydrate taken with water in the form of a sports drink can be highly effective and can be used in conjunction with hydration strategies.

Carbohydrate intake during performance

Carbohydrate feeding in the form of sports drinks has been shown to delay fatigue (Coyle *et al.*, 1986) by sparing liver glycogen and maintaining blood-glucose levels, thereby improving endurance performance (Jeukendrup *et al.*, 1997) and even

reducing perceptions of effort. It is recommended that we consume 30–60 grams of carbohydrate per hour (Williams, 1995). For example, an athlete should attempt to consume a 5–10 per cent solution containing 15–20 grams of carbohydrate every 15–20 minutes. Concentrations above this level may cause gastric distress that may hinder performance. Most sports drinks adhere to these guidelines.

Carbohydrate intake after performance

Replenishing carbohydrate stores following exercise is an essential part of the recovery process, especially if an athlete intends to perform again over the course of a day. In the 15 minutes immediately following intense exercise our body is geared towards replenishing energy stores, with digestive enzymes being super-efficient. In this first 15 minutes the athlete should try to consume approximately 50 grams of carbohydrate (e.g. two slices of bread and a banana, 85 grams of dried fruit, three small bananas, 0.5 litre of fruit juice) and a further 50 grams over the next 2 hours. Addition of some protein (approx. 15 grams) to this food will increase carbohydrate uptake by causing an increased insulin response (Zawadzki, 1992; Roy *et al.*, 2001).

After this 2-hour period the athlete should aim to have a low-glycaemic-index, high-fibre meal that will allow for slow release of carbohydrate and that will completely replenish their energy stores. Research has demonstrated that ingestion of protein in combination with carbohydrate (Tipton *et al.*, 1999; Rasmussen *et al.*, 2000) after weight-training exercise stimulates protein synthesis, aiding hypertrophy (muscle gain) (Figure 15.3)

This makes taking on board food immediately after exercise absolutely essential for good recovery and maximum gains in muscle.

CARBOHYDRATES AND THEIR EFFECT ON BLOOD SUGAR

Glucose is the only fuel that the brain can use. If we allow our blood-sugar levels to fall we suffer a condition known as *hypoglycaemia*. We become tired, lethargic and our physical and mental performance deteriorates. If blood-sugar levels fall too far the brain could be damaged. Our body has important hormones to ensure this does not occur and that the brain is always supplied with energy.

Insulin and glucagon

Blood-sugar levels are regulated by the hormones *insulin* and *glucagon*. *Insulin* is the body's storage hormone, stimulating the storage of glucose in the muscles as well as promoting the formation of fat when blood sugar exceeds the body's needs. As sugar is released into the bloodstream the pancreas secretes insulin, which causes a shunt of the blood sugar into the muscles and liver, ready to be used by the muscles to fuel movement. If carbohydrate is consumed in excess, insulin stimulates conversion of these excess calories into fat, to be stored by the body as subcutaneous (under the

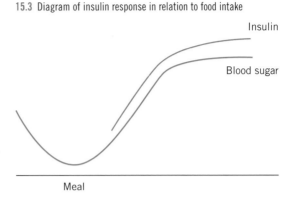

15.3 Diagram of insulin response in relation to food intake

skin) fat. If we eat too much in one sitting or eat foods that release sugar too quickly into our blood (see fast-release carbohydrate), the rapid rise in blood sugar stimulates excessive insulin production in response. The result is a rapid fall in blood sugar, causing *hypoglycaemia* (excessively low blood-sugar levels) and the usual deficits in performance associated with low blood sugar. Feeling sleepy after eating a large meal is often a good indication that you have over-consumed carbohydrate.

KEY POINT

Insulin	Insulin is a storage hormone. Excess insulin release causes an increase in fat storage and a fall in fat use to fuel movement. Therefore strategies to balance insulin levels can help in a fat-loss programme.

Glucagon has the opposite effect to insulin: it stimulates release of glycogen from the liver to raise blood-sugar levels. Glucagon counteracts the effect of insulin under normal conditions so that blood-sugar levels do not fall too low. It increases during exercise with other hormones that stimulate breakdown of glycogen, such as *adrenaline* and *cortisol*. Cortisol is released from the adrenal gland. It stimulates breakdown and release of amino acids from muscle to be used by the body to provide energy.

15.4 Daily fluctuations in blood sugar with eating

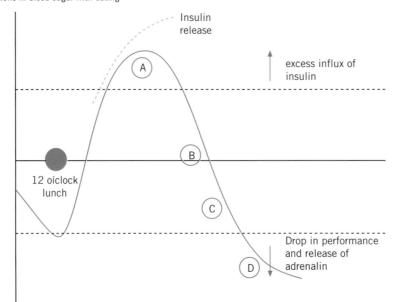

Blood sugar and daily life

Imagine you have eaten breakfast and are at work. You have lunch about 1 o'clock and do not intend eating again till you get home, which may be around 6 or 7 o'clock. This is a typical eating pattern for many people. After lunch, blood-sugar levels rise, and insulin is released to stimulate the uptake of sugars from the blood into the muscles (Figure 15.4, point A). Depending on the type and quantity of carbohydrate we consume, blood-sugar levels will remain elevated for about three hours (Figure 15.4, point B). After this, blood-sugar levels start to fall below levels where performance deteriorates (Figure 15.4, point C). We are noticeably less alert and less able to concentrate on work around 4 o'clock. The brain recognizes low blood-sugar levels and stimulates sensations of hunger, causing sensory changes that make food look, smell and taste more appealing. It is at this time that we often snack on something sweet such as chocolate, biscuits or sweet tea or coffee. If we don't, blood-sugar levels continue to fall.

At this stage the body reacts by stimulating the adrenal gland to release adrenaline, our 'fight or flight' hormone, that will help elevate our blood-sugar levels by stimulating the breakdown of glycogen in the liver, releasing glycogen into the bloodstream. Other side effects of adrenaline are an increased heart rate, drawing of blood to the core of the body. We go slightly pale, our skin may be slightly clammy, we may become irritable and short-tempered. These symptoms are commonly experienced at this 4–5 o'clock time with this type of eating pattern. Someone asks you to do a small job near the end of the working day and all hell breaks loose! If the adrenaline influx is a frequent occurence it places added stress on the body. There may also be other negative effects on your immune system caused by the hormone cortisol, which acts as an immunosuppressant, making you susceptible to illness. This is the consequence of not eating over an extended period of time. We need to balance our calorie intake over the day to prevent this from happening (see 'meal timings').

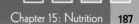

Fast-and slow-release carbohydrates

The speed at which carbohydrates are broken down and the speed at which sugars are released into the blood are not the same for all foods. For various reasons some are broken down and digested faster than others. This speed of digestion and release of sugar have important metabolic and hormonal consequences.

To oversimplify the story we can break foods into two categories: *fast-release foods* that result in a fast influx of sugar into the blood and *slow-release foods* that cause a less dramatic rise in blood sugar. Foods are classified as fast- or slow-release according to their effect on blood-sugar levels in the body after they are eaten. In Figures 15.5 and 15.6 we look at a classic example by comparing the effects of eating white bread (fast-release) and baked beans (slow-release) on blood glucose levels.

White bread is a fast-release food (Figure 15.5). The increase in blood sugar is steep and this stimulates an increased release of insulin which causes a steep fall in blood-sugar levels well below the original baseline level. This can cause a situation in which blood sugar falls to levels close to hypoglycaemia, stimulating sensations of hunger and resulting in a loss of performance. The increased insulin levels drive these calories into muscles to be stored as fat.

Now imagine that the same individual ingests an equivalent amount of carbohydrate calories but of the slow-release food, in this case baked beans (Figure 15.6). Note that the actual weight of food may differ because of differences in calorie density in the two foods. Here the curve is a lot less steep and takes a far greater time to drop. The area

15.5 Fast-release food

15.6 Slow-release food

underneath each graph in this case represents the total amount of calories, so will be equal in both cases. In this instance the release of insulin is a lot less steep and more controlled. The individual's blood-sugar levels will remain much more stable, meaning the person will feel satiated for longer.

Scientists originally thought that simple sugars found in fruits and table sugar were fast-release and the starchy carbs found in potatoes, pasta and rice were slow-release. This was why the traditional advice was to reduce simple sugars in favour of a more starchy diet. With further study this was found not to be universally the case and in fact the story is far more complex than that.

GLYCAEMIC INDEX

The glycaemic index (GI) is a ranking of foods (0–100) based on their immediate effect on blood-sugar levels. It is a more accurate tool than simply trying to label foods as fast- and slow-release. Carbohydrate foods that are broken down quickly and cause steep increases in blood sugar have high GI scores (e.g. white bread, jacket potato). Carbohydrates that break down slowly, releasing glucose slowly into the bloodstream have a low GI score (e.g. wholegrain bread, beans, pulses, legumes).

The effect of a food on blood-sugar levels is influenced by many factors, including the degree of cooking (processed foods are digested more quickly, increasing their GI), the fibre content (the 'bits' in food act as a barrier to digestion, decreasing their GI), the fat content (fat slows digestion), and the type of starch (viscous, soluble starch such as that found in oats slows the digestive process).

Glycaemic index and weight reduction

The GI is a scientifically validated tool in weight reduction, management of diabetes and performance enhancement. Fast-release, high-GI foods cause us to pump insulin continually into our systems, training our bodies to store fat, increasing our chances of putting on weight. As with any other drug, the body starts to build up a resistance to insulin. Therefore, for every meal, more insulin has to be pumped into the system in order to regulate blood sugar; and the more likely the body is to store food as fat. As the body preferentially stores calories as fat, weight increases and the levels of insulin have to increase further in order to compensate for an increased body mass. The result is a self-perpetuating spiralling of weight gain.

Pronounced insulin resistance is known as **type II adult onset diabetes** and is thought to be the underlying cause of a group of symptoms (obesity, high blood pressure, increased abdominal fat) called **syndrome X**. Levelling out hormone levels can be extremely important in achieving results in terms of weight loss and controlling these chronic diseases.

Consuming lower-GI foods avoids the dramatic peaks in blood sugar. This can have two effects: blood-sugar levels take much longer to fall, making us much less inclined to snack and crave for sweet foods, and the low insulin levels encourage the body to metabolize fat as a fuel.

Glycaemic index and performance

In general, by choosing lower-GI options in our diet we can maintain blood-sugar levels, which is essential for physical and mental performance. There are times when a fast influx of calories can be useful to performance. During exercise, particularly of long duration, you may require a lot of calories quickly. This would be an ideal time to make use of moderate- or fast-release foods. The orange or banana you see tennis players eating at intervals is the classic example, or the simple carbohydrate drinks carried by distance runners. After a training session when muscles are depleted of fuel and need fresh glycogen stores there is a 15-minute 'window of opportunity', during which time the muscles are desperate to take energy on board. After a weights session carbohydrates are required for the protein-synthesis process to begin. These are situations in which high-GI foods, which provide rapid influxes of sugar, are ideal. They will enhance recovery, increase muscle gain and improve subsequent performance.

Glycaemic index guidelines

Table 15.2 lists the GI scores for some common foods. To optimize your carbohydrate intake,

---

GUIDELINES FOR IMPLEMENTING LOW-GI EATING

- Limit intake of foods with a higher GI.
- Try to have some protein with every meal or snack for its satiating qualities.
- Eat carbohydrate-rich meals earlier in the day, to match energy-requirement patterns.
- Eat protein, vegetable and salad-rich meals later in the day when the requirements for repair are greater.
- Eat seven or more servings of fruit and vegetables per day.
- Include green leafy vegetables.
- Try to have a salad each day.
- Snack on fruit and low-fat yogurts.
- Eat wholegrain breads and cereals with a low GI.
- Choose breakfast cereals based on oats.
- Eat grainy breads.
- Eat pasta or noodles in place of potatoes.
- Use basmati rice instead of long-grain.
- Eat more pulses (beans, peas and lentils).
- Use nuts frequently although sparingly (whilst high in saturated fats they are nutrient-dense).
- Eat higher-GI foods during or immediately after exercise.

Table 15.2 Glycaemic index scores

High		Moderate		Low	
Breakfast cereals					
Rice Krispies	82	Mini Wheats	58	All Bran	42
Coco Pops	77	Muesli, untoasted	56	Muesli, toasted	43
Corn Flakes	84			Porridge	42
				Special K	54
				Sultana Bran	52
Grains and pasta					
Brown rice	76	Basmati rice	58	Buckwheat	54
White rice	87			Noodles	46
				Egg fetuccine	32
				Ravioli	39
				Spaghetti	41
Bread					
Bagel	72	Croissant*	67	Fruit loaf	47
White bread	70	Crumpet	69	Heavy grain bread	46
Wholemeal bread	69	Pitta bread	57		
Vegetables					
Parsnip	97	Beetroot	64	Carrots	49
Baked potato	85	New potatoes	62	Peas	48
French fries	75	Sweetcorn	65		
Swede	72				
Legumes					
Broad beans	79			Baked beans	48
				Butter beans	31
				Chick peas	33
				Haricot beans	38
				Kidney beans	27
				Lentils	28
				Soya beans	18

Table 15.2 continued

High		Moderate		Low	
Fruit					
Watermelon	72	Banana	55	Apple	38
		Pineapple	68	Apricot	31
		Raisins	64	Cherries	22
		Sultanas	56	Grapefruit	25
				Grapes	46
				Orange	44
				Fresh peach	42
				Canned peach (in natural juice)	30
				Pear	38
				Plum	39
Dairy foods					
		Ice cream (full-fat)	61	Milk whole*	27
				Skimmed milk	32
				Yoghurt	33
Beverages					
Lucozade	95	Fanta	68	Apple juice	40
		Squash	68	Orange juice	46
Snack/conveniance food					
Crisps	72	Popcorn	55	Peanuts*	14
Jelly beans	80	Mars bar	68	Chocolate*	49

*High in fat so low GI but high in calorie content so not recommended.

simply take your diet at present and adapt it by selecting lower-GI foods, preferably those below a GI of 55.

When you talk to your client about their diet, it is a good idea to have a few low-GI snack and menu suggestions to give them. For example:

- porridge with yoghurt
- oat-based muesli with nuts and seeds
- poached eggs on rye toast
- low-fat humus with crispbread.
- oatcakes/crispbread with cottage cheese
- yoghurt with nuts and seeds and fruit
- apple or pear with handful of nuts and seeds
- salmon or smoked mackerel with mixed salad and portion of brown rice
- tuna and pepper salad with half a baked potato
- chicken breast with roast Mediterranean vegetables and baked sweet potatoes.

MEAL TIMINGS

The time of day when we eat can have a large effect on our performance. We have already seen how allowing blood sugar to fall can cause a rapid deterioration in physical and mental function. If we do not provide our body with the appropriate fuel we cannot expect to perform optimally.

Figure 15.7 illustrates the way many professional people eat over the course of a day. Breakfast tends to be light, maybe toast or cereal with a light lunch

of sandwiches, and the main meal of the day is usually in the evening. Most people consume a large proportion of their daily calories in the evening, many of the calories coming from alcohol, puddings and after-meal snacks. The overall result is long periods of low blood sugar during the day broken up by occasional, sugar-driven peaks.

The consequences of eating in this way can be devastating. Performance drops in line with blood sugar during long periods without food in a similar way to that described above. Metabolism invariably drops as the body attempts to conserve energy, sending the body into a *starvation mode* (see Chapter 6) during times when energy and mental concentration are most required. When we do eat we consume large quantities of calories and reward our effort with comfort foods low in nutrients and high in calories. This invariably happens late in the evening when there is no chance that the calories will be used during activity. Any excess calories are stored as fat, a process driven by the large peak in insulin created by the large influx of blood sugar. This type of eating drives weight gain and hinders any progress we attempt to make in our training.

Dietary plan: little and often

By spreading calorie intake over the day, eating every 3 hours, blood-sugar levels can be balanced and thus hormonal fluctuations moderated. What you need to do is to take the amount of calories that your client is consuming throughout the day, or more importantly the amount of calories required by them to achieve their goal, whether weight loss or gain, and spread them throughout the day, ideally a breakfast, lunch and early tea, split by two smaller snacks (Figure 15.8).

This means that energy is available when the body is doing most work and not at night when the body is asleep. The gaps between meals will also have less chance of exceeding 3 hours. It is also important to cycle the macronutrients so that carbohydrate is consumed in greater quantities when the body is being active and proteins are emphasized during periods of recovery when activity is going to be low: think, 'What am I doing

15.7 Daily fluctuations in blood sugar with eating

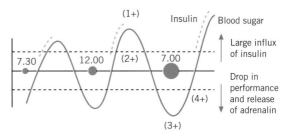

15.8 Diagram of five-meals-a-day eating plan

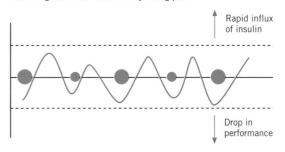

in the next three hours?' – the more activity, the more carbohydrate we should consume.

NUTRIENT DENSITY

The concept of nutrient density refers to the nutritional value of a food: how much protein, vitamins and minerals food contains in relation to its calorie content. Some use the term 'quality calories' to describe calories gained from nutrient-dense foods. For example, if you compare tuna with chocolate, you gain far greater quantities of protein, vitamins and minerals from tuna than you do from an amount of chocolate that would contain an equivalent amount of calories. The key to healthy diet is to pack your meals with nutrient-dense foods and reduce those foods with high calorie densities in comparison to their nutritional benefit. By doing this and eating a varied diet you ensure that you ingest all the nutrients the body requires to remain healthy and have a greater chance of achieving a desirable weight.

Your role as a personal trainer is to identify foods with high calorie density and low nutrient density and to reduce the frequency and/or the volume in which they are consumed in a client's diet. The foods you choose to eliminate first may vary from client to client. Prioritize which foods are having the greatest negative effect on their diet and the ones that the client will least miss from their diet.

Foods with a high calorie density but little nutritional benefit are known as 'nutrient-empty' foods.

EXAMPLES OF NUTRIENT-EMPTY FOODS

- Alcohol
- Highly processed or junk food
- Sweets, fizzy drinks, cakes, chocolate etc.
- Saturated fats from foods in the form of butters, mayonnaises, salad dressing and visible fats in meats

We can increase the nutrient density of meals by:

- changing cooking methods from frying meat and boiling vegetables into grilling and steaming
- cutting visible fat off meat
- adding less sugar to foods
- choosing low-fat dairy options
- choosing leaner meats (chicken, pork) or fish to replace red meats higher in fat (lamb, beef, duck).

THE CLIENT-CENTRED APPROACH TO NUTRITION

Unfortunately, educating people about healthy eating is not enough to make long-term changes to dietary habits. If this was the case we would not have the current massive problems with obesity and weight-related chronic disease (heart disease, diabetes) in Western society. In general, people know what they should be eating but they do not have the skills and control over their eating habits to implement a healthy-eating plan.

Without taking into account a person's lifestyle, tastes, likes, dislikes and possible barriers to success, any dietary plan is likely to fail on a long-term basis. This explains why many commercial 'diets' don't work on a long-term basis. They are highly prescriptive and make very little allowance for a person's routines, their eating habits, and their individual tastes. People can stick to such diets for a short period of time and generally experience good results to begin with, but as their motivation dwindles they return to their old habits and their weight returns with interest.

Programmes have to be *individualized* to match the needs of the client, with psychological strategies in place to encourage adherence. The client's current diet has to be assessed and the interventions you make have to be prioritized with the client's behaviour. *Modelling* should be used to give the client the maximum opportunity for success (see Chapter 16 for more details on these techniques).

The first step is to assess your client's current dietary behaviour. There are a variety of ways of doing this. The method you choose is down to personal choice, but generally the more information and detail that you can obtain, the better.

Methods for assessment of dietary habits

We can simply ask our client for a typical day's food or ask them to perform a *24-hour recall* of their eating. This can then be used to highlight key issues and areas for improvement. A *diet history questionnaire* can be used to find out about general food habits. Likewise a *food frequency questionnaire* can assess how often certain foods are eaten. The problem with these modes of assessment is that they are subjective and rely on the client's own memories about what they have eaten. Often these perceptions are wrong, causing these reports to be misleading. Far more effective is a *food diary*, in which the client has to record what they have eaten and drunk over a set period of time, typically a week. This can often highlight some key issues to the client that they have never perceived before filling out the diary.

15.9 Food diary

Exercise and diet diary						
Goals:						
Please detail your exercise (minutes cardio/PB). Please detail the food and drink you consume for the next 7 days. Please include details of times and quantities.						
Monday	Tuesday	Wednesday	Thursday	Friday	Saturday	Sunday

ANALYSIS OF FOOD DIARIES

Once your client has completed a food diary, you can use the following steps to analyse and provide advice based on it.

- Check that the balance of macronutrients in the meals is in accordance with the food plate (see Figure 15.1).
- Check there is adequate vegetable, salad and fruit intake (seven portions per day), especially green leafy vegetables.
- Is simple sugar and saturated fat intake low?
- Check water intake (over 2 litres per day).
- Check eating frequency and meal timings.
- Ensure overall calorie intake represents calorie requirements.
- Check whether calorie intake is spread throughout the day.
- Check the glycaemic index of the foods.
- Make sure there is a wide variety of foods to ensure recommended daily intake of all nutrients.
- Identify intake of anti-nutrients – those foods with little nutritional value (alcohol, coffee and tea, nicotine, saturated fats).
- Check whether foods are wholefoods (cooked from basic ingredients) or processed foods (pre-prepared).

- If a client's goal is weight loss, the number of calories must represent a negative energy balance, so you cannot have five meals of the same size as before.
- Check pre- and post-exercise nutrition.

This information provides the basis for the nutritional interventions that you can safely make with your clients. The aim when analysing a food diary is to build a mental list of interventions you can suggest to aid the client's progress towards their goals and to improve their general health and wellbeing.

IMPLEMENTATION OF DIETARY CHANGE

The implementation of this dietary plan has massive motivational, organizational and logistical problems for many of the people you will encounter. The elite athlete may have the discipline and control over their behaviour to implement these dietary interventions without much effort or even any great change in their routine. This is unlikely to be the case for some clients, who may have struggled with their dietary behaviours or their weight for many years and have to date been unsuccessful.

In Chapter 16 we look at strategies to reinforce correct behaviour and improve our clients' chances of success. In the meantime here are some tips.

- Enquire about your client's 'readiness for change'. Which changes do they think will be the easiest for them to make?
- If the person does not have a regular eating pattern and has a tendency to snack or binge, make regular eating a first priority.
- Make the changes in the diet slow and step-by-step.
- Set goals only two or three at a time, making success more realistic.
- Having three meals a day and snacking on fruit on two occasions is a realistic first target for many individuals.
- Look at the glycaemic index tables and start making small changes in diet to lower GI (e.g. change white bread to wholegrain bread, long-grain rice to basmati rice) in order to help satiety and reduce sensations of hunger if weight loss is the goal.
- Make sure your client's diet has plenty of variety. This will help to ensure the full recommended daily intake of vitamins, minerals and essential amino acids.

CASE STUDY: NUTRITION

A new female client came to me looking to lose weight and tone up. As well as giving her a resistance and cardiovascular programme I also asked her to complete a food diary. I explained that this involved writing down exactly what she had eaten and drunk for at least 5 days over the course of a week, including information about the weekend.

Her immediate reaction was to ask if she could start after this weekend because she was expecting a big weekend out with friends. I asked her to record this, as her social eating may be an important factor in her new regime. I asked her to include times when she ate and also some information about quantities of food. Also when she had exercised, including any walks or other light exercise.

This is the diary I got back:

Monday	7.30am Toast, butter and marmalade with coffee 1 cup	12.30pm Tuna sandwich, tea, packet of crisps, apple and chocolate biscuit	4.00pm Cup of coffee and biscuits (2 choc digestive)	Workout at gym. Bottle of water	8.00pm Spaghetti Bolognese with glass of red wine, small bowl of ice cream
Tuesday		12.30pm Cheese, sandwich, cup of tea, packet of crisps, apple and chocolate biscuit	Bottle of water		7.30pm Chicken and vegetables with gravy, 2 glasses of red wine
Wednesday	7.30am Toast, butter and marmalade with coffee 1 cup	12.30pm Sandwich, cup of tea, packet of crisps, apple and chocolate biscuit	4.00pm Chocolate bar, bottle of water		8.00pm Vegetable soup
Thursday	7.30am Toast, butter and marmalade with coffee 1 cup	1.00pm Pub lunch: ploughman's, 1 glass of wine	4.00pm Cup of tea and apple	Workout at gym	Glass of wine
Friday	Apple (late for train)	1.00pm Pre-packed sandwiches on train, coffee	Cup of coffee and chocolate bar	Several glasses of wine	Chinese take-away, noodles and chicken
Saturday	7.30am Toast, butter and marmalade with coffee 1 cup	1.00pm Vegetable soup		8.00pm Pizza out, 4 glasses of wine	Other alcohol?
Sunday	10.00am Scrambled eggs on toast	1.00pm Sunday lunch: chicken, potatoes, parsnips, broccoli	Glass of wine	7.00pm Tea piece of toast and butter	9–11pm Coffee sweets whilst watching film

This is quite a typical food diary. As well as wanting to tone up and lose weight the client also complained of having low energy levels. She takes a vitamin tablet in the morning but always seem tired and does not sleep particularly well.

I always start by trying to draw on some positives. I explained to the client that it was good that they got two sessions of exercise in and it was good to see they were eating reasonable regular meals without an excess of snacking. She explained that she tried not to snack but always felt very low on energy at about 3 or 4 in the afternoon and that others in the office always bring round a hot drink and some sugary snacks.

In my own mind I then drew up a list of interventions that would help achieve her goals of losing weight, toning up and increasing energy levels. Although there were many changes that we could make, I always try to prioritize by asking which changes will make the most impact on a client's diet without making big changes to their habits and lifestyle.

I pointed out that there were a lot of simple sugars in her diet, for example the bread, pasta, potatoes and sugary snacks. I explained about glycaemic index and what effect this would have on her blood-sugar levels, insulin and therefore her energy levels. I gave her a simple rule to help this: cut out the bread. Because this would have the effect of changing her breakfast, I suggested some lower-GI alternatives, such as muesli, bran flakes or porridge, but always allowed her an element of choice so she could choose something that suited her taste. Cutting out bread would also require her to change her lunch, so I suggested some alternatives using salad or cous-cous but again allowing her to generate her own meals as long as they remained healthy.

Next I explained how important hydration is for her energy levels and for weight loss. I explained that she is not drinking nearly enough water and the drinks she is having are diuretics and may be dehydrating her further. It is very common for people to associate drinks such as coffee, tea and alcohol with relaxation. Every time they want to relax they reach for their favourite drink. We need to break this habit and replace it with a more productive one. I suggested she could try a herbal tea to replace her coffee and tea, and if she could find a more palatable alternative, all the better. This was a good start for week 1.

In week 2 I explained that low blood sugar due to long periods without eating causes the desire to have a coffee and sugary snack about four o'clock. We needed to add a couple of healthy snacks to stop her blood-sugar levels from falling. I asked her to take a fruit bowl into work and maybe even some dried fruit and nuts to have as a snack at 10am and 3pm. This should stop her feeling the need for a sugar hit at these times. Again, if she can generate some other food options, even better.

Lastly, I asked her to reduce her alcohol intake. I explained that although her intake is not excessive, this would help her lose weight by reducing her calorie intake and also help her energy levels because alcohol can both interfere with sleep patterns and cause dehydration. We talked about the best ways of doing this, maybe having a smaller glass, having water first thing when she gets home from work and so on, and I set her a target of halving the alcohol intake.

If she is successful I will continue to set new targets as the weeks progress. Other interventions could be:

- increasing vegetable intake
- adding more variety
- never skipping meals especially breakfast
- reducing carbohydrate in the evenings
- eating more fish
- eating earlier in the evening
- snacks to aid recovery from training.

This list could go on. As we see from Chapter 16, the important thing is to make changes gradual and possible for the client to adhere to.

CHAPTER SUMMARY

Correct macronutrient intake is one of our most powerful ergogenic performance aids. Performance tends to drop dramatically if we are deficient in any one of these macronutrients, and muscle gain will not occur without sufficient essential amino acids. Performance also drops dramatically if our water intake is too low. Weight loss or weight gain is essentially impossible without considering diet. Sound nutritional guidance is therefore at the heart of good exercise advice and has to be one of the first considerations when we design a client's programme. Having read this chapter you should be clear as to what constitutes a healthy diet and what basic recommendation you can make to move your clients towards a position of improved health through dietary modification.

REFERENCES AND RECOMMENDED READING

1. American College of Sports Medicine (1996) Position stand on exercise and fluid replacement. *Medicine and Science in Sports and Exercise* 28.
2. Brand-Miller, J. (2001) *The Glucose Revolution – GI Plus.* London: Hodder and Stoughton.
3. Chyssanthopoulos, C. and Williams, C. (1997) Pre-exercise carbohydrate meal and endurance-running capacity when carbohydrates are ingested during exercise. *International Journal of Sports Medicine* 18:543–548.
4. Clarkson, P.M. (1998) Nutritional supplements for weight gain. *Sports Science Exchange* 68.
5. Coyle, E.F., Coggan, A.R., Hemmert, M.K. and Ivy, J.L. (1986) Muscle glycogen utilization during prolonged strenuous exercise when fed carbohydrate. *Journal of Applied Physiology* 61:165–172.
6. Gibala, M.J., Tipton, K. and Hargreaves, M. (2000) Amino acids, proteins and exercise performance. *Sports Science Exchange Roundtable* 42. www.Gssiweb.com.
7. Lemon, P. (1991). Effect of exercise on protein requirements. *Journal of Sport Sciences* 9:53–70.
8. Jeukendrup, A., Brouns, F., Wagenmakers, A.J. and Saris, W.H. (1997) Carbohydrate-electrolyte feedings improve 1-h time-trial cycling performance. *International Journal of Sports Medicine* 18:125–129.
9. Gonzalez, Alonso, J., Calbet, J. and Neilson, B. (1999) Metabolic and thermodynamic responses to dehydration-induced reduction in muscle blood flow in exercising humans. *Journal of Physiology* 520:577–589.
10. Hubbard, R.W., Szlyk, P.C. and Armstrong, L.E. (1990) Influence of thirst and fluid palatability on fluid ingestion during exercise. In: Gisolfi CV, Lamb DR, eds. *Perspectives in Exercise Science and Sports Medicine: Fluid Homeostasis during Exercise.* Indianapolis, IN: Benchmark Press, pp. 39–96.
11. Leeds, A., Brand-Miller, J., Foster-Powell, K. and Colagiuri, S. (1996). *The Glucose Revolution.* London: Hodder and Stoughton.
12. Maughan, R.J., Shirreffs, S.M. and Leiper, J.B. (1996) Rehydration and recovery after exercise. *Sport Science Exchange* 9:1–5.
13. Nose, H., Mack, G.W., Shi, X. and Nadel, E.R. (1988) Role of osmolarity and plasma volume during rehydration in humans. *Journal of Applied Physiology* 65:325–331.
14. Rasmussen, B., Tipton, K., Miller, S., Wolf, S. and Wolfe, R. (2000) An oral essential amino acid-carbohydrate supplement enhances muscle protein anabolism after resistance exercise. *Journal of Applied Physiology* 88:386–392.
15. Roy, L., Jentjens, G., Van Loon, C., Mann, C.H. and Anton, J.M. (2001) Addition of protein and amino acids to carbohydrates does not enhance postexercise muscle glycogen synthesis. *Journal of Applied Physiology* 91:839–846.
16. Rowell, L.B. (1986) *Human Circulation:*

Regulation During Physical Stress. New York: Oxford University Press.

17. Tarnopolsky, M. (1992) Evaluation of protein requirements for trained strength athletes. *Journal of Applied Physiology* 73:1986–1995.

18. Tipton, K., Ferrando, A., Phillips, S., Doyle, D. and Wolfe, R. (1999) Postexercise net protein synthesis in human muscle from orally administered amino acids. *American Journal of Physiology* 276:E628–E634.

19. Wee, S.L., Williams, C., Gray, S. and Horabin, J. (1999) Influence of high- and low-glycemic-index meals on endurance running capacity. *Medicine and Science in Sports and Exercise* 31:393–399.

20. Williams, M.H. (1995) *Nutrition for Fitness and Sport*, 4th edn. Madison, WI: Brown and Benchmark.

21. Yoshida, T., Takanishi, T., Nakai, S., Yorimoto, A. and Morimto, T. (2002) The critical level of water deficit causing a decrease in human exercise performance. *European Journal of Applied Physiology* 87:529–534.

22. Zawadzki, K.M., Yaspelkis, B.B., III and Ivy, J.L. (1992) Carbohydrate-protein complex increases the rate of muscle-glycogen storage after exercise. *Journal of Applied Physiology* 72:1854–1859.

16

PSYCHOLOGY AND BEHAVIOUR CHANGE

Getting a client to stick to your programme is one of the hardest challenges you will face as a personal trainer. Roughly half the people starting an exercise routine will drop out within the first six months (Dishman, 1982). Whilst most exercise plans or fad diets work in the short term they are often doomed to failure because most people cannot maintain them over longer periods of time. Many people looking to lose weight have been dieting and exercising on and off for years. This causes fluctuations in weight that place stress on the heart and predispose them to further weight gain. Psychological intervention involves manipulating your client's environment and the way they perceive that environment to make them stick to your programmes.

A psychological programme designed to maintain motivation must go alongside the exercise and dietary plan that you prescribe. It is the psychological and behavioural interventions underpinning adherence to a programme that are likely to be key to an individual's success, not just

over five weeks but for the next five years. In this chapter we will look at motivation, how we can help to motivate individuals, how we can remove barriers to success and what simple psychological tools are available to us to help clients achieve their goals.

MOTIVATION

Motivation or lack of it is a common reason for failing to stick to a programme. Many people will come to you saying, 'I haven't achieved my goals because I have no motivation, I need you to motivate me.' But what is motivation and how do we go about increasing the motivation of our clients?

Motivation is a vague term and will mean different things to different people. A simple psychological definition of motivation is 'the direction and intensity of effort' (Weinberg and Gould, 1999)

motivation: the direction and intensity of effort (Weinberg and Gould, 1999).

The direction of effort refers to what the person wants and intensity of effort refers to how much the person wants it. Therefore, to be motivated a person must have a 'present state', where they are or what they have now, and a 'desired state', where they want to be or what they want, also known as a goal.

We have to assume that people who approach us about personal training are already inherently motivated. They generally have a goal; they also have the drive to seek you out and invest money in achieving these goals. Unfortunately there are inherent barriers and obstacles to people achieving their goals. If these barriers outweigh our desire to reach our target then our motivation is likely to fail. This balance can be demonstrated by a set of scales that may explain their failure in the past (Figure 16.1).

If our *barriers* for exercise, which include factors such as time, energy, work commitments, lack of knowledge etc. outweigh our *motivation* we are unlikely to succeed. When a potential client comes to you asking you to increase their motivation, start by asking, 'What do you want to achieve?', 'How important is achieving this goal to you?', 'How far away are you from achieving this goal?' and 'What obstacles are in your way?' This will provide an excellent initial insight into their levels of motivation.

16.1 Motivation scales

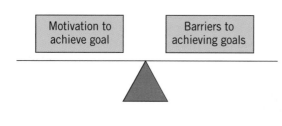

SEVEN STEPS TO MAINTAINING MOTIVATION

These are seven simple steps, based on scientifically proven theories, for increasing motivation and ensuring that motivation exceeds the barriers to success.

1. Enhance motivation
2. Set effective goals
3. Remove barriers
4. Build confidence
5. Achieve results
6. Help cope
7. Provide tools.

ENHANCING MOTIVATION

We start to tip the scales in a positive way by highlighting or increasing the client's motivation. Finding out a client's true motivation, or their **primary motive**, is a key first step because this will be the psychological driving force behind their efforts. Sometimes finding a person's primary motive is simple – an athlete may want to improve his performance at a particular event, for example – but for many their motives are far more complex. During the consultation process we have to probe for their motives and understand what is truly behind their desire to exercise. For some there may be strong emotions linked to their goals, and discussing them may be a difficult process. For example, the client's perception that they are overweight may be seriously affecting their self-esteem and self-confidence. The key question to ask when doing this process is, 'Why?'

Conversations often follow this pattern:

Trainer: 'What is your reason for exercising, what is your goal?'
Client: 'I want to lose weight and tone up.'
Trainer: 'Why do you want to lose weigh and tone up?'
Client: 'I want my clothes to fit better.'

Trainer: 'Are you unhappy with the way your clothes fit?'

Client: 'I have a really nice pair of jeans that I can't fit into and this is really frustrating.'

Trainer: 'How important is it for you to look good in those jeans?'

Client: 'Very important.'

Once we understand their primary motive we can reinforce it using simple reminders. For example, we can keep checking how the jeans are fitting; if the client is looking to lose weight for a wedding having the outfit hanging out at home may be an important reminder of why they have to work so hard; a picture of their holiday destination or a few choice words written in their diary may be enough to keep them focused. If you remind them during a session it may be enough to get that little bit of extra effort. Use this motivation if they are finding things hard going.

People have many reasons why they start exercise or diet. These other reasons to exercise may be called *secondary motives* (Figure 16.2). We should be aware of these various factors so that we tap into each and every one.

As a personal trainer we should highlight these other motives and encourage the client to monitor their performance in a variety of different ways. For example, your client might say, 'I want to lose weight, tone up, get a bit fitter and look better in

my clothes.' People often make the mistake of then only using one criterion to judge their progress. For many the scales are their best objective measure of performance. But if the scales say their weight is the same, a client who uses this as their only form of feedback may feel that they are making no progress even though they are fitter, their body shape has changed because they are more toned (remember that muscle is more dense than fat and hence weighs more) and they look better in their clothes. Even though they have achieved all their goals other than their scales target weight, they still appraise their progress as being poor.

The benefits of exercise are numerous. Your client will almost certainly improve their fitness, especially early in their training, they will sleep better, their health will be better etc. Accentuating these benefits at every possible opportunity will help to maintain motivation.

GOAL SETTING

In the 1980s a study by Harvard University looked at the performance of graduates from a particular year group. It revealed that 2 per cent of the graduates earned more than the rest of the graduates put together. To understand why this was, the researchers looked at some of the

16.2 Secondary motives

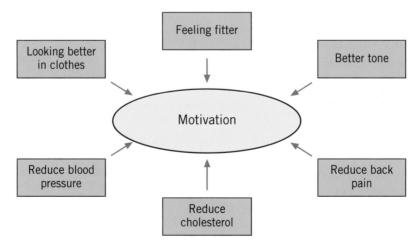

common characteristics and behaviours of this top 2 per cent. The one outstanding feature of these individuals was that they wrote their goals down upon leaving university. Goal setting was seen as the key distinguishing factor between the Harvard graduates.

---

goal setting: a simple yet effective approach to motivation that requires you to set your clients effective *goals*, *monitor* their progress, provide *feedback*, *reinforce success* and help them *cope* with setbacks.

Locke and Latham (1990) describe goals as 'something we consciously want to obtain'. Goal setting has been shown to be a successful method of aiding motivation and improving performance in both industrial and sport settings (Kyllo and Landers, 1995). Goals are thought to positively influence performance in one of four direct ways. Appropriately set goals may direct attention to important elements of the skill being performed, mobilize effort, prolong persistence or foster the development of new learning strategies (Locke and Latham, 1985). By definition, a motivated person must have a goal. By manipulating and redefining their goals we can increase a client's likelihood of success. We start by setting *SMARTER* goals.

SMARTER GOAL SETTING

- **Specific:** Clearly stated and understood.
- **Measurable:** The goals must be objectively (not subjectively) quantifiable.
- **Action-orientated:** Process and outcome goals.
- **Realistic:** Realistic but challenging.
- **Timed:** Place a time frame on the goal. Use short- and long-term (yearly, outcome) goals.
- **Enjoyable:** Enjoyable, varied and socially rewarding modes of exercise.
- **Rewarded:** Reinforcement of correct behaviour.

Specific

Goals enhance our chances of success by highlighting key elements of performance. To do so effectively, they must be clearly stated and understood by both the instructor and the client (Locke and Latham, 1990; Kyllo and Landers, 1995). Just saying, 'I want to be fitter' or 'I want to look better' is too vague and leaves too much room for interpretation when progress is assessed. We have to clarify what aspect of fitness we want to improve or exactly what the client needs to achieve to feel satisfied that they have met their target.

Measurable

The goal must be objectively, not subjectively, measurable. This means that you should be able to place an exact numerical measure on the goal. A subjective goal means that improvement is open to opinion and interpretation. For example, if the goal is to improve body shape then it is demonstrable, however much their weight, or fitness has altered, that their body shape has improved. This leaves the amount of progress open for discussion. A specific goal would be to increase aerobic fitness; a specific and measurable goal would be improve the time they can run 5 km by 30 seconds. If a goal is not measurable progress cannot be assessed and objective feedback cannot be given to the client.

Action-orientated

There are two types of goals: *outcome goals* that describe the end result (e.g. to lose 12 kg in weight or to come first in a specific race) and *process goals* that describe what actions must be taken to ensure progress towards the outcome goal (e.g. exercising three times per week and cutting down on fats in the diet, or three track-running sessions per week). Both types of goals are important. Outcome goals provide motivation and process goals provide the strategy by which results will be achieved. Your skills as a trainer will determine how successful your process goals will be at achieving the outcome goals in the context of the ability, time and commitment levels of the client.

Realistic

The difficulty of the goals you set greatly determines their effectiveness. The harder the goal is without seeming unrealistic, the greater impact it will have on performance (Kyllo and Landers, 1995). If goals are perceived to be overly difficult or improbable then the client is unlikely to commit to them and the goal will fail to be motivating. Failure to achieve goals can be demotivating. Failure can erode a person's self-confidence and when goals are perceived as being overly challenging, people, especially those with lower self-confidence, tend to lower their levels of effort in order to cope mentally with any failures they experience (Kyllo and Landers, 1995). On the other hand, unchallenging goals will fail to motivate and will only cause a reduction in effort. In my experience, goals that are perceived by the client as 'challenging but realistic' are the most effective.

Timed

Placing a realistic time frame on the goal is an extremely important step. Without a completion date a goal will fail to mobilize effort. Teachers will be familiar with the use of deadlines: most schoolchildren only start writing an essay the week before the date it is due in.

It is also important to set more than one timed goal with varying *goal proximity*. Clients will often come to you with a target that is a long way off. For example, they may want to lose 12 kg in weight, run a marathon next year or fit into an outfit that is presently a couple of sizes too large for them. These *long-term goals* can often seem overwhelming and therefore demotivating. Because they are so distant there is no urgency, which means they can be put to one side and forgotten, while the person focuses on more urgent issues such as finishing a project at work, shopping or any number of day-to-day tasks.

Long-term goals have to be broken down into bite-size pieces that appear more realistic and manageable. These smaller targets should then be allocated reasonable completion dates to create urgency and the need for action. These are called *short-term goals*. Short-term goals have a time frame of weeks or months rather than years and must be process-orientated as well as outcome-orientated. Short-term targets will keep our clients on-task, will keep them focused on important elements of their training and will make the realization of long-term goals more manageable (Hall and Kerr, 2001).

Successful completion of short-term goals will increase confidence and provide a source of satisfaction that will make their efforts appear worthwhile. Assessment of progress alongside short-term targets will provide valuable feedback regarding a client's progress. The use of short-term goals in conjunction with long-term has been scientifically shown to lead to a better performance than long-term goals alone (Locke and Latham, 1985; Tenenbaum *et al.*, 1991).

Enjoyable

Without reward for doing something we will generally stop it very quickly. Reward can be *intrinsic*, we enjoy it for itself, or *extrinsic*, we gain something else for doing it. Socializing with friends is intrinsically rewarding: we do it because we enjoy it. We go to work not necessarily because we enjoy it but because we need to earn money – this is an extrinsic reward. Training is generally extrinsically rewarding: we do it because of the rewards we will receive, whether those are weight loss, muscle tone or increased fitness. This is why programme design is so important. If a client is working hard and fails to see the results, motivation can soon fade.

If we increase the intrinsic reward of exercise we will increase the likelihood of our clients adhering when the results are not coming. We do this by making the exercise as enjoyable as possible – introducing exercise classes, encouraging participation in sports or exercise outside if the client prefers. In my own personal training sessions I vary aerobic exercise by using 'box-ercise' techniques, ball games and runs outdoors. We should encourage our clients to introduce a social element to their exercise – going to the gym with friends, making friends in exercise classes, encouraging the support of spouse or partner and finding a training partner. This will increase the intrinsic value of exercise and help keep our client motivated.

Rewarded

Rewarding exercise will help encourage and motivate our clients. Reward works through the process of *reinforcement*. Reinforcement is a concept often used in behavioural psychology. Every day we experience negative and positive reinforcement. If we receive something pleasurable for our actions then we will likely repeat that same action in the future (reinforcement). Likewise if we lose something pleasurable (negative reinforcement) or experience something unpleasant following an action (punishment), the likelihood of us doing it again will reduce. This is why adhering to exercise can be an extremely difficult motivational challenge because it is often painful (punishment) and stops us from enjoying other pastimes (negative reinforcement), and the benefits of shape change, weight loss and increased fitness (positive reinforcement) are not guaranteed and may only come after weeks of hard work.

We can increase the extrinsic reward of exercise by giving ourselves gifts if we successfully achieve our goals. Remember that praise and encouragement for good performance can act as a powerful reward, especially if the praise comes from a significant other such as a friend, partner or respected fitness professional (i.e. you!).

OTHER TIPS IN GOAL SETTING

In addition to being SMARTER, goals should also adhere to the following guidelines.

Written

By writing the goals down you make them clearer for both you and your client. Ask your clients to write down their progress towards a goal and write this progress down in an exercise diary, for example. This form of *self-monitoring* is valuable feedback. Ask a client about what exercise they perceive they are doing and it may be very different to what they are in reality doing. Ask a person to say what they think they eat then compare that with what they actually consume after they have completed a food diary and the two things can be completely different. Very often a client is shocked when they see what they actually eat, not realizing that the odd glass of wine or chocolate biscuit is actually a much more regular occurrence than they think. For this reason an exercise or food diary will provide a valuable source of feedback and will also act as a reminder to exercise.

Without self-monitoring we cannot assess what is going wrong in a programme that you set. We cannot determine whether it is your programme that is at fault or that the client is just not doing what you ask.

Agreed

The client's goal-commitment is an extremely important factor in determining their success. Unless they are fully committed to their goals, they are likely to give up as soon as obstacles are placed in their way. With a decline in commitment there is a corresponding decline in performance (Erez and Zidon, 1984). To make sure that your client is committed to their goals, make sure that you arrive upon the goals together and that the client agrees the goals are realistic, and have them sign a written contract saying they agree to commit to them (Hall and Kerr, 2001).

Reviewed

There will always be obstacles that crop up that change the difficulty of a goal. Injury, increased work commitments, holidays taken on short notice, for example, can all make the original targets unrealistic. Continuing to pursue the goal in the face of such obstacles will inevitably result in failure, which is demoralizing and can reduce the motivation of your client.

Goals that are overly challenging can actually create stress. The pressure of work deadlines, children to look after and other daily challenges can create negative pressure. If this is combined with an inability to cope it may start to affect an individual's health. An overly challenging gym programme can become an additional stressor. For this reason allow clients to review their goals regularly and make reasonable adjustments if need be in order to keep targets realistic. This process will allow them to cope better with the disappointment of failing to reach targets for reasons not under their control, and stop the gym being a negative, stressful part of their life.

Feedback

Feedback is essential is goal setting is to be effective (Locke and Latham, 1985; Weinberg and Gould, 1999). Imagine you are running a race and have a goal to finish in under a certain time. This would, under normal circumstances, be an effective goal, but if when you run the race you do not have a watch and are not provided with information about your times, then you have no way to gauge your performance. If you knew you were behind the pace you could put more effort in; likewise if you are ahead of time, you would know to conserve energy and not burn yourself out. Without feedback this process is not possible and performance suffers as a result.

Review your client's progress and provide feedback on a regular basis. The end of each session is an excellent time to review their performance in that workout and assess their progress towards their next short-term outcome goal.

Negative feedback has to be given at times and this has to be presented in a way that will not reduce the motivation or self-esteem of your client. Always ensure that negative feedback is sandwiched between positive feedback and that you also provide guidelines for your client to

respond positively to negative feedback, so that they feel they can get back on track.

PROVIDING FEEDBACK

When providing feedback the order is important:

1. positive feedback
2. negative feedback
3. solution
4. further goal setting
5. positive feedback

For example: 'Your treadmill run was good today, Sue. We still need to cut out those late-night snacks and I want you to work hard at that for next week, but the exercise in the gym is going really well.'

Controllable

Avoiding social comparison is a strategy I employ when setting goals and providing feedback. Often clients will ask questions such as, 'Am I fit for my age?' or 'What times *should* I be running?' or 'Am I the correct weight for my height?' and so on. They are asking you to compare them to other people and make conclusions about their ability or condition. Clients entering into competition with other individuals in this way lose the element of control over their performance; clearly they cannot control how well the other individual performs or improves.

If your client's progress falls below that of other individuals, they may feel dissatisfied with their own improvements, good though they may be. ***Controllability*** of goals is extremely important; emphasize goals in which greater effort will almost certainly lead them to experience rewards in terms of success. Always focus on their previous experience, placing emphasis on them achieving ***personal bests*** when and where you feel it is realistic. This will ensure that their targets are always self-referenced and that they will always be ***realistic but challenging***. For some, social comparison may not be avoidable: those looking to win a race, for example. For these athletes select a speed or time likely to be sufficient to win the race or a time challenging but realistic for the athlete and emphasize movement towards this benchmark rather than focusing on what times the other athletes are performing.

REMOVING BARRIERS

Whilst a person may be motivated there may be factors acting against them that hinder their progress. If these barriers are too great the person is likely to fail. The more barriers we can remove or overcome, the more likely the person will be to succeed.

Factors to be considered by a trainer include initial fitness levels, current exercise and dietary habits, injuries, availability and ease of access of facilities, financial limitations and other demands on a client's time such as children and work. After making a client aware of the barriers that are relevant to them we must then provide them with strategies to overcome them. The trainer must account for these *practical restrictions* when they design a programme, as they may undermine the client's efforts. Providing alternative modes of exercise, recommending the client pre-plans babysitting and diarizes times for exercise are example strategies for dealing with these practical restrictions, but each person's barriers and therefore each solution will be different. Ask the client from the outset what has stopped them achieving results in the past. Find ways around these factors.

Along with practical restrictions there may be many *perceived barriers* that the client sees as hindering their efforts. A perceived barrier is one in which there is no physical barrier to them achieving their goal. Time, energy and motivation are three perceived barriers that are most commonly used to explain failure to adhere to exercise. In these instances their time, energy and motivation are obviously being invested in other activities, perhaps work or socializing with friends, for example. For this individual there is a simple

choice: 'What do you want most – to socialize with friends or to reach the goals we have discussed above?' Reaffirming the reason they started exercise, their primary motivation, is important in these cases.

Strategies that may help this process when you are not there include *exercise reminders*, *decision balance sheets* (writing lists of benefits for each action) and *goal setting*. But the client has to realize that unless they prioritize the exercise they will not achieve their goals.

Very often the client will claim they had no control over the factors that stopped them sticking to their targets for the week. A lack of time is the classic excuse. Asking the question *why* is often useful in making people realize that they have control over their own behaviour. For example;

Client: 'I didn't train last week. I didn't have enough time.'
Trainer: 'Why do you not have enough time?'
Client: 'Work got in the way.'
Trainer: 'Why did work get in the way?'
Client: 'I had to work late.'
Trainer: 'Every night?'
Client: 'No.'
Trainer: 'Was there no time to get training in?'
Client: 'There was if I trained first thing or maybe came in at the weekend.'
Trainer: 'Is this something we could do next time you are working late?'
Client: 'Possibly.'
Trainer: 'How about we say if you miss a session in the week you have to come in at the weekend?'
Trainer: 'I would rather come in first thing.'
Trainer: 'That sounds great.'

This is just one example, but there may be a variety of solutions your client will come up with if you ask the right questions. There are many hours in the week that can be used for exercise, especially if we make exercise our priority.

BUILDING CONFIDENCE

When dealing with beginners to the gym or those who have been unsuccessful in sticking to an exercise programme in the past, we have to consider any possible negative associations to exercise they may have. They may feel they are unable to use the gym equipment, unable to stick to a programme or, alternatively, if they do stick to a programme they may feel it is not likely to bring them results. These negative associations in themselves create a barrier to exercise and may undermine a client's success.

In some cases there may be underlying psychological factors such as low self-esteem, low self-confidence, body-image issues, and many other psychological associations tied in with their eating and activity patterns that should be addressed by another professional (psychologist, counsellor etc.). Whilst we cannot act as counsellors or psychologists, simply building the confidence of these clients can have dramatic benefits.

Self-confidence is the term we use to refer to the poise and assurance with which an individual generally approaches any given situation. The confidence with respect to a specific task is known as their *self-efficacy*. If a person is confident in using the gym, their self-efficacy for using the gym is high.

---

self-efficacy: Task-specific self-confidence.

Self-efficacy greatly affects the way a person will approach a specific situation. It will determine the degree by which an individual will engage or avoid an activity.

Highly efficacious individuals approach more challenging tasks, expend greater efforts in the task, and persist longer in the face of aversive stimuli (McAuley and Mihalko, 1985).

In other words, the greater the person's belief that they can do something, the more effort they will put in and the longer they will keep trying. Self-efficacy has a huge effect on motivation. If you want to help motivate your client use the gym, increase their confidence.

Bandura (1977) identified four major sources of self-efficacy: (1) *mastery accomplishments*, the success or failure at a task in the past, (2) *vicarious experience*, watching the success of others performing a task, (3) *verbal persuasion*, being told you can perform the task, and (4) the correct *interpretation of physiological status*, in which sensations of increased heart rate, sweating and nerves are interpreted positively (a 'rush' from exercise) rather than negatively (nerves). A personal trainer can use this information to enhance the self-efficacy of a client using the gym. This can be achieved by accurately demonstrating an exercise (increasing vicarious experience), letting the client try the exercise for him- or herself on a relatively easy weight (increasing performance accomplishment), whilst verbally encouraging and providing feedback (verbal encouragement) and explaining symptoms of exertion such as sweating and increased heart rate.

Mastery accomplishment is the most powerful source of self-efficacy. A classic example is the person who goes parachuting for the first time and finds that, although they were initially petrified by the thought of jumping out of a plane, they cannot wait to do it again after they have had their initial jump. I apply the principle of *small successes* when training my clients, to increase mastery accomplishment.

Small successes

I allow clients to start their exercise programme using weights and exercises that they feel are only moderately challenging. The proviso for this is that they make small improvements or personal bests with every session. With each 'PB' the client is reassured that they are improving, they revel in the congratulations and praise you provide as their trainer, and they strive for the next challenge. With every new success self-efficacy increases. Whilst initial intensity may be low, if the client continues to increase the challenge with each success, they will soon have to push themselves to achieve their next PB.

I often use *preferred rate of exertion* when setting cardiovascular goals with new deconditioned clients. This means that the client can set their own intensity levels (speed or resistance) but they have to go a little bit faster or do a little bit longer each time they come in. Preferred rate of exertion is associated with higher levels of adherence; it provides many opportunities for small successes that increase efficacy and give the client a sense of control. They are allowed to start in a comfort zone but are then progressively pushed harder and harder and further out of that comfort zone. These small successes should be highlighted and praised at every opportunity, as they will get fewer and fewer as the client progresses.

Modelling

Asking a client to make dramatic changes overnight in the way they live, eat and exercise can be overwhelming and is unlikely to be successful in the long term. A better strategy is to mould your client's lifestyle in a gradual, step-by-step process. The changes you make should have minimal impact on the client's lifestyle whilst still achieving their goals. This step-by-step process is known as *modelling*. Modelling increases the client's likelihood of success and makes the changes in their life easier to maintain.

A good guideline is to set only two or three new realistic but challenging goals each week.

ACHIEVING RESULTS

Achieving results is always the cornerstone of exercise adherence because it is the strongest extrinsic reward for the client. Without an effective programme of diet and exercise the client will not achieve the results that they invested so much time and effort to get. No matter how motivated an individual is, without any reward for their effort, they will eventually drop out.

HELPING COPE

There will be times when the client is unsuccessful. Whether it is their own fault or because of an external factor such as injury or illness, there will be times when their performance plateaus or their shape stays the same. These failures can be highly demotivating. When motivation falls, perceived barriers increase and the danger is that the client drops out of exercise. This is what happens for around 50 per cent of people within the first six months of starting an exercise routine (Dishman, 1982, 1994). Part of your job as personal trainer is to make sure this does not happen; your client must be taught how to deal with these failures and lack of reward.

RELAPSE PREVENTION STRATEGIES

- Emphasize a return to routine as quickly as possible.
- Don't overcompensate or make up for a break with harder work. This may lead to **over-training** and **burnout**.
- Provide flexible goals that allow for lapses.
- Provide positive thought processes that will help a client; for example:
  - 'Missing one week doesn't set us far back.'
  - 'If you put 2 kg on during your holiday it will only take three weeks to get that back off.'
  - 'Appreciate that the body needs a break at times and that you get stronger when you rest, not when you train.'
- Provide alternative goals to work on if a client is unable to train for a period of time. Successes in these tasks will maintain motivation and provide a sense of control.
  - Focus on diet if they are unable to exercise.
  - Provide a home programme if they are unable to attend the gym.
- Contact your client by phone and provide encouragement.

Managing expectations may be the first step in this process. Making the client understand that progress is never linear and that there will always be undulations with periods of plateau is important in helping them deal with such stagnant periods. Highlighting alternative areas of success may also help them remain positive. If your client does have a break in training, ***relapse prevention strategies*** can be used. These are just strategies to minimize the frequency and impact of relapse.

There will be times of high risk when a client is less likely to follow your exercise or dietary programmes. If you arm them with the relapse-prevention strategies and positive thought processes, these interruptions will be less likely to cause significant gaps in their training.

PROVIDING TOOLS

As well as the strategies already discussed (goal setting, self-monitoring etc.) these are the other tools that have worked well with my clients.

Stimulus control

Our environment can affect our behaviour. For example, have you ever looked in the fridge, seen a cold beer or a bottle of wine and suddenly felt like a drink – even though the thought was never in your mind before? Alternatively, have you ever walked past a bakery or restaurant, smelt the food being made and and suddenly started feeling peckish? Stimulus control is the manipulation of an individual's surroundings to ensure that environmental cues encourage the behaviour that you want. Some simple tips you can use with your clients are as follows.

Positive cues for exercise and good diet:

- make sure your training kit is always in the car
- put exercise reminders in your diary
- always keep healthy foods at the front of cupboards or fridge
- put stickers in the car or at workstation as reminders about good posture and correct sitting position

- have a shopping list to ensure you purchase healthy foods
- stick to that list and don't add sugary or fatty snacks to the trolley
- always do a weekly shop to ensure healthy food is available.

Negative cues for exercise and good diet:

- turn your mobile phone off so work can't get in the way
- organize a crèche for children in advance
- don't buy inappropriate foods or bottles of wine at the start of the week.

Although these small tricks may seem inconsequential, they will go a long way to helping your client stick to their plan.

Positive self-talk

Inner dialogue (the things you say to yourself as you exercise) influences performance. If you are continually saying to yourself that you are not able to achieve a task, whatever it may be, you are continually wearing down your own self-confidence and reducing your chances of success. Often these negative thoughts have little real backing or proof. Saying things like, 'I don't have time to exercise' or 'I could never run for 5 km without stopping' are negative thoughts that have no truth in them and only serve to undermine and sabotage our efforts. When we use the words 'never', 'always' and 'can't', there is rarely evidence to back them. They can be described as irrational and maladaptive thoughts because they reduce our ability to cope with situations.

Positive self-talk can be used to restructure these thoughts and reduce maladaptive, irrational and unhelpful thoughts. Self-talk should be positive and rational in nature and should include self-reward in order to increase effort.

Changing self-talk can:

- emphasize more positive feelings about performing exercise
- reduce tension about failure to lose weight
- reduce tension and inner conflict when exercise goals are not met

■ reinforce realistic goals (1 kg is enough weight to lose in a week).

As a trainer you should identify negative self-talk and maladaptive statements. You can then either confront your clients, asking them to identify the rationality in their own statements, or you can offer alternative statements that may be more positive. A process of education about exercise and diet is key in this process.

CHAPTER SUMMARY

The use of basic psychological tools to underpin adherence and help clients to maintain motivation is vital in helping them to achieve long-lasting results. Hopefully we are not only there for the quick fix, we are attempting to make meaningful changes to our client's lifestyle. This chapter has hopefully equipped you with the tools to enhance a client's motivation, set them effective goals and provide them with a range of ideas designed to maximize their chances of success.

REFERENCES AND RECOMMENDED READING

1. Bandura, A. (1977) Self-efficacy: Toward a unifying theory of behavioural change. *Psychological Review* 84:191–125.
2. Cox, R.H. (2001) *Sport Psychology: Concepts and Applications*, 3rd edn. Madison, WI: Brown and Benchmark.
3. Dishman, R.K. (1982) Health psychology and exercise adherence. *Quest* 33:166–180.
4. Dishman, R.K. (1994) *Advances in Exercise Adherence*. Champaign, IL: Human Kinetics.
5. Erez, M. and Zidon, I. (1984) Effect of goal acceptance on the relationship of goal difficulty to task performance. *Journal of Applied Psychology* 69:69–78.
6. Hall, K. and Kerr, A.W. (2001) Goal-setting in sport and physical activity: Tracing empirical developments and establishing conceptual direction. In: Roberts, G.C. (ed) *Advances in Motivation in Sport and Exercise*. Champaign, IL: Human Kinetics.
7. Kyllo, B.L. and Landers, D.M. (1995) Goal setting in sport and exercise: A research synthesis to resolve the controversy. *Journal of Sports and Exercise Psychology* 17:117–137.
8. Locke, E.A. and Latham, G.P. (1990) *A Theory of Goal Setting and Task Performance*. Englewood Cliffs, NJ: Prentice Hall.
9. Locke, E.A. and Latham, G.P. (1985) The application of goal setting to sports. *Journal of Sport Psychology* 7:205–222.
10. McAuley, E. and Mihalko, S.L. (1998) Measuring exercise related self-efficacy. In: Duda, J.L. (ed) *Advances in Sport and Exercise Psychology Measurement*. Morgantown, WV: Fitness Information Technology.
11. Roberts, G.C. (1992) *Motivation in Sports and Exercise*. Champaign, IL: Human Kinetics.
12. Roberts, G.C. (2001) *Advances in Motivation in Sports and Exercise*. Champaign, IL: Human Kinetics.
13. Tenenbaum, G., Pinchas, S., Elbaz, G., Bar-Eli, M. and Weinburg, R.S. (1991) Effect of goal proximity and goal specificity on muscular endurance performance. *Journal of Sport and Exercise Psychology* 13:174–187.
14. Weinberg, R.S. and Gould, D. (1999) *Foundations of Sport and Exercise Psychology*, 2nd edn. Champaign, IL: Human Kinetics.

SALES AND MARKETING

THIS CHAPTER CONTAINS

- Business plan
- Professionalism (medical model)
- The sales chain
- Marketing and lead generation
- From lead enquiry to consultation

- Networking and effective communication
- From consultation to sale
- Useful tips
- Benefits of exercise
- References and recommended reading

It does not matter how good your knowledge of exercise is or how good your sessions are, without clients your career as a personal trainer will be short-lived. It would be nice if there were an abundance of people who just approached us in the gym that had seen a poster or advert and automatically knew they wanted personal training. Unfortunately it simply does not work this way. Whether we find ourselves working freelance, visiting people's homes or working as an employee of a large private health club, we need to understand how to find clients. If we want to be successful we have to understand about sales and marketing.

BUSINESS PLAN

Whether you are a new personal trainer starting your own business or an established trainer looking to expand into new areas it is vital to start with a business plan. A business plan helps us build a strategy for building our business. We have

---

STRUCTURE OF A BUSINESS PLAN

Mission statement

- Make a long-term goal that incorporates a vision of what you want to achieve and where you want to be.
- It may be, 'To be the most successful personal trainer in the UK', or 'Trainer to the stars', or simply to earn a good living.
- The vision will dictate how you market your business.

Statement of intent

- Broadly speaking, how will you achieve these goals?

Product

- What is your title (personal training, personal coaching, strength and conditioning coach, life coach etc.)?
- What skills and qualifications do you offer?
- What do your sessions involve?
- How long is each session?
- How much does each session cost?
- Will you sell the sessions in blocks?
- Will there be a discount for buying larger blocks?

Unique selling point

- What will make you stand out?
- Why will you better than the rest?

Customers

- Who will be your market?
- How many people can you market to that will be potential clients?
- How many clients do you need?
- Identify and give reasons for whom you will target and why.
- Ask whether this is realistic.

Marketing

- How do you intend to reach these potential clients?
- Provide example scenarios on how you plan to connect with potential clients.
- How will your marketing appeal to the particular clients you are looking for?

to treat our business in the same way as our training. We need short- and long-term goals that describe our desired outcome and also the processes by which we are going to get there.

If you are starting a new business there are numerous factors to consider:

Costs

- What equipment do you need to set up (equipment, weights)?
- What are the costs of marketing (business cards, posters, leaflets etc.)?
- What other costs per client will you incur (petrol, paper, forms etc.)?
- What other costs will you incur (insurance, legal fees etc.)?

Viability

- What do you need to earn based on the cost of living?
- How many sales do you need to make or sessions perform to reach this?
- Is this realistic based on your projections of how many clients you will have?

Branding

- What will your image be?
- How will you brand marketing materials and stationery?
- Does your branding connect with the market that you are aiming at?

This list represents just the tip of the iceberg and it is definitely advisable to seek professional help before embarking on starting your own personal training business. Most banks have small business advisors who offer free advice. Even if you are already operating your own business or if you work as an employee of a large health club, building a business plan is a useful start in planning your steps to success.

PROFESSIONALISM (MEDICAL MODEL)

Professionalism is the foundation upon which we build our business. There are presently no industry requirements for qualifications needed to be a personal trainer and for this reason we need to move beyond the traditional image of a muscle-bound meathead who shouts and harangues their clients to work harder and lift more weight. We need to move towards an image of knowledge and professionalism. When we say the word 'professional' we think of doctors, dentists, lawyers or teachers. We need to have the same attitude to our profession as these people do to theirs. We need to be working with the same professional standards and ethics as a physiotherapist or sports therapist.

SUMMARY OF PROFESSIONAL STANDARDS

Qualifications

- Every trainer needs to be qualified with a universally recognized organization.
- The trainer should never misrepresent his or her skills, qualifications or experience.

Registration

- The trainer needs to be affiliated with an industry-recognized organization, such as the Register of Exercise Professionals (REPs).

Insurance

- The trainer must be insured to work with the general public.

Appearance

- The trainer should always appear professionally presented to clients or potential clients (e.g. dressed in some sort of appropriate uniform, jewellery kept to a minimum, clean).

Time keeping

- The trainer should always be on time for sessions, and ready to greet their client at a pre-agreed time.

Paperwork

- All clients should have completed a Physical Activity Readiness Questionnaire and received written clearance from a medical professional if any medical conditions are flagged.
- The trainer should keep records of all financial transactions.
- Session content, progressions should be logged and recorded in case an accident does occur and the trainer is held accountable for his or her actions in a court of law.

Ethics

- The trainer must be honest to the client about the likely benefits he or she will experience.
- The trainer must provide safe and effective exercise sessions, not just sessions designed purely to make the client keep coming back.

PHYSICAL ACTIVITY READINESS QUESTIONNAIRE (PAR-Q)

Anyone starting an exercise routine with you or in a gym must complete a PAR-Q. These are the questions included on the PAR-Q.

If you are planning to become more active and are between 15 and 69, answer the questions below with a yes or no response:

1. *Has your doctor ever said that you have a heart condition and that you should only do physical activity recommended by the doctor?*
2. *Do you feel pain in your chest when you do physical activity?*
3. *In the past month, have you had chest pain when you were doing physical activity?*
4. *Do you lose your balance because of dizziness or do you ever lose consciousness?*

5. *Do you have a bone or joint problem that could be made worse by a change in your physical activity?*
6. *Is your doctor currently prescribing drugs (for example, water pills) for your blood pressure or heart condition?*
7. *Do you know of any other reason why you should not do physical activity?*

An answer yes to any of these questions would require your client to seek written medical clearance before starting an exercise routine. Your client should complete a questionnaire such as this and you should check their blood pressure prior to them starting an exercise routine with you. An example PAR-Q can be found in the ACSM Guidelines for Exercise Testing and Prescription (American College of Sports Medicine, 2000).

If you are unsure whether a type of conduct is acceptable, use the medical model. You would look a little strangely at a doctor or physiotherapist if they were chewing gum, slouching on their table or couch, wearing their shirt untucked or chatting to someone else in the middle of an assessment. Expect the same standards from yourself as these medical professionals do.

THE SALES CHAIN

Finding clients is essential if you are to be a successful personal trainer. It is no good having mountains of knowledge if you cannot find clients to apply it to. There is a definite chain of events that has to occur for you to sign up a new client for a block of sessions. This process, from marketing to enquiry/lead to consultation to sale, I call the *sales chain*.

Step 1. Marketing and lead generation

The first step is called lead generation. A *lead* is someone who has expressed an interest in purchasing personal training from you. The first step in lead generation is *marketing*. You have to advertise your skills as a personal trainer to as many people who might be interested as possible. This will increase their awareness of your skills and the services that you offer.

Step 2. From lead enquiry to consultation

After you have successfully marketed yourself this should generate a number of leads that are potentially interested in personal training. You have to talk to these people and convince them that a trainer is a wise investment of their money. I always found it effective to arrange a time to sit down, free of charge, and have a talk with a prospective client. The idea is to get to know them better and to explain better the benefits of personal training. I call this a consultation.

Step 3. From consultation to sale

During the consultation you can discuss the goals and aspirations of the potential client and determine whether personal training is a viable option for them. If the person is convinced that they want a trainer, then you need to close the sale. I recommend selling personal training in blocks of at least three sessions to allow you time to achieve some sort of result with your clients. If you have a contract, this can be completed at this point, along with any other relevant paperwork (health questionnaires, personal details etc.). Payment can then be taken for a block of sessions and you can book in their first official session.

At each link of the chain there is the potential to gain or lose leads. If your marketing is not good you will fail to generate leads. If you do not have the relevant skills to convince them to have a consultation it is unlikely you will make any sale. It is a good idea to keep a record of the number of leads you generate, how many leads sit with you for a consultation and how many consultations you convert to sales. This will provide you with a better understanding of what stages of the sales chain you are performing well and at which stages you are losing prospective clients. The weak areas can then become a focus point in which you need to gain training of some description. For independent trainers the best advice would be to ask other successful personal trainers how they communicate with their clients and how they have been successful.

The following sections break down and analyse each stage of the sales chain, giving you advice and tips on how to be successful.

MARKETING AND LEAD GENERATION

Without effective marketing we cannot expect to generate enough leads to be successful. The types of marketing you use will be dictated by your individual situation and environment but I have listed below many of the most common methods.

- *Posters and flyers:* Advertising using a branded format giving information about your skills is a good starting point. These can be put into gyms or handed out in flyer drops door-to-door.
- *Internet site:* With the World Wide Web becoming so popular the Internet should be a useful port of call. Design a website advertising your skills or commission a professional website designer to set one up.
- *Business cards:* After talking with someone a business card is a useful way of leaving them with your contact details, along with some branded information about the services you provide.
- *Information leaflets:* It is useful to provide information leaflets about various health and exercise topics, with your contact details available for further help.
- *Seminars:* You may find it profitable to provide free seminars that people can attend on health and fitness topics in which you specialize.
- *Sample sessions:* Free taster sessions will give

people a chance to experience your workouts before they book up your services.
- *Workshops:* You might like to run stretching, core or Swiss ball workshops so that people can experience what you do in groups.
- *Exercise classes:* Group exercise classes, such as circuits or aerobics, will expose you to large numbers of prospective clients.
- *Question and answer evenings:* Advertising Q and A sessions in gyms will give people a chance to come and talk to you about their training or what you do.
- *Word of mouth:* One of the most effective forms of advertising is from other people talking about you. If you get results for your clients and conduct yourself in a professional manner your clients and work associates will pass on good feedback to those around them.

This is certainly not an exhaustive list. Depending on whether you are working in people's homes or working out of a gym, there will be numerous ways of advertising to prospective clients. The key is to have a definite strategy and to follow your strategy through.

Networking

Networking is probably the most important form of marketing. Talking to people about what you do and what results you can achieve is your most powerful form of advertising. If you work in a gym environment the best thing you can do is simply offer people help and make them aware of who you are and what you do. Talk to other members of staff and even offer them free sessions. Talk to local physiotherapists, chiropractors, gym instructors – in fact, anyone who has contact with your market.

FROM LEAD ENQUIRY TO CONSULTATION

Have a clear strategy by which people can contact you for further information. This may be a telephone number, an interest sheet left at a gym reception, email address or a tear-off slip that people can fill in to leave you their details. It is essential for people to be able to contact you easily. Ideally you should be available to talk immediately. Remember that although a person may be interested one day their motivation may very quickly go as other things become a priority. This is why if you are just starting out in a gym a lot of your time may be spent simply interacting with people and networking. This may seem like a lot of work for no pay but it is essential if you want to build your business.

As soon as you talk to someone about personal training your key aim at this point should be to book a consultation. Whether it is over the phone or in person I recommend sitting down face-to-face before you talk over the details of personal training. If they have time you should do a consultation straight away while the thought of having a trainer is fresh in their minds. If they have not got the time or you are talking over the phone make it your only goal to book a consultation session. This will allow you to talk in more depth about the individual's motivation and will make it far easier to build rapport with that person.

When people approach you about training, their first question is usually, 'How much is it going to cost?' This is natural, but you should avoid answering it until later in the conversation. The idea of paying £300 for a block of ten £30 sessions can be very daunting if the person does not yet know what they will get for their money. To get past the issue of money until you know more about your potential client you can say something like: 'There are various different packages I offer but the best idea is to sit down and talk a bit more about exactly what it is you are looking for. Have you got time to do that now or should we book something for later in the week?'

You do not even have to call it a consultation. But once you sit down you will have more time to talk and find out about their motivation.

NETWORKING AND EFFECTIVE COMMUNICATION

The most effective form of lead generation is through networking, talking to people about the service you provide. These communications come in a variety of forms: you may be helping people with their exercise programme in the gym, giving them advice about diet, or telling them what you do as you hand out flyers door-to-door. The advantage of lead generation through networking is that you can arrange an appointment for a consultation if they are interested in buying sessions there and then, or even do the consultation straight away. This sounds simple but the communication skills involved are highly complex. You may be a natural sales person who has no problem talking to people or in bringing up the option of buying personal training. Most people, however, find it much harder to approach people and sell their skills.

First impressions

Your first impression is vital as it will form the basis of how your potential client will perceive you. You have only 2–5 seconds to create a great first impression. The basic keys are:

- smile
- be well groomed with appropriate dress and jewellery (see medical model, above)
- keep good eye contact maintained 80 per cent of the time
- smell good (do not overdo overpowering aftershaves or perfumes)
- introduce yourself by name on first meeting
- use the person's name if you know it or ask them their name for future reference
- shake hands firmly but not too firmly.

Build rapport

Rapport is the level of connection you have with an individual. To connect with someone you have to demonstrate that you understand where that

person is coming from, their interests and their motivation. This is extremely important in selling personal training. We have to establish common ground and common interests. Ask **open-ended questions** to gather information about a person. An open-ended question allows a person to expand on the information they are giving and does not naturally lead to a yes/no answer. Find out what issues are important to them; their children, training, sports are good examples.

Build commonality by finding and talking about common areas of interest. Show empathy with the way the person feels in certain situations that you have both experienced. The more time spent doing this the more rapport you will build and the more likely your client will listen to you if you choose to offer advice. It is interesting that people tend to seek advice from those people with whom they have good rapport rather than those who are technically the most qualified. The same can be said for selling. A person will buy from someone they trust and with whom they feel good rapport.

Another useful tip is to **paraphrase** if you want to demonstrate understanding. Paraphrasing is simply confirming what a person has said but using your own words.

If you want to confirm decisions the person has made, use **closed questions**; these are questions that naturally lead to a yes or no answer. Remember to use a person's name: it is their favourite word. Most importantly, listen. This is the only way to find out what is important to them.

Remember the saying, 'It is better to use two ears and one mouth.' In other words, listen more than you speak. The best sales people listen more than they talk. These tips can be used in any number of situations. It is harder when we want to lead the person towards talking about personal training in order to generate a lead.

Leading into personal training

How do we raise the topic of personal training? Whilst we are talking and chatting to people and building rapport we might casually ask them about their training and how it is going. We might ask

key questions such as, 'How is your training going?', 'What is it you want to achieve?', 'Why do you want to achieve this?' During this conversation you can look out for what I call **flag phrases**. These are phrases that naturally lead you to talk about how you can help this person. They may include:

- 'I'm not getting the results that I want.'
- 'I need help with a new programme.'
- 'I'm working hard but getting nowhere.'
- 'I haven't got the time to train.'
- 'I'm lacking motivation.'
- 'I'm looking for that little bit extra out of my training.'
- 'Training is ok but I keep straining my back.'

When you hear a flag phrase, take the opportunity to probe to understand more about what it is the potential client wants and what is stopping them getting there. Paraphrase and continue to build rapport by empathizing with them. Ask if there are any ways you may potentially help them. If you can help you may offer some potential solutions; one of these may be some personal training. At this point I may offer my time to sit down and help them overcome the difficulties they are having and if they are interested they might want to talk about personal training. If they have expressed interest in personal training I may even call the session a consultation in which the main aim is to determine whether personal training is for them.

FROM CONSULTATION TO SALE

Selling is an art as much as a science. Although people working in the fitness industry are often good communicators, they are often not the most natural sales people. This is why it is essential to have a tried and tested format to stick to that helps you through the sales process. In Figure 17.1 I have provided an example of a questionnaire that can be used to structure a consultation. Refer to this when reading the following consultation guidelines.

17.1 Exercise consultation

EXERCISE CONSULTATION

NAME: DATE:

What exercise/sports have you participated in previously?

....
....
....

What physical activity/exercise do you currently participate in?

....
....
....

What are your specific fitness goals and why are these goals so important to you?

....
....
....
....
....

What obstacles have prevented you from achieving these goals in the past?

....
....
....
....

How do you feel personal training can help you overcome these obstacles?

....
....
....

How many times per week have you available to exercise (circle one)?

                       1   2   3   4   5

How many times per week would you like to benefit from personal training to achieve your goals?

                       1   2   3   4   5

Which times and days are most suitable for you to train?

....
....

Do you have any illness, injuries or medical conditions that may affect your exercise programme?

....
....

Have you any pending commitments that would affect when you started?

....
....

Do you want to sign up today for personal training?

....

Make a good first impression

We talked above about how important it is to make a good first impression. Start every consultation with a warm handshake and a smile. Introduce yourself, sit the person down somewhere inviting and offer them a drink if you are able. Choose somewhere private and relaxing.

Rapport building

If your consultation session is with someone you do not already know you should spend time building rapport. You may initially ask some light questions such as 'How was your journey?', 'Did you find the place OK?' or 'How has your day been?' Try to strike up a little conversation to help them relax and get used to their environment. Remember that a person might be quite nervous about the situation, especially if they do not use gyms regularly.

Explain the process

The first serious topic is to confirm their reasons for sitting down with you, maybe explaining that the consultation session is a chance for you to get to know each other better. It is a chance to find out about their goals and motivation and a chance to see whether personal training is a viable solution for them.

Understand their motivation

We talked about motivation in Chapter 16. We have to understand what the person is motivated by. What is it they want to achieve? What is the emotion that is driving them to spend money on a personal trainer? People tend to buy because of pleasure or pain – **pleasure** from feeling good about what they will achieve or **pain** caused by how they will feel if their condition stays the same or even gets worse. We have to understand which one it is.

A useful start is often 'What motivated you to talk to me today?' This might be followed by 'What are your goals?' or 'What do you want to achieve?'

The factors motivating someone are often quite personal and they might not be forthcoming initially. In which case you have to probe for more detail.

When you ask a person about their goals they often say, 'I want to lose a bit of weight, tone up and maybe get a little fitter.' Is this the pleasure or pain that is really motivating them to seek you out – no! The key question at this point is 'Why?' Why is it the person wants to lose weight and tone up? Whilst being sensitive to how the person feels, asking the question 'Why' can reveal the real emotional motivation. Is it because they feel overweight and do not like the way they look in clothes (pain)? Is it that they have a wedding to go to and want to look great in the photos (pleasure)?

Always probe for details, asking them to elaborate. Keep it conversational using lots of open-ended questions. If there is more than one goal ask which of them is the most important.

If a person is mostly motivated by pleasure they will probably talk positively about what they want to achieve, how good they will feel and how great it will be. With these people find out what their image of success really looks like. I often ask, 'If you got the results you wanted what would be different?' People often have a mental picture in their heads about how they would look, how they would feel and how their life would be different if they got the results they wanted and achieved their goals. Help the person build that mental image. Ask them to explain to you this mental image. Ask them how important it is for them to feel and look like this.

If the person is mainly motivated by pain they will often talk about how badly they feel at the moment. The may talk about a lack of self-esteem and dissatisfaction with their present condition. Ask these individuals, 'How would you feel in three months if things had not changed or even got worse?' and 'Are you progressing towards your goals at the moment?' This might be a very uncomfortable process for a person, which is why it is so important to have good rapport with them.

By going through this process you can build your potential client's levels of motivation and their desire to do something about their present situation. Paraphrase back to them how they feel and what conclusions they have come to. This is all ammunition for you and reasons why they should invest in your services. At this point it is useful to highlight the results you may expect given a reasonable time frame. For example:

> 'I usually expect a weight loss of between 1 and 2 pounds a week (depending on initial weight and the time the person is willing to commit). This level of weight loss is thought to be safe without being damaging to your health. If over a course of 10 weeks you were to lose 10 pounds would you be satisfied with that?'

Notice that at this stage I will have spent 20–30 minutes talking to the prospective client about things important to them. I have not talked about what personal training is, how it works and how much it costs. Talking about these things at this stage is an easy mistake and one we make to try to fill some of the silences. The best solution is to fill silences with questions.

Tipping the scales

An analogy I often use is of a set of imaginary scales with which the person is weighing up whether they should spend their hard-earned money on personal training. On one side you have all their obstacles, the cost, time, work commitments, whether they will get on with you, whether you have the knowledge to get them results and so on. On the other side of the scales is their motivation to change and achieve their goals. The more we can increase their motivation by making more powerful their sense of pleasure and pain, the more we tip the scales in our favour.

We can also build a picture of what they feel their obstacles are and systematically try to overcome them. Ask, 'What are you doing in the gym at the moment?' This might highlight inadequacies in their training and barriers they are not even aware of. Ask, 'What is stopping you achieving these goals at the moment?' This will provide you with an insight into why this person feels they have been unsuccessful in the past.

Imagine if you could immediately provide the answer to all these barriers: how valuable would that be?

I might start to build a picture of how personal training can be an answer to their problems. For example, if time is an obstacle, 'Personal training can optimize your time by making sure each workout is as effective as it can be in the time that you have. We can also provide you with ways of making sure exercise fits into your lifestyle.'

Closing the sale

At some stage you will hopefully understand your potential client's motivation. On the consultation sheet provided, the next question asks how the person sees personal training helping them overcome their obstacles. You can now let the person convince himself or herself that personal training is the answer. You might ask how many times the person is available to exercise, then ask how many times a week they would like personal training. This automatically prompts the person to choose at least once per week. I usually explain that this is the minimum number of sessions I book for a client each week. Anecdotally, I feel this achieves the best results, with less than once per week making the effect of personal training far less beneficial. I explain that if the client's motivation is not good, I often recommend more than once per week.

Having established the frequency, you can then negotiate a time that works for both of you and find out about any injuries or medical conditions that might affect your potential client's training. Only at this point do I ask if personal training is going to work for them and whether they would like to book some sessions. If they say yes, I ask them to complete any paperwork, such as contracts and health questionnaires, take payment for the sessions and only then book in the first session.

Upon signing a contract, if you have one, it is important to make clear any guidelines or rules of the sessions. For example, do you have a 24-hour cancellation policy (i.e. if they cancel less than 24 hours in advance they lose that session). Explain how long each session lasts, explain if they

are late and you have another client straight after that you cannot extend their session. Explain how you keep track of how many sessions they have had if they are making payment up front and so on.

USEFUL TIPS

Money

Do not talk about money until you have made perfectly clear what you are offering and what you can achieve for your client. In general, if you have built up their sense of pleasure or pain and convinced them that you can achieve their goals in a reasonable time frame, money is not normally an obstacle. People will pay a lot of money if they think we can help them to achieve their goals. I once asked how much a client would pay if I guaranteed him a six-pack in ten weeks. He said he would pay £3000. Although I could not guarantee the six-pack at the start of the training we achieved good results over a 10-week period for just a tenth of the price, a bargain.

Most people are aware that personal training costs money and if this is likely to a major barrier would not have approached you in the first place. If you do not believe it is worth £30, neither will they. Be confident in yourself and your service.

Do not tell, ask

Someone very wisely told me that *giving advice builds resistance to change*. If a personal trainer tells a client that buying sessions will help them lose weight they may seem like a pushy sales person. But if the person tells the personal trainer that buying sessions will help them lose weight that is, of course, far more powerful. This is why we have to let them come up with the answers and then reinforce those answers using closed questions and paraphrasing. Questions such as 'What do you need to do to achieve your goals?' and 'How do you think personal training can help you?' are very important.

Use a prompt sheet

It is all too easy to dry up and forget what questions to ask. Use a prompt sheet like the consultation form provided so that if you need some help you have a structure to return to.

Mirroring personalities

Different people approach situations very differently and want to be communicated with in very different ways. Some people will be shy and reserved, others very direct and confident. Some will want to know every minute detail, others will want to get on with things. We have to respond to these differences and treat people as individuals, being sensitive to their personality. I call this *mirroring personalities*. Try to match the person's body language, voice style and attitude. For example, if a person has a very direct attitude, with lots of eye contact and a small personal space, try to match these qualities. If someone is quite shy, nervous and closed in their body language, match your communication by talking slowly and calmly, giving them lots of personal space and limiting any flamboyant hand gestures. If someone is direct and to the point, do not waste his or her time with every minute detail, get straight to the point. If someone wants to take their time and wants answers to lots of questions, do not rush them, give them answers and explain in detail. The key is to be sensitive to the personality of the person and mirror their qualities.

Use their language

Make sure that you use the language of the person in front of you, avoiding your own technical jargon, which they may not understand. They do not need to know the science, only that you can help them. For example, although I know that 'tone' means the tension held by a muscle, most clients use the word tone to describe the visual appearance of their muscles. I would always use their terminology, making sure they understand what I mean.

A client can also empower us with their language. For example, although we cannot refer to someone as 'overweight', because that would be rude and offensive, as soon as they have called themselves overweight we can start to use their language. Getting someone to admit that they are overweight and that they need to do something about it is very powerful and good for you because you are perfectly placed in terms of knowledge and training to help them.

Client confidentiality

Never disclose any personal details about your clients to anyone else unless you have permission from the clients themselves. This should include contact details or details of anything involved with your sessions.

Dual roles

Never become overly familiar with your clients. I advise keeping your relationship strictly professional at all times. Where possible, avoid dual roles. You will find that you will become friendly with clients, but becoming too close can blur the lines of your professional relationship. I avoid training people with whom I already have a close relationship. Being a personal trainer is very different from giving someone health and fitness advice; this I give for free.

Communication

Communicate with your clients as if they were your employer. Obviously we are on first name terms with our clients but it is not appropriate to start slapping them on the back and calling them 'mate'.

BENEFITS OF EXERCISE

Many people, when thinking about becoming a personal trainer, find it difficult to justify charging large amounts of money for helping people with exercise. Many others find it hard to justify using sales techniques to try to convince people to buy personal training. Nevertheless, when you simply look at the array of benefits of developing an exercise habit you will appreciate that personal training is well worth the money.

Moderate exercise on a regular basis can:

- aid in maintenance of ideal weight
- improve muscle tone and definition
- improve self-confidence and self-esteem
- improve posture
- reduce chronic pain syndromes such as lower-back pain with correct exercise prescription
- reduce the risk of coronary heart disease
- decrease the risk of diabetes
- reduce blood pressure
- improve immune system function
- reduce the risk of colon cancer
- decrease the risk of breast cancer
- reduce or relieve depression
- increase bone density, decreasing the risk of osteoporosis.

Physical inactivity can lead to:

- high blood pressure
- chronic fatigue
- premature ageing
- poor musculature
- lack of flexibility (causing)
- lower-back pain
- mental tension
- obesity
- coronary heart disease.

Imagine the benefits your clients are going to experience if with your help they can adhere to a programme of regular exercise. Never think that personal training is overpriced. The results of your training can be life-changing for an individual.

CHAPTER SUMMARY

Sales and marketing are an important part of any business. This is more so for personal trainers as those in the fitness industry are not always natural sales people. This chapter should have provided some useful tips in how to generate sales, making you an all-round fitness professional.

REFERENCES AND RECOMMENDED READING

1. American College of Sports Medicine (2000)
    *ACSM's Guidelines for Exercise Testing and
    Prescription*, 6th edn. Philadelphia: Lippincott,
    Williams and Wilkins.

BRINGING IT ALL TOGETHER

Upon completing this book you should have all the skills to be able to design effective and enjoyable workouts for your clients.

When you start taking sessions, it may be that you design a sheet to record all your client's information. This should be kept in your client's personal file along with any contracts, medical questionnaires and consultation forms. These documents should be available to you every time you have a session and should always be kept up-to-date. They will act as a record of what you have done with your client should your professionalism ever be called into question. For example, it is essential you have a record of the preparation you have done for more advanced exercises in case the clients were ever to injure themselves.

For each client you should have:

- the client's long-term outcome goals
- the short-term outcome and process goals
- an analysis of the client's requirements in relation to any sports or activities they may do
- the client's periodized plan, outlining the macrocycle and the mesocycle they are presently in with the current acute exercise variables they are working to (reps, sets, volumes, tempos, rest) and any other exercise considerations
- any dietary goals the client may have and food diaries they have completed
- the results of their postural analysis with your recommendations and exercise guidelines.

For each session you should have:

- the dates of your sessions
- the exercises they performed
- their performance on each exercise
- points to work on and develop.

An example of the exercise sheets I use to record a client's exercise are shown in Figure 18.1. Remember that for each client you should have:

- gained a signed contract if required and gained payment for sessions
- performed an initial consultation to assess their goals and any obstacles to achieving these goals
- received a completed PAR-Q health questionnaire and gained medical clearance if needed prior to beginning an exercise programme.

When designing the client's programme you should have:

- designed their periodized plan based on their goals and present condition
- designed their microcycle and provided them with advice and guidance about the exercise programme they will do when they are not training with you
- provided the client with their own programme card and coached them on how to do the exercises, making sure they feel totally confident

give your client things to work on when they are not in the gym (e.g. increasing activity levels, holding a good posture, addressing bad habits)

analysed their diet based on a food diary and set them a series of dietary goals

analysed their posture, determining what factors are influencing their posture, which muscles are tight and weak, and provided a programme to improve posture based on this

assessed core function and determined level of core conditioning and designed a core programme to develop this to be done at the end of your sessions prior to stretching

designed a resistance programme based on goals, our periodized plan and postural analysis

designed a cardiovascular programme to develop cardiovascular fitness and complement our resistance programme

given psychological tools to aid exercise adherence and programme maintenance. I always recommend an exercise diary and a written contract that you both sign, making clear their commitment to the goals you have agreed.

Remember:

Make sessions flow by always giving the client a task even when they are resting. This might just be focusing on posture while sitting on a Swiss ball, for example.

Include some assisted stretches at the end of the session to add that personal touch.

Use the Swiss ball when appropriate to keep an element of fun.

Try to improve your client's movement as you train them to achieve their goals. Do this by improving posture and prescribing exercises that are relevant to their everyday movement.

Always act with energy and enthusiasm, making your spotting appear as professional and involved as possible. Remember – anyone could be watching.

Always have a reason for whatever you do.

Try to keep an element of fun by introducing new ideas and exercises and thinking beyond the norm.

Be interested in your client, learn things about them, names of family members, interests. If it helps you to remember, write these things down on your exercise sheet. You do need a good working relationship with your client.

Never:

progress exercise too quickly just to keep the client interested

forget that what happens outside the gym (activity and diet) can be far more important than what happens inside the gym

turn spotting into glorified rep counting, with the emphasis on shouting and bullying your client

look or act unprofessionally

appear bored or uninterested

forget that your client's results are your responsibility.

18.1 Exercise sheets

Name:					
Training Phase					
Ex. variables					Sets, rep range, rest, tempo, RPE
CV goal					Time and type
Date					
Weight					
Other					
Full body					
Lower body					
Chest					
Back					
Shoulders					
Triceps					
Biceps					
Core					
Cardiovascular	Time, level, RPE, format (interval ratio, fartlek, LSD etc.)				
Treadmill					
Row					
Eliptical					
Crosstrainer					
Stepper					
Bike					
Stretch focus					

18.1 continued

Client profile	
Client goals	
Postural notes	Includes static amd dynamic postural assessment, flexibility and core assessments
Dietary goals	

Periodisation					
Phase					
Date from-to					
Focus					
Other					
Other					
Other					
Other					
	(including smart exercise and dietary goals)				
Program written					
Additional notes					

GLOSSARY

Abdominal brace A mild contraction of the abdominal muscles in order to maintain neutral alignment of the spine against external forces (i.e. core stability).

Active range of motion (AROM) The sum total of angular movement in which muscles are actually working (full ROM minus passive ROM).

Active recovery (in periodized plans) Periods of reduced-intensity exercise of a nature different to that usually performed by the athlete/client to allow recovery and supercompensation.

Active recovery Reduced-intensity exercises performed during rest periods to aid recovery by increasing blood flow back to the heart.

Active stretching Movement into and out of a stretch.

Acute exercise variables The different ways we can alter exercise intensity or challenge of an exercise.

Aerobic base A basic level of aerobic conditioning or cardiovascular fitness that supports cardiovascular performance at higher intensities.

Agility A combination of acceleration and deceleration combined with our ability to change direction.

Agonist The main force-producing muscle of a movement at a joint, also known as the prime mover.

Amino acids The chief structural material of protein.

Amortization phase The time between the eccentric and concentric phases of the stretch-shortening cycle, or the time between landing and take-off during running, jumping or bounding.

Anabolism Constructive metabolism in which we build or repair body tissue.

Anaerobic endurance The time we can work under anaerobic (without oxygen) conditions or at high intensities.

Anaerobic Energy production in the absence of oxygen, important for short-term (up to 180 seconds) performance.

Anaerobic threshold The point at which lactic-acid production exceeds removal, causing an accumulation of lactic acid in the muscles resulting in a burning sensation and eventual fatigue; also known as lactate threshold.

Anatomical plumb lines Lines drawn through the body with which we can compare the position of postural landmarks.

Antagonist The opposing muscle group to the prime mover or agonist required to relax to allow optimal force production and movement.

Ascending pyramid A stepped increase in intensity or workload – an excellent way to warm up a client.

Assisted stretching Exercises in which the trainer is actively involved in the stretching process, also known as partner stretching.

ATP (adenosine triophosphate) A high-energy

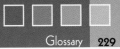

phosphate compound used as an initial source of energy by the body.

Autogenic inhibition The reflex relaxation of muscle caused by the Golgi tendon organs in response to excessive muscular tension; also known as the inverse stretch reflex.

Balance Controlling centre of gravity so that it always remains within our base of support. Failure to do so causes momentum and movement.

Ballistic stretches Powerful movements that utilize momentum to take the joints into increased range of motion and stretch.

Base of support The area around which we stand or balance our body weight.

Bilateral loading Loading through both legs (e.g. squatting).

Burnout An exhaustive psychophysiological response to repeated unsuccessful efforts to meet the demands of training stress.

Carbohydrate loading The practice of consuming meals high in carbohydrate in the days leading up to an endurance event in order to increase muscular stores of glycogen.

Carryover The extent by which training leads to improvements in other tasks or improves performance.

Catabolism Destructive metabolism in which the body breaks down and loses tissue.

Centre of gravity The point at which our body weight is balanced on all sides.

Cheat mechanism The use of synergistic muscles to perform an exercise from the outset of a set.

Cheat repetitions Those reps performed at the end of a set using synergistic muscles to assist a fatigued prime mover as the person becomes fatigued.

Circuit training Alternating between a series of different exercises.

Closed chain An exercise in which we cannot overcome the resistance against which we are working, the result being that our body moves away or towards it during exercise (e.g. pull-ups, squat, lunge).

Closed questions Questions that have a yes or no answer.

Complete proteins Those proteins containing all eight essential amino acids and said to have high biological value.

Complex carbohydrates Foods such as breads, cereals, and vegetables that are high in starch.

Compound exercises Exercises involving movement at more than one joint at the same time.

Concentric contraction Muscular work in which the muscle overcomes the resistance against which it works and shortens, lifting the weight.

Conditioning A preparation of the kinetic chain for increased intensity of work.

Contraindicated Used of an exercise deemed to be dangerous and that should be avoided.

Cool-down Cardiovascular exercise with steadily decreasing intensity designed to provide a steady transition from a working state back to a rest.

Core stability Maintaining ideal static postural alignment of the lumbo-pelvic hip complex against external forces.

Core strength The ability of muscles to produce forceful bending or twisting movements of the trunk.

Core The centre of the body. The core is the foundation of movement.

Counter movements Eccentric muscle action that precedes concentric muscle action in order to increase force production.

Creatine phosphate A high-energy phosphate compound found within the cells of the body and used to regenerate ATP; also known as phospho-creatine.

Delayed onset muscle soreness (DOMS) The post-workout muscle soreness felt 24–72 hours following training.

Descending pyramid A stepped decrease in intensity or workload. Excellent as a way to cool down a client.

Developmental stretches Static stretches held for 30 seconds or more, causing long-lasting changes in muscle length and range of motion.

Disaccharides Simple sugars containing two monosaccarides.

Drop sets Reducing the load immediately after the point of failure has been reached so that more repetitions can be performed, thereby optimizing muscular fatigue.

Drop out The choice to discontinue exercise.

Eccentric contraction Muscular work in which the load against which we work is greater than the force we produce, so that the muscle contracts whilst lengthening or lowering the weight.

Eccentric loading Giving the client a weight that they can lower with good technique but that is marginally too heavy for them to lift. The trainer will then help them through the lifting/concentric phase of each repetition.

Electron transport chain A stage of aerobic metabolism.

Energy systems The different ways the body can metabolize sugar gained from food to produce energy.

Equilibrium reactions Postural reflex movements involved in maintaining control over centre of gravity to keep it over our base of support so that we do not lose balance and fall.

Essential amino acids Those amino acids that cannot be synthesized by the body.

Essential fatty acids (EFAs) Unsaturated fats that cannot be synthesized by the body, so have to be consumed in the diet.

Excess post-exercise oxygen consumption (EPOC) The number of calories burnt after exercise finishes due to the recovery process.

Extrinsic reward A reward given for an act.

Fartlek 'Speed play' involves spontaneous variation in exercise type and/or intensity to challenge all the energy systems of the body.

Faulty movement The inappropriate use of muscles or incorrect movement patterns characterized by loss of performance and increased incidence of injury.

Fibre Complex carbohydrate found in plant material that is resistant to digestive enzymes.

Flexibility The range of motion available at one joint or a series of joints.

Forced reps The trainer assists the client in lifting the weight after the point of failure, reducing the load and allowing more repetitions to be completed, thus increasing the level of muscular fatigue the client achieves.

Full pyramid A stepped increase in intensity followed by a stepped decrease in intensity.

Functional carryover The degree by which training in an artificial setting, the gym for example, carries over to our performance at daily tasks.

Functional range of motion Range of motion available under muscular contraction without assistance.

Functional training Training that utilizes exercises that reproduce and therefore improve everyday movements.

General warm-up Usually a cardiovascular exercise aimed at elevating body temperature and preparing the body for exercise.

Generalized motor programmes Templates for muscle action for particular movements found within the brain.

Glucagon Metabolic hormone that stimulates release of glycogen from the liver to raise blood-sugar levels, having the opposite effect from that of insulin.

Glucose A monosaccharide or simple sugar.

Glycaemic index A ranking of foods (0–100) based on the immediate effect on blood-sugar levels.

Glycogen The storage form of glucose mainly found in the muscles and liver.

Goal proximity Relative time required to achieve a goal .

Goal setting A simple yet effective approach to motivation that requires you to set your clients effective goals, monitor their progress, provide feedback, reinforce success and help them cope with setbacks.

Golgi tendon organs Mechanoreceptors sensitive to changes in muscular tension and the rate of change of muscular tension. If tension levels rise too high Golgi tendon organs stimulate muscular relaxation called the autogenic inhibition.

Gross stabilization Maintaining the natural soft S-shape of the spine.

Ground reaction force The force created when we land on the ground whilst walking, running or jumping.

High responders Individuals predisposed to adapt quickly in response to a training stimulus.

Human growth hormone Hormone linked with the development of muscle mass.

Hypermobility A condition in which there is too much range of motion at a joint, causing loss of stability and support.

Hyperplasia An increase in the number of muscle fibres.

Hypertension High blood pressure.

Hypertonic Overly strong, tight muscles with excess muscle 'tone'. Have an increased likelihood of recruitment by the nervous system.

Hypertrophy An increase in the size of muscle fibres.

Hypoglycaemia A fall in blood sugar.

Incomplete proteins Proteins without all eight essential amino acids; said to have low biological value.

Individualization The training principle that states that each individual will have different training requirements and will respond differently to specific training stress.

Inhibition Loss of strength in a muscle due to reciprocal inhibition from a hypertonic antagonist.

Inner unit muscles Muscles whose primary function is segmental stabilization of the lumbar spine.

Insulin Hormone that controls the storage of sugar, stimulating the storage of glucose in the muscles as well as promoting the formation of fat when blood sugar exceeds the body's needs.

Intensity The level of training stress.

Interneurons Nerves that allow communication between other nerves.

Interval training Periods of high-intensity work interspersed with periods of low-intensity work to allow recovery and subsequent work periods.

Intra-abdominal pressure The internal pressure created by the co-contraction of deep stabilizing muscles such as the transverse abdominis, diaphragm and pelvic floor, which aids in stabilizing the spine against external forces.

Intrinsic reward Inherent reward in doing something.

Inverse stretch reflex See autogenic inhibition.

Isolation exercise Exercise that involves movements at only one joint and utilizing only one prime mover.

Isometric contraction Muscular work whilst staying at the same length or holding the weight.

Kinaesthetic sense Our ability to interpret proprioceptive information to give us an awareness of where our body is in space.

Kinetic chain The sum total of the nervous action and muscular action to move bones and joints involved in any particular movement.

Krebs cycle A stage of aerobic metabolism that produces ATP.

Lactate clearance The ability to convert lactic acid into lactate and remove this from muscles in order to prolong performance.

Lactate threshold The point at which lactic acid production exceeds a body's ability to remove it, and acidity levels rise within muscle tissue; also known as anaerobic threshold.

Lactic acid The waste product of anaerobic metabolism linked with fatigue.

Lactic tolerance The ability to withstand raised concentrations of lactic acid and hydrogen ions in the blood.

Lead generation Increasing the number of people you know that are interested in personal training.

Lipoprotein lipase Enzyme responsible for regulation of fat storage.

Load The resistance or weight used.

Long slow distance (LSD) training High-volume, low-intensity training without rest periods, designed to stress the oxidative system.

Long-term goals Goals with a large time scale.

Low responders Individuals predisposed to respond slowly to a training stimulus.

Lumbo-pelvic hip complex (LPHC) The shorthand for the bones and joints associated with the core of the body.

Macronutrients Nutrients required by the body in large quantities (grams per day) such as carbohydrate, proteins, fats and water.

Manual resistance (MR) The use of your own body weight to provide resistance to a client's movement.

Maximal force production The most force our muscles can produce in one effort.

Maximal steady rate The maximal speed that can be worked at below lactic/anaerobic threshold.

Maximal steady rate The maximum pace someone can maintain below the lactate threshold.

Maximal strength The highest level of force an individual can produce or the heaviest weight they can lift.

Maximum aerobic power (VO$_2$max) The amount of oxygen that can be supplied to and used by working muscles for aerobic metabolism; also known as maximum oxygen uptake.

Maximum rate of force development (mRFD) The most force that can be produced in the least amount of time.

Mechanoreceptors Sensors within the body detecting mechanical changes such as load or tension.

Metabolic demand The requirement for the body to produce energy via its different energy systems for movement.

Metabolic stress A level of work exceeding the body's ability to supply muscle with oxygen via the cardiovascular system, causing build-up of waste materials such as lactic acid. The body attempts to cope with this by removing lactic acid via the cardiovascular system.

Micronutrients Nutrients required by the body in small quantities (less than grams per day) such as vitamins and minerals.

Mobilization The slow and deliberate movement of a joint through its full range of motion.

Modelling Moulding your client's lifestyle in a gradual, step-by-step process to aid adherence and success.

Momentum The force acting to keep us moving in the same direction.

Monosaccharides Simple sugars.

Monounsaturated Fats that have a single double bond.

Motivation The direction and intensity of effort.

Motor learning The process of learning new movements and skills.

Motor neurons Nerves connecting the brain with the muscles of the body.

Muscle energy techniques Collective name for techniques that use physiology of reflex muscle action and relaxation to aid in stretching.

Muscle spindles Mechanoreceptors found along the length of muscle fibres sensitive to changes in length of muscle and of rate of change of muscle length. If muscle length increases excessively, muscle spindles activate a stretch reflex.

Muscular synergy The process in which many muscles work together to produce movement.

Musculo-tendinous junction (MTJ) The point at which the muscle and the tendon join together.

Negative adaptation Catabolic response to over-training, or overly high training stress with insufficient recovery.

Negative reinforcement Motivation provided by fear of losing something pleasurable.

Neural demand The complexity of or skill required in performing an exercise.

Neural drive The degree by which the nervous system stimulates the muscular system to produce muscular force; also known as neurological drive.

Neuromuscular coordination The nervous system's ability to coordinate muscle action.

Neutral Position of ideal alignment, the position in which the body is best able to absorb external stress and produce muscular force in order to move.

Neutral spine The position of ideal spinal alignment characterized by a smooth S-shape, the position of greatest strength and stability for the spine.

Neutralizer Muscle acting to limit unwanted movement.

Ninety-ninety position Resting on the ground on one foot and one knee with legs bent at right angles.

Non-linear periodization A method in which each workout within a microcycle is different, challenging different properties of muscle.

Nutrient density The nutritional value of a food.

Open chain An exercise in which we can overcome a resistance in order to create movement, i.e. when we push something away or pull something towards us. For example, a bicep curl.

Open-ended questions Those questions that can

be expanded upon and encourage more than a yes or no answer.

Optimal overload The maximal stress placed on the client for optimal training gains without increased risk of injury.

Outcome goals Goals that describe the end result desired.

Outer unit muscles Muscles that generate dynamic movement around joints.

Overload The training principle that states we have to expose the body to more stress than it is used to in order to stimulate a training effect.

Overpronation Excessive pronation can increase the potential for injury during walking and running due to a lowered capacity to absorb ground-reaction forces.

Over-training An excessive training stress without sufficient rest, leading to a negative-adaptation syndrome.

Oxygen debt The lag in oxygen uptake we experience upon starting exercise.

Paraphrase Repeating back what someone has said to you but using your own words to demonstrate understanding.

Partial range of motion When range of motion is limited to alter the intensity of the exercise.

Passive range of motion (PROM) Range of motion in which there is little muscular work being performed. These may be described as rest points.

Pattern overload The overexposure to similar movement patterns, causing damage and eventual injury.

Peaking The practice of ordering training to ensure that key physical attributes are highest at the most important times of the competitive season or for the most important games.

Periodization The systematic cycling of exercise variables with periods of planned rest to ensure maintenance of training gains.

Peripheral heart action The practice of alternating between upper- and lower-body exercises to place more stress on the cardiovascular system to supply working muscles with blood; also known as vascular shunt.

Plateau A levelling-off of training gains.

Plyometric muscle action The additional

concentric force created by muscles after an eccentric or lengthening contraction.

Point of failure The point at which form and technique deteriorate and the risk of injury increases during resistance training.

Polysaccharides Sugars containing many monosaccharides.

Polyunsaturated Fats that have more than one double bond.

Positive adaptation Anabolic response to correct training stress and recovery.

Positive energy balance A situation in which we are consuming more calories than we are using. This will cause a storage of excess calories in the form of fat deposits.

Post-activation potentiation The phenomenon that muscles can produce more power immediately following a high-intensity strength exercise.

Post-isometric relaxation (PIR) A muscle energy technique that utilizes autogenic inhibition to create a state of relaxation in the muscle to be stretched.

Postural stress The stress resulting from chronic exposure to poor posture and prolonged static body position.

Posture The way a person holds themselves.

Power The rate at which work can be done.

Pre-exhaust Fatiguing a muscle using an isolation exercise before working that same muscle again during a compound exercise.

Primary motive The main reason for participation.

Prime mover The muscle primarily involved in producing force during an exercise; also known as the agonist.

Process goals Goals that describe actions that must be taken to ensure progress towards the outcome goal.

Progression The training principle that states we have to increase training stress in order to maintain overload, or the manipulation of acute exercise variables to increase the challenge of an exercise.

Pronation Movement that involves a combination of dorsiflexion, adduction and external rotation.

Proprioreception Sum total of sensory feedback.

Punishment Experience something unpleasant following an action.

Quickness Ability to accelerate or the time taken to reach maximal speed.

Range of motion The angular distance travelled by joints during an exercise.

Rapport The level of relationship between two individuals.

Rating of perceived exertion (RPE) Scale rating the perceived level of work intensity.

Reactive strength Another way to describe power, particularly plyometric power.

Reciprocal inhibition The natural reflex relaxation of a muscle when its opposing muscle group contracts.

Refined foods Foods that have gone through increased levels of processing (i.e. have been cooked, prepared with added sugars, salt, preservatives colouring etc.).

Regression Manipulating acute exercise variables to decrease the challenge of an exercise.

Relapse prevention Techniques used to minimize the impact of failure to adhere to a programme.

Relative flexibility The comparative chain of flexibility of muscles involved in a certain movement; for example, in touching our toes, movement will come from the spine, hip and ankle, with a large number of possible muscles effecting movement.

Relative timing patterns The patterns of muscle action for particular movements.

Repetition One complete movement of an exercise.

Rest The time between sets given to the client to recover.

Resting metabolic rate (RMR) The energy required to maintain all the physiological processes of the body at rest.

Righting reactions Involved in maintaining head position and drawing the body back into alignment.

Saturated fats Fats fully saturated with hydrogen ions. They tend to be solid at room temperature.

Scapular retraction The drawing together of the shoulder blades.

Secondary motives Alternative reasons for participation other than the primary motive.

Segmental stabilization, Maintaining the optimal position of each vertebra in relation to adjacent vertebrae.

Self-efficacy Task-specific self-confidence.

Self-monitoring A self-tracking of performance (e.g. food or exercise diary).

Self-talk Inner dialogue – the things you say to yourself as you exercise.

Semi-unilateral loading Loading predominantly on one side but with some weight also taken through the second leg (e.g. lunge).

Sensory neurons Nerves supplying the brain with sensory information.

Sets A group of consecutive repetitions.

Short-term goals Goals with a time frame of weeks or months rather than years and that are also process- as well as outcome-orientated.

Simple carbohydrates Also known as mono- or disaccharides, they are short chains of sugars.

Somatosensory feedback Proprioreceptive information obtained from mechanoreceptors found within muscle, skin and joints.

Specific warm-up Exercises designed to mimic the elements and movements found in the main workout, aimed at preparing the body for increased-intensity work.

Specificity The training principle that states that we experience training adaptation specific to the type of training we perform.

Speed endurance The ability to maintain speed over distances greater than 60 metres.

Speed Maximal velocity independent of acceleration.

Spinal reflexes Involuntary movements that occur without conscious effort.

Split routine The practice of exercising different muscle groups on different days of a week (or microcycle) to allow sufficient recovery.

Spot reduction The theory that exercising a specific part of the body will result in fat loss from that same area.

Stabilization Maintaining good alignment of joints against external forces.

Stabilizer Muscle providing solid base on which movement can be produced.

Staleness An initial failure to adapt to the training stress.

Starvation mode The adaptations of the body in response to a negative energy balance.

Static dynamic posture The position of the kinetic chain without movement.

Static stretching Taking a muscle to the point of comfortable tension and holding.

Sticking points Points during a lift in which the person is at a mechanical disadvantage and the muscular work required to produce movement is greater.

Strength The ability to be able to produce muscular force.

Stress Any potentially catabolic (i.e. breakdown) influence on the body (e.g. training stress, emotional stress).

Stretch reflex Reflex activation of muscle in response to excessive stretch.

Stretch reflex The reflex contraction of muscle in response to excessive or sudden stretch.

Stretch-shortening cycle The cycling between concentric, isometric and eccentric phases of muscular loading, characteristic of rhythmic movements such as running.

Stride frequency The number of strides in a given time.

Stride length The distance covered in each stride.

Super-compensation The increase in performance seen with sufficient training stimulus and adequate rest.

Supersets One set composed of two different exercises.

Supination Movement that combines plantarflexion, abduction and internal rotation.

Synergistic dominance The use of synergistic muscles to complete a movement in preference to a prime mover that may be at a disadvantage due to fatigue, injury or faulty posture.

Synergists Muscles that assist the prime mover in creating movement.

Synovial fluid The lubricating fluid released around synovial joints.

Talk test Inability to finish complete sentences during cardiovascular work generally indicates that the client has reached lactic threshold and is working at an intensity somewhere near 85 per cent maximum heart rate.

Tempo The speed of movement at which an exercise is performed.

Tempo training Work at speeds slightly above those of race speeds or slightly above the lactate threshold.

Testosterone The male sex hormone linked with promotion of muscle mass.

Thermic effect of food (TEF) Energy used to digest, absorb, transport and store food.

Thermic effect of physical activity (TEPA) The burning of calories during activity or whenever we move.

Thoracic breathing/abdominal breathing Stomach pushes forwards and back as the diaphragm moves up and down.

Thoraco-lumbar fascia (TLF) Connective tissue stretching across the lower back with attachment points to the spine. Many muscles have attachments into this fascia enabling them to influence the alignment of the spine.

Thoraco-lumbar fascia gain The slight force into extension felt through the spine when the thoraco-lumbar fascia is pulled taut due to contraction of certain muscles (e.g. lats and TVA). This helps stabilize the spine during movements pulling the spine into flexion.

Thyroid gland An endocrine (hormone) gland that regulates resting metabolism.

Time under tension The total time in which muscles have to produce force during a set of repetitions.

Tone The low level of muscle activity present at all times that helps us maintain posture.

Touch training The use of physical contact to give your client feedback and improve their training.

Training phase A planned period of training usually lasting 6–8 weeks.

Training-sensitive zone The recommended target heart-rate range for the client for maximum benefit, dependent on the condition of the client and their goals.

Training volume The total number of reps performed throughout the workout, or the total distance travelled during a cardiovascular workout.

Transverse abdominis (TVA) A muscle that wraps around the middle of the body almost like a corset. When it contracts it pulls the stomach in, creating internal pressure that helps stabilize the spine, especially the lumbar spine.

Tri-planar movement Movement that combines all three planes of motion: sagittal, frontal and transverse.

Type I muscle fibres Fatigue-resistant muscle fibres.

Type II muscle fibres Muscle fibres with low resistance to fatigue but high force production.

Unilateral loading Loading through one leg only (e.g. hopping).

Unsaturated fats Fats that contain a double bond, meaning they are not fully saturated with hydrogen ions. They tend to be liquid at room temperature.

Valsalva manoeuvre A holding of the breath causing an isometric contraction of the diaphragm. This aids in providing spinal stability but also causes large increases in blood pressure that can be potentially dangerous for high-risk groups such as individuals with hypertension.

Variation The training principle that states we have to change a training stress to avoid plateau.

Vestibular feedback Proprioceptive information obtained from fluid balance in the inner ear.

Visual feedback Proprioceptive information obtained from our sense of vision.

Warm-up Cardiovascular exercise with a gradually increasing intensity at the beginning of the workout, designed to increase readiness to exercise.

INDEX